Alan Clarke

of related interest

WOODY ALLEN ON WOODY ALLEN
edited by Stig Björkman

ALMODÓVAR ON ALMODÓVAR
edited by Frédéric Strauss

BURTON ON BURTON
edited by Mark Salisbury

CRONENBERG ON CRONENBERG
edited by Chris Rodley

DE TOTH ON DE TOTH
edited by Anthony Slide

FELLINI ON FELLINI
edited by Costanzo Costantini

HAWKS ON HAWKS
Joseph McBride

HITCHCOCK ON HITCHCOCK
edited by Sidney Gottlieb

KIEŚLOWSKI ON KIEŚLOWSKI
edited by Danusia Stok

LEVINSON ON LEVINSON
edited by David Thompson

LYNCH ON LYNCH
edited by Chris Rodley

MALLE ON MALLE
edited by Philip French

POTTER ON POTTER
edited by Graham Fuller

SCHRADER ON SCHRADER
edited by Kevin Jackson

SAYLES ON SAYLES
edited by Gavin Smith

SCORSESE ON SCORSESE
edited by David Thompson and Ian Christie

SIRK ON SIRK
Conversations with Jon Halliday

Alan Clarke

edited by Richard Kelly
foreword by Stephen Frears

ff
faber and faber

First published in 1998
by Faber and Faber Limited
3 Queen Square London WC1N 3AU

Typeset by Faber and Faber Ltd
Printed in England by Clays Ltd, St Ives plc

A CIP record for this book
is available from the British Library

ISBN 0-571-19609-8

2 4 6 8 10 9 7 5 3 1

Contents

Acknowledgements

This book does its best to be accurate about the major events of its subject's life. In order to convey the personality of the late Alan Clarke across the nearly fifty-five years of his life, I needed to allow witnesses to speak in their own voices. Over sixty people were interviewed across a period of three months. The transition from tape to print has required a certain measure of trimming and chronological re-ordering. I have taken the liberty of smoothing bits of syntax here and there, purely to ensure that the testimony is accessible and that the narrative structure is maintained.

I would like to express a deep gratitude to the following people who gave their time, and in many cases threw open their filing cabinets, for the good of this project:

Anna Scher, Arthur Ellis, Barry Hanson, Bronco McLoughlin, Christopher Morahan, Clive Parsons, Corin Campbell Hill, Danny Boyle, David Hare, David Jones, David Leland, David Rudkin, David M. Thompson, David Yallop, Davina Belling, Douglas Livingstone, Eleanor Bron, Gary Oldman, George Costigan, George Fenton, Graham Benson, Grenville Middleton, Irene Shubik, Jacqui Lyons, Jane Harris, Janine Duvitski, Jehane Markham, John Ward, John Willett, Juliet Middleton, Ken Loach, Kenith Trodd, Lesley Manville, Lesley Sharp, Margaret Matheson, Mark Shivas, Michael Jackley, Michelle Holmes, Mike Leigh, Molly Clarke, Mossie Smith, Norma McMinn, Pam Brighton, Patsy Pollock, Paul Knight, Phil Daniels, Philip Davis, Ray Winstone, Richard Broke, Rosilyn Heller, Roy Minton, Sandy Lieberson, Sean Chapman, Siobhan Finneran, Stella Richman, Stephen Frears, Steven Berkoff, Stuart Griffiths, Stuart Walker, Susanna Capon, Tariq Anwar, Tim Roth, Tony Garnett, Verity Lambert, Vicky Murdock, William Armstrong.

For help in gathering additional research materials, many thanks to Geraldine Higgins of The British Council Film & Video Department; Kathleen Dickson of The National Film & Television Archive; everyone in the office of David M. Thompson at BBC Single Films; Bobbie Mitchell of the BBC Photographic Library; John Henderson of Euro London Films Limited; Graham Fuller of Interview; Gavin Smith of Film Comment; and everyone at BFI Stills, Posters & Designs.

Special thanks to: Mike Jackley, for proposing the title of Chapter One; Lizzie Francke, Director of the Edinburgh International Film Festival, for her boldness in honouring Clarke with his first retrospective on British cinema screens; Jacqueline McCann, for support and advice throughout; Justine Willett, for attention to detail; and Kevin Macdonald and Walter Donohue, for guidance and patience.

Cast of Principal Characters

(*In order of appearance. Descriptions refer to individuals' principal activities as discussed in the text.*)

NORMA MCMINN – Sister of Alan Clarke.

DAVID YALLOP – Screenwriter and author. Wrote the screen adaptation of his own book, *To Encourage the Others* (1972).

ROY MINTON – Dramatist and screenwriter. Wrote numerous plays for Clarke, including *Goodnight Albert* (1968), *Horace* (1972), *Funny Farm* (1975), and *Scum* (1977).

JANE HARRIS – Partner of Alan Clarke, mother of Gabriel Clarke and Molly Clarke.

PAUL KNIGHT – TV producer.

SUSANNA CAPON – Friend of Alan Clarke.

CHRISTOPHER MORAHAN – Film and theatre director. BBC Head of Plays 1972–1976

GRENVILLE MIDDLETON – Film and TV cameraman. Photographed *Bukovsky* (1976).

DAVID JONES – Film and theatre director. Producer of *Danton's Death* (1978)

STELLA RICHMAN – TV producer, Head of Scripted Series at Associated Rediffusion 1966–1968.

STUART GRIFFITHS – Co-adaptor of *Danton's Death*, script editor of *Baal* (1982)

GRAHAM BENSON – TV producer. AFM on several Clarke productions, including *The Hallelujah Handshake* (1970).

DAVINA BELLING – Co-producer of *Scum* (1979).

VERITY LAMBERT – TV producer/executive. Produced *Achilles' Heel* (1972).

MARK SHIVAS – TV producer/executive. Produced numerous Clarke plays, including *Horace*, *To Encourage the Others*, *Diane* (1975), *Funny Farm*.

MIKE LEIGH – Film and TV director.

MICHAEL JACKLEY – BBC production manager on numerous Clarke plays, including *Horace*, *Diane*, *Scum* (1977).

KEN LOACH – Film and TV director.

IRENE SHUBIK – Producer of several Clarke plays, including *Sovereign's Company* (1970) and *Everybody Say Cheese* (1971).

TONY GARNETT – TV producer/executive.

DOUGLAS LIVINGSTONE – Screenwriter. Wrote *I Can't See My Little Willie* (1970) and *Everybody Say Cheese* (1971).

JEHANE MARKHAM – Poet and writer. Wrote screenplay of *Nina* (1978).

RICHARD BROKE – Script editor on *Diane* and *Funny Farm*.

BARRY HANSON – TV producer/executive. Worked on *Penda's Fen* (1974), produced *Fast Hands* (1976).

MARGARET MATHESON – TV producer/executive. Produced *Scum* (1977), *Nina*, *Made In Britain*.

BRONCO MCLOUGHLIN – Film and TV stuntman. Worked on *To Encourage the Others*, *A Life Is Forever* (1972), and others.

PAM BRIGHTON – Theatre director, TV and radio producer.

DAVID HARE – Dramatist and director. Author of *Man Above Men* (1973).

DAVID LELAND – Writer, director and actor. Played 'Nemov' in *The Love Girl And The Innocent*. Wrote *Beloved Enemy* (1980), *Psy-Warriors* (1981) and *Made In Britain*.

STEPHEN FREARS – Film and TV director.

DAVID RUDKIN – Dramatist and screenwriter. Author of *Penda's Fen*.

JANINE DUVITSKI – Actress. Played the title-role in *Diane*.

PHIL DANIELS – Actor. Plays 'Richards' in *Scum* (1977) and *Scum* (1979), 'Billy Kid' in *Billy the Kid and the Green Baize Vampire* (1985).

RAY WINSTONE – Actor. Played 'Carlin' in *Scum* (1977), and *Scum* (1979).

STUART WALKER – Production designer of *Danton's Death* (1978) and *Road* (1987).

JULIET MIDDLETON – Friend of Alan Clarke.

ELEANOR BRON – Actress. Played the title-role in *Nina*.

CLIVE PARSONS – Co-producer of *Scum* (1979).

SEAN CHAPMAN – Actor. Played 'James' in *Scum* (1979), 'Barry Giller' in *Made in Britain*, 'The Platoon Commander' in *Contact* (1984).

SANDY LIEBERSON – Film producer/executive. Produced *Rita Sue and Bob Too* (1986).

ROSILYN HELLER – Film producer/executive. Worked with Clarke on the unmade 'Assassination on Embassy Row'.

STEVEN BERKOFF – Actor, writer and director. Played 'Koslov' in *Beloved Enemy*.

JOHN WILLETT – Author and Brechtian scholar. Co-authored TV adaptation of Brecht's *Baal*.

TIM ROTH – Actor. Played 'Trevor' in *Made In Britain*.

CORIN CAMPBELL HILL – BBC production manager on *Contact*, *Christine* (1986), *Road* and *The Firm* (1988).

GEORGE FENTON – Composer. Wrote music for *Billy the Kid and the Green Baize Vampire*.

ARTHUR ELLIS – Screenwriter. Co-wrote *Christine*.

JOHN WARD – Lighting cameraman and Steadicam operator. Worked on *Rita Sue and Bob Too*, *Road*, *Elephant* (1988) and *The Firm*.

VICKY MURDOCK – Actress. Played the title-role in *Christine*.

TARIQ ANWAR – Editor of *Beloved Enemy* and *Christine*.

MICHELLE HOLMES – Actress. Played 'Sue' in *Rita Sue and Bob Too*.

SIOBHAN FINNERAN – Actress. Played 'Rita' in *Rita Sue and Bob Too*.

LESLEY SHARP – Actress. Played 'Michelle' in *Rita Sue and Bob Too* and 'Valerie' in *Road*.

GEORGE COSTIGAN – Actor. Played 'Bob' in *Rita Sue and Bob Too*.

DAVID M. THOMPSON – BBC TV producer/executive. Co-produced *Road*, produced *The Firm*.

MOSSIE SMITH – Actress. Played 'Carol' in *Road*.

WILLIAM ARMSTRONG – Actor. Played 'Eddie' in *Road*.

DANNY BOYLE – Film and TV director. Produced *Elephant*.

GARY OLDMAN – Actor. Played 'Bex' in *The Firm*. Made debut as writer–director with *Nil By Mouth* (1997).

PHILIP DAVIS – Actor and director. Played 'Yeti' in *The Firm*.
LESLEY MANVILLE – Actress. Played 'Sue' in *The Firm*.
ANNA SCHER – Founder of The Anna Scher Theatre School, whose students appear in many Clarke productions, including *Scum*.

Foreword

I got to hear about Alan Clarke when I went to Halifax in 1972 to make my first film for the BBC (also, incidentally, the first thing Alan Bennett wrote for television). Generally, when you were new to making films, crews would put you at your ease by talking about 'Stanley' (they all seemed to have spent their lives working with Kubrick) or 'Joe' (Losey). On this occasion they had recently been to Halifax with a man rather more wonderful than God, who, quite apart from his prodigious and effortless talent, had spent the time womanizing and drinking until he had ended up in jail. Marginally less hooligan behaviour on my part would mark me as a failure. Nowadays, when people rabbit on about 'Quentin', I turn a hardened face. Then I hated Alan.

When at last I met him, it was on a Saturday morning outside the lifts on the Fifth Floor of the Television Centre. He said, 'You know Jehane,' and looked at me suspiciously. Not much talk about 'Whither the Wednesday Play?'

In an essay, David Hare describes going to interview Hugh Carlton Greene; the conversation turned to mischief. 'Ah! Mischief,' said the great man who, during his time running the BBC, had allowed the one-armed gateman at the Television Centre to let in the post-war scepticism of young people as a counter to the complacency and excludingness and unspeakable boringness of the people who ran Britain. I can see that finding a cure for cancer would have been of greater value but, at the time – the sixties – it was good to be young and alive.

God decided to make Alan Clarke young at this time – and he was the beneficiary and product of this rare period in British history. He was sceptical, cynical of authority, rebellious but not ideological, instinctively principled but also practical and canny, solitary but the best company, authoritative but not in search of power, serious and frivolous, as serious and as funny as anyone I've ever met. He was, in other words, his own man. No one wanted to change him or indoctrinate him or spin-doctor him. That was how – at their best – things were at that time.

Alan's early work – I imagine – was done for the drama departments of the various television companies (principally for the BBC). Ken Loach and Tony Garnett had inventively and mischievously devised a way of getting films made at the BBC which meant they could show – literally – the real world rather than the inside of a studio. Clarkey made – as did I – a lot of films under this system. They were made on 16mm negative and were generally shown once or, if they were very good, twice. They weren't much to do with Glamour or Show Business; they weren't shown at festivals. But for a time people liked to see films that gave an accurate account of their lives, both emotional and social. Most of what I've learnt came from my time working in this way.

After his death, I said of Alan, 'He was the best of all of us.' I find it difficult to think of him as anything but the fine and attractive man I knew, so maybe that's what I meant. But, for what it's worth, I also think that, as he developed after the fiasco of *Scum*, his films and his way of making films became increasingly singular, mysterious, visionary; angrier and more committed. Kids used to pass nicked copies of *Scum* around in the schoolyard just as I hope they do now *Trainspotting*.

Above all, he was funny. For some reason he turned up at the Los Angeles première of *Dangerous Liaisons*. God knows what he thought of the film but he put his thumb up. 'Great,' he said. 'It's a Three-Erection movie.'

And that – as he would drive me mad by saying – that's a wrap!

Stephen Frears, 1998

Introduction: 'This Is Your Man'

'Any form of authority requires justification; it's not self-justified. And any time you find a form of authority illegitimate, you ought to challenge it. It's something that conflicts with human rights and liberties. And that goes on forever.'

Noam Chomsky

'I don't know that I ever had a profound political discussion with Alan, in the sense of theoretical politics. But he's of the anarchist left, I'd say – and by personal example. He's just on the side of the people who are getting a raw deal. So he's of the poetic left, and the anarchist left – the 'Fuck You' left, basically. And especially so as the Eighties go on. He's a profoundly anti-establishment artist, that's his stance, and that's his glory.'

David Hare

Alan Clarke enjoys a cuppa on location in Easington for *Road* (1987)

Alan Clarke is, we may safely contend, the most important British film-maker to have emerged in the last thirty years – the most productive, the most prodigious, the most restlessly innovative, the most impulsively radical, the most redoubtable. And yet it would be pushing it to claim that he enjoyed even so much as a 'large, vague renown' in his working life, even though by its late stages he was widely regarded as the professional's professional, the *non pareil*. Clarke's premature death in 1990 prompted many eulogies, none more striking, perhaps, than the verdict of his colleague Stephen Frears: 'He became the best of all of us.' But Clarke remains an enigma, because he was a master of that ephemeral dramatic form, the single television play. Many of his finest productions survive only in the archives of the BBC. Some of them didn't make it so far, the broadcast tapes having been quietly recycled for some frugal purpose in the seventies. And one, *Scum* (1977), served fourteen years in the BBC's legal vaults, labouring under a broadcast ban. So if there is a cult of Clarke already afoot, its keenest votaries are perhaps the younger viewers who grew up with his late works, some of them extant on commercial video. These titles include *The Firm* (1988), in which Gary Oldman is Bexy, 'top boy' in a band of parvenu football hooligans; *Made in Britain* (1983), wherein Tim Roth is a young jobless skinhead spraying spleen and repellent all about him; and the feature remake of *Scum* (1979), a bleak drama of borstal life, in which the trapped animosity of the warders rains down upon the heads of hapless young 'trainees', and is inculcated in 'the daddy', Carlin (Ray Winstone). These are all clamorous, bristling films, studies of the kind of atavistic male violence that our society inevitably encourages, while sanctimoniously trying to condemn it. They are not comfortable films to watch, either, unless one is comforted by the slash of a Stanley knife, the heft of an iron bar, the crunch of a kick in the bollocks. But then Alan Clarke always worked most effectively when he positioned himself right up at the pointed end of a social problem.

In David Leland's *Made in Britain* (1983), the sixteen-year-old skinhead Trevor finds no real justification for a 'juvenile assessment centre' to keep classified files concerning his character. He challenges that authority one night by urinating on said files, and urging his friend Errol to go one better. Trevor is no more impressed by the 'tacky jobs' on offer at his local DHSS office, and therefore he throws half of a paving slab through the window of said office. 'You don't invite leniency, do you?' says the judge when Trevor is brought to heel. 'No,' says Trevor. Dramatic cruces such as this are very Clarkey – to borrow a term which will recur. This is not to neglect that high among Clarke's gifts as a director was his facility to find collaborators who shared his ungovernable spirit, his urge to carry awkward and unpalatable news to a television audience. David Leland was one of the most vital of Clarke's creative accomplices, providing two other incendiary scripts for him (*Beloved Enemy* in 1980, *Psy-Warriors* in 1981), having previously taken the lead in his production of Solzhenitsyn's *The Love Girl and the Innocent* (1973).

Another major co-conspirator was the writer Roy Minton, with whom Clarke produced a brilliant sequence of plays – *Horace* (1972), *Funny Farm* (1975), *Scum* – which constitute a fierce championing of some of the most neglected and despised members of our society: the backward and the afflicted, the uneducated and the institutionalized. These films are both harrowing and very funny, rich in pathos and lined with knife-edge anger. There are moments in *Scum* which are resonant of Trevor's later protests, and suggestive, in their handling, of Clarke's anarchic tendencies. Most of these *frissons* are provided by Archer, an over-aged inmate determined that the screws won't get a piece of him. In one riveting scene, he calmly engages a warder in a dialogue about the merits of the punitive system. 'My experience of borstal convinces me that more criminal acts are imposed on prisoners than by prisoners on society.' The warder is, of course, personally offended. 'You may be a smartarse, Archer, but you're nothing but a fool to yourself.'

But in truth we are always very lucky if we have such fools among us. One of the tenets – if we may use so binding a word – of anarchism, is that the problem of humanity is not the will to command but the urge to obey. Clearly Alan Clarke found both predilections distasteful, and he dedicated his directorial career to giving them both a good pasting.

Clarke could press this case incisively even without the ammunition supplied by articulate, firebrand protagonists, such were his finical skills – rigour in preparation, humour and openness to the play of ideas among cast and crew, and a hard-edged mastery of *mise-en-scène*. *Contact* (1984), my own favourite of Clarke's films, is adapted from A. F. N. Clarke's published account of serving at the head of a paratroop patrol on border duty in Crossmaglen, Northern Ireland. A detailed script was prepared with the author: a study of a crisis of command which afflicts a young Platoon Commander as he leads his callow charges on a series of lonely and hazardous operations in 'bandit country'. The cast were drilled within an inch of military discipline, and in the process of production Clarke gradually stripped the piece of exposition and dialogue. He elected to 'retouch some real with some real', as Robert Bresson would put it. He left the big lights at home, and filmed the nocturnal manoeuvres with an infra-red night-sight. And in daylight he framed these soldiers as figures in a landscape where they have no mission, no prayer and no place. The film is punctuated by close-ups of Sean Chapman as the Commander, crouched behind cover and caught in what seem to be quite terrifying moments of mental absence. Illegitimate authority, indeed.

Clarke was a great political film-maker, though his personal convictions were often unpredictable. He was no Ken Loach (though he greatly respected Loach's work). The true anarchic temper tends to be at odds with that study of the evolution of society and production which the sincere Marxist must commit to. But Clarke was free of that right-wing taint in those who profess 'anarchic sympathies', all the better to feel themselves unfettered in defending their own property, or expressing their contempt for lower-class rabble. As Tony Garnett contends, Clarke was 'on the left in his gut'. Once, when asked as bluntly as you please why he became a socialist, the writer Christopher Hitchens cited an early reading of Richard Llewellyn's *How Green Was My Valley* which brought him forcibly to the realization that working-class people have lives and minds of their own. 'You can't be a socialist', Hitchens pointed out, 'if you don't think that.' You're not a socialist *de facto* if you do. But Alan Clarke had this conviction in his bones, and his body of work is a searing testament to what can be achieved when supreme dramatic intelligence is harnessed to such a belief. The backdrop of his work in the eighties, of course, was years of horrendous government-engineered mass unemployment. Those films are haunted by enforced inertia, the desperate things people are driven to do when there's nothing to do. Emblematic among them is his inspired filming of Jim Cartwright's play *Road*, shot on location in 1987, in the vicinity of Easington Colliery and amidst the dire ramifications of the defeat of the Miners' Strike.

Clarke's early death from cancer in 1990 was felt by everyone who knew the man and his work to be excruciatingly untimely. What would have been his reaction had he lived to see a book compiled in his honour? A book which, not incidentally, rates his severest accomplishments against those of Robert Bresson, and which attempts to traverse the full stretch of his riotous and rigorous life – from the Liverpool reminiscences of his sister Norma McMinn, through the unruly escapades at the BBC which begat the legend of 'Clarkey', to his final sojourns in Los Angeles and Cuba, working on a cruelly curtailed feature project, *Assassination on Embassy Row*. In truth, one imagines Clarke's response would have been a bit of Trevor-speak – something of the sort considered 'unprintable', albeit very much at home between these covers. This, after all, was a man with a rudely healthy dose of the demotic about him. But Clarke was also a man with a 'sound ego', uncommonly serious about how he went about his work, and what that work was for. At least, one imagines, nothing of the testimonies gathered herein would have greatly surprised him, because they are the words of many of the people who knew him best. And if Alan Clarke was finally an intensely private man, among his many strengths of character was an enviable honesty and directness in his dealings with those who came closest to him.

Critical consideration of Clarke was on the sparse side throughout his life (though W. Stephen Gilbert was clearly one critic deft enough to discern the gathering force of his work). A few years ago, Paul Schrader mused aloud that perhaps the future of film scholarship, for those so luckless as to retain an interest, would reside in the study of TV movies, and the identification and taxonomy of 'TV auteurs'. Clearly Schrader was imagining a gang of small-screen Sam Fullers and Budd Boettichers, somewhere at large within the police procedural series and Disease-of-the-Week weepies which constitute American television drama. In Britain there is, of course, a rightly more robust sense of what is the Great Tradition on telly – broadly, it began with Loach and Garnett, it may be identified with the rubric of *Play for Today*, and it had what seemed to be its last savage throw in the later works of Dennis Potter. Its concerns were marginal, working-class, and left-wing. Its achievement may be measured quite precisely by the cavils of many in the trade who considered that the stuff was, for all its irritating brilliance, simply not sufficiently cinematic, not enough like *Mean Streets* or *Apocalypse Now*, to merit very detailed writings.

But the torch has been carried for Clarke. Corin Campbell Hill, production manager on his late films, later a director in her own right, made a documentary tribute for the BBC in 1991, and accompanied a touring retrospective to the United States. The background to this publication is a more extensive retrospective of Clarke's films, planned for the Edinburgh Film Festival in August 1998. And let's not forget the many rowdy friends made by Carlin, Trevor, and Bexy. It would be a grave misreading of Clarke, however, if his reputation were to endure only on the strength of those ferocious films, formidable as they are. Much else in his sprawling body of work is as abstruse and pensive, still and soulful, as moving images get.

So, is Alan Clarke the Robert Bresson of British television? The conceit is floated partly for mischief, because it is not actually possible to imagine two more dissimilar characters plying their trade with the same set of tools. Bresson's personal mythology, such as it is, describes a man who worked at agonized intervals, who hid behind chairs rather than submit himself to photographers, and whose name conjures the critical byword for box-office poison – 'austerity'. Buttressing that legend is his published collection of horse sense, *Notes on the Cinematographer*, the more elliptical lines of which might usefully be applied to the films of – well, just about anybody. What of the Alan Clarke legend? Rarely did he fail to manage two films a year, and yet what he had to say about his own work survives mainly in recordings of baffled appearances on BBC 'talkback' editions, where he gazes patiently into studio lights and tries to explain to testy callers why he makes films about such unattractive people. Clarke's personality? This was a man with an astounding libido and an equally prodigious thirst, who loved a laugh and squared up unstintingly to petty officialdom by taking off all of his clothes. 'Uninhibited' is the word, I think. And whilst Clarke was certainly a cinephile in his own unshowy way, there is no explicit homage to cinema in his work, certainly not after the late sixties.

And yet, and yet. It is very clear that for all his gregariousness, Clarke drew his reserves for work from a core quite solitary, almost disturbingly so in later years. Bresson was fond of identifying with Racine's reproach to his more thoughtless critics: 'They think this simplicity is a sign of meagre invention.' Of course it was nothing of the sort. And several of Clarke's late pieces are just as spare and taxing. *Contact* we have already considered. *Elephant* (1988) and *Christine* (1986) are films built on repetitions and minor variations – 'several takes of the same thing', as Bresson counselled, 'like a painter who does several pictures or drawings of the same subject, and each fresh time progresses towards rightness'. Their acute concern is with intensifying everyday life – where that everyday happens to be sectarian shootings in Belfast, or the perambulations around a housing estate of a teenage girl with a plastic bag full of drugs. In both cases, the repetitions create a sense of disparity, between the banality of the visual surface and the submerged bulk of its awful implications. Film-making of this order forces self-scrutiny upon the viewer; it demands closer attention than the most convoluted thriller plot. Such a method – winnowing away at most of the things that people like about movies – always sounds a bit inhuman on paper. And there's no point in denying that some people will find this kind of stuff powerfully boring, a waste of space.

But as with Bresson, Clarke's love of life and of people is at its most evident when his means are most sparse. Vicky Murdock as *Christine* – taciturn, her demeanour downcast in the patented manner of the Bressonian heroine – is among the most loveable of Clarke's screen ensemble. Her twin star in Clarke's work is Janine Duvitski as *Diane* (1975), another naturalistic and massively endearing performance assisted by an uncommonly overt and entirely Bressonian piece of direction from Clarke. He instructed her (albeit by way of a small deception) to lower her eyes and intone her lines at the moment of a dreadful emotional admission. The effect is intensely saddening, and points up a truth in Bresson's expressed consideration of his own 'models': 'What they lose in apparent prominence during the shooting, they gain in depth and in truth on the screen. It is the flattest and dullest parts that in the end have the most life.' Here, we are some distance from Trevor's principled pissings, his crunching kicks and four-lettered assaults on authority. But this too, it seems to me, is very Clarkey.

The title of this introduction is borrowed from Tim Roth's characterization of the actor-centred impetus behind those long, propulsive Steadicam sequences which became Clarke's signature: 'This is your man. Go with him.' It's also a way of underscoring the claims made in these pages for the relative stature of Clarke's work – if you're looking for a worthy exemplar of British film-making, you can stop here. Finally, it's a way of offering up the book to the individuals whose words comprise it. I never met Alan Clarke, I only grew up as an avid fan of his work. But this volume is respectfully presented in the sincere hope that its portrait of an artist is faithful at least in spirit.

Richard Kelly, March 1998

1

The man from Everton: Early years and roamings (1935–1962)

NORMA MCMINN: The family? Well, our mother was born in Liverpool in 1911. She had lost both her parents when she was very small, just a baby really. Her mother Annie O'Neill died suddenly in 1912 and her father was so upset he volunteered straightaway for the war in 1914. So she and her brother were looked after by an old aunt while their dad was away fighting. He went right through the war and he was due to come home when a sniper got him, on Armistice Day. Mum's name was Annie Bailey, but she got the name Cissy off her brother; he called her 'Sis', so everyone else did. Jack Clarke was our father, he was born in Seacombe in 1913. He was an insurance salesman when he and Mum met. There was a bit of a problem because Mum was Protestant but Dad was Catholic. He never went to mass or anything, but his family were staunch Catholics, especially his mum, Grandma Clarke. There's a lot of Irish in the family; Grandma Clarke's family came over after the potato famine. In fact, they wanted Mum to raise me and Alan as Catholics, but she wouldn't. And my dad just fell in line with her; he went, 'OK, then.' The Clarkes weren't very happy, but there was nothing they could do, so they all seemed to stay friends.

Alan was born on 28 October 1935 at 24 Edgmond Street, Seacombe, Wallasey. I was born on 4 July 1938, so Alan was three years older than me. Just after that, the war started. Dad got based in the Isle of Man and we moved there and stayed for a year or so. When we got back, about 1941, our house in Edgmond Street was uninhabitable really – bombs had blasted it to bits. So we moved to Gorsdale Road not far away; that was a bit more posh, all semi-detached. After Dad was called up, Mum was always at work – it was usual in those days. She was a customs officer based in Castle Street, inspecting all the parcels that came into Liverpool. After that she worked issuing the ration books. So Alan always had to

Alan Clarke and his sister Norma

look after me, and we spent most of our school holidays together. Dad would send us postcards and birthday cards from wherever he was: France, Italy, a lot from Belgium around 1944. But when he came home he wasn't well, he'd had a bad chest all through the war. And he'd seen some terrible things. He'd talk about a landing where a lot of his friends had been killed. He always remembered them lying dead on the ground around him. So he needed some time to adjust. But he managed to get to work again eventually as a plasterer.

When he was about ten, Alan joined the Pathfinders Boys Club in Seacombe. It was like an army cadets thing. He played in their football team, he was excellent. I remember my dad and Alan trying to repair the lace-up leather ball when it burst – always quite a traumatic scene, that. Alan's boots had the screw-in studs that kept going missing, and he would go mad. We were all a bit football-oriented; my dad was a keen supporter – it might have been Accrington Stanley back then. But Everton became Alan's team, and that never changed. I was in the junior school when Alan was taking his eleven-plus in 1946–47. And he passed his scholarship and went to Wallasey Grammar School in 1947–48. It was a big thing then, he was a clever lad. And he got on excellent, won a school prize for Latin. The book he picked was *The Kon Tiki Expedition* by Thor Heyerdahl, he was really into that. He had his favourites too: *The Saint*, *The Thirty-Nine Steps*, and *Dick Barton Special Agent* on the wireless.

About 1949 we moved to 27 Castleway North, Leasowe. It was pretty bleak, very isolated, not much there: about two shops, one bus stop, one bus. We moved into one of the first corporation houses they'd put up, and most of the neighbours were people who were working on the building sites. In about five years it was a big estate. Then Cadburys built a factory around 1955 and they became the big employer.

Me and Alan weren't very friendly when he got into his teens, we just used to ignore each other. He was a bit of a rebel, y'know – thought he was dead hard. He got into weight-lifting a lot, him and his mates. They bought a set of weights, put them up in the shed in our back garden, and they'd get together and do the whole muscleman routine – showing off, as lads do. They used to go to the Tower Ballroom in New Brighton for their Saturday nights, it was quite a ride away. He was an excellent dancer, Alan, he went for lessons, passed all his exams – fox-trot, tango, quickstep, waltz, samba. I started going to the Tower myself when I was about fifteen and he was eighteen. We'd see each other there but we never spoke. He'd look through me, just carry on dancing with his girl. Later on I'd see them smooching. Last bus would be eleven o'clock, right after the ballroom shut. By the time he came home I'd usually be in bed trying to get to sleep, but he'd go into the bathroom and start singing – if he'd had a happy night.

At grammar school he passed the right exams and he stayed on until 1953, when he was 18. Then he got called up for his National Service. But he enjoyed it, spent some time in Hong Kong. He'd come home on leave and joke with my mum that she probably had lots of grandchildren out there. He'd say, 'Ah, if these here army boots of mine could say where they've been, Mum, you'd never let me in the house again.' He surprised me too, because he had some excellent presents – he got me a manicure set. I was a bit of a tomboy, into horse riding and all that. I suppose he was trying to tell me something.

DAVID YALLOP: When we got to know each other later, Alan and I would compare our earlier lives, which were in many ways similar. He was very funny about his National Service, I used to get him going on that stuff. He was stationed in Hong Kong, the Great Fear of that moment in the 1950s being the prospect of the Chinese hordes invading.

Alan would talk about a Maltese guy, who'd been pro-British all his life, and now he'd joined the British army. I think they'd given Clarkey a stripe, so he was a lance-corporal, and this guy somehow came under his charge. And he was told: 'You have to look after this man, he's your responsibility in everything he does' – because in everything he did, this man was a walking disaster. At one point Alan went off to the fleshpots of Hong Kong for a thirty-six-hour R & R and left this fellow in charge of a tank. When he came back, the lads said, 'Oi, Nobby' – that was what they called him, Nobby

Clarke – 'Have you seen what he's done, your boy? Go have a look at your tank.' He went outside, and this fella had parked the tank right in the middle of the parade ground. And he was standing to attention beside it, very proud of himself, because he knew Alan was coming. He had painted the entire fucking tank pink. He said he 'thought it would look pretty'.

NORMA MCMINN: Alan came home in 1955 and got a job at the State Assurance in Dale Street, Liverpool. But he wasn't very keen on it, getting the bus from Leasowe to the ferry to the office and back. And the nine-to-five, the mundane routine, all that. He had his twenty-first birthday in the house at Leasowe, 1956. That was a good one. The lads got all the crates of beer in, and we found Alan the next day sleeping in the bath. Some of his mates were in the greenhouse. He did a funny little drawing of himself as he was that morning – sort of buried under these crates of beer, all you could see was his fist in the air with a bottle in it. I still have the picture. And on the back of it he had written a little reading list for himself, philosophy books mostly, Kant and Hegel.

In 1956 Alan suddenly told us he wanted to make arrangements to emigrate to Canada. Dad wasn't very happy about it. He said, 'Why? You've got a job. You're going to leave your mum on her own.' He never discussed his reasons for going with me. But he'd saved the money up, and he wanted more than what was on offer in Liverpool. And for Mum, anything Alan did was all right by her. Not that she liked him going, but he was his mummy's boy, he couldn't do wrong. In the middle of all this, December 1956, our Dad died. And I suppose Alan felt a bit bad, he hadn't really got his dad's blessing to go. But sure enough, early 1957 he was off, with three mates. Mum went to the docks to see Alan off, very upset. I didn't go, I was at work and couldn't get time off. And he'd have thought it was a bit strange to see me waving him away. He'd have probably said, 'Oh, so you're glad to get rid of me?' Though at least that way we might have spoken to each other – maybe I should have gone. But when I got home I had to console our mum, she was very upset. 'Alan's gone!' she kept saying. 'He's gone!'

ROY MINTON: Al always said that, on the day they left, the boat was barely ten minutes out of the Mersey docks and they'd all got Canadian accents. And, of course, they already had their big lumberjack jackets on and all that.

NORMA MCMINN: We didn't hear from him – not a word. But Mum and I were both working, and I was seeing my soon-to-be-husband John McMinn. 1958 came and went. So did 1959. Still no word. We weren't on the phone, of course. 'Oh, he'll write soon,' Mum used to say. But she was worried, obviously. She asked the mothers of the other lads, and they'd written. So she got an address and wrote to Alan, gave him the news and that. In 1959 I married John. A telegram showed up from Alan, to me and John: 'Love to you both, sorry I can't be there but I'm there in spirit.' Then Alan wrote to Mum and asked for his birth certificate. He'd met a young French-Canadian girl and was going to marry her, but she wanted him to convert to Catholicism – which he did, it wasn't a problem because he wasn't religious. But that only lasted about six months. What we found out later was that Alan had been working in a gold mine and he'd injured himself, and a nurse in the hospital where he was treated told him about a college he might like. He said it changed the course of his life.

JANE HARRIS: I never know how much Alan embroidered on this, or how much was just lost in recollection. But the way he always told the story, he and his friends from Liverpool had planned to make their fortune as lumberjacks, but he fell in with a gold-mining company instead. He was up near Wawa in north Ontario, close to Lake Superior. Then he damaged his hand and was hospitalized, they had to do a graft on his thumb. And it was while he was in hospital that he heard about the Ryerson Institute of Technology in Toronto. He found out they were doing a course in Radio and Television Arts. I don't know if there was anything else quite like it then, certainly not in Canada. So he just decided to apply and he got in. It was a three-year course, he was there from 1958 to 1961. And that's where he and I met.

I just loved theatre and television. I had been too self-conscious to get on in acting, but I thought this production course sounded good. Ryerson had its own radio station and they broadcast on FM every day. And this course was big enough that they ran two parallel classes: there were forty, forty-five people in all. In the second year, 1959–60, Alan and I were in the same class. I'd noticed him already – you would see people in the corridors – and his English accent stood out a lot. He was slightly older than a lot of us, nearly six years older than me – I'd gone up straight from high school like most of the students. So it was probably a bit tricky for Alan to get into the routine of writing essays and so on, as well as trying to earn money and find digs. He had nearly flunked his first year.

And sometimes they couldn't cope with Alan. He didn't see the necessity for all the rules and regulations, particularly anything relating to dress, which didn't concern him at all. At Ryerson the guys had to wear ties, one of those silly collegiate rules. You could wear a crew-neck sweater, and if you had a shirt on it wasn't necessarily clear whether or not you were wearing a tie. But the tutors had a habit of tugging at the neck of these sweaters to see if the tie was there. That happened once with Alan: 'Where's your tie, Clarke?' He said, 'S'all right, sir, I've got it here.' He lifted up his sweater and the tie was knotted round his waist, holding up his pants instead of a belt. Lateral thinking, I suppose. Alan played soccer for Ryerson, but he could only ever play forty-five minutes, then he'd be worn out by it. So the manager always had this tricky tactical choice of whether to play him from the start or save him for the second half. Physically he was sort of – weedy really, in those days. We had the usual university drama productions, and Alan was in some of those; he was a very good actor. Now Alan had to earn money while he was studying – he had taken a loan, but he was supposed to pay it back. And we had very long holidays, from June through August and part of September. So in 1959 he went to Buffalo to do summer stock. It was a Melody Fair, quite popular then; they had various musical productions running in a tent. We have a picture of him in costume, dressed as a genie, arms folded, trying to make his biceps look bigger by pushing them up from the underside.

Clarke soaks up some rays in Toronto, 1959

Clarke in 'genie' costume during a stint in summer stock in Buffalo, 1959

ROY MINTON: Al said Buffalo was when he knew acting wasn't for him. He was a great bunny, you know – great raconteur, lot of fun to be with. But getting on stage and doing it was something else, and he realized that wasn't his game.

JANE HARRIS: In his last year at Ryerson, Alan produced *Huis Clos*, or *No Exit*, by Sartre, his first real directorial effort. Sartre and Camus were very big at the time; Alan was very fond of *L'Etranger*. The male lead was a guy called Robin Brewer, a very good actor. And *No Exit* was very sharp, a good show. Alan ended up taking it to Western University for one of those college drama competitions. We had high hopes for winning, but it was pipped. There was only one judge, an actor, and he criticized Alan's handling of the love scene in the play, rather weirdly on the grounds that the actors' feet didn't move. But the piece had a stillness to it; Alan didn't move people unless he had to. He hated that unnatural proscenium stage set-up with people sitting round a table but facing out and speaking to the audience. In *No Exit* he sometimes had the actors sitting quite naturally sideways on, backs to the audience, and as long as they could be heard, he thought that was fine. That's why he worked so well in the round later on – he could move people around more naturally.

In the last year at Ryerson, Alan and I became a couple. We'd go to the cinema all the time, there was one movie house in Toronto which showed the good European films of the period. Truffaut's *Les Quatre Cent Coups* came out, we were both stunned by that. *Jules et Jim* Alan liked as well. I remember us seeing *Last Year at Marienbad*, and Alan was completely taken with those long, elegant dolly shots through the hotel. The very first thing he said when he came out was, 'God, that tracking shot was really something.' I think everything that he saw and enjoyed, he logged it away inside himself. Kurosawa was another one he thought was brilliant, because of his grittiness. He loved *Ikiru* and *The Seven Samurai*, especially the great battle in the rain. His other big favourite was Antonioni, he'd see them all: *La Notte*, *L'Avventura* he thought was a stunner – partly because of Monica Vitti, I'm sure. But he loved Antonioni's kind of slow deliberate pacing and the strange relationships in the piece. And the use of space, that sense of people rather wandering through the film. But also the stunning close-ups, he liked those. And I suppose Antonioni didn't make any great effort to endear the characters to a general audience, and that was impressive to Alan. Cassavetes was another favourite – Alan liked the raw, improvised acting.

He graduated from Ryerson in 1961 with a prize as one of their top creative students – quite an achievement, having nearly flunked out in the first year. Robin Brewer ended up coming to England with Alan at the end of the course in June. Then they had one of the quickest tours of Europe ever during that summer, Alan on the back of Robin's motorbike. And they ended up in London. I followed him over in August 1961. We were in Liverpool for that Christmas.

NORMA MCMINN: In the winter of 1961 John and I were living with Mum and I was expecting my first child. There was a knock at the door one night and there was Alan. Mum just went 'Ahhh!' He had a big case and he said, 'Can I come in?' Mum was concerned about the way he looked – he was a bit of a sight, beard and all that. And he was apologizing profusely because he had odd socks on. Then he said, 'Can she come in too?' And behind him was Jane – a very tall, very attractive Canadian girl. So that was it, he was back, and we mucked in together for a bit. I went into hospital November 1961 and had my daughter Gillian. Visiting hours were very strict, but Alan came down and put on a Canadian accent, said, 'I've come to see my sister, and I've got to get the plane back to Canada tomorrow.' Then he and my husband John went out on a big binge to wet the baby's head. That was about the time when Alan and I got closer, we started speaking as if we'd never not spoken. We'd both grown up, I suppose: I was twenty-three and he was twenty-six, it was like we were two different people. He seemed more relaxed, more together. It was a very bad winter, that one, and Jane and Alan stayed with us until early 1962, then they went down to London. And he started it all over again. He was never in touch with us.

2

Bare boards and a passion: Life in the theatre (1962–1966)

JANE HARRIS: We lived in Earl's Court then. Alan was looking for work, money had run out and he was desperate to earn some. For a while he and Robin cleaned the Eros Cinema in Piccadilly Circus. I got an office job, writing promos for Wales and West Television in Knightsbridge. And eventually Alan got his first work in television on the floor at ATV.

PAUL KNIGHT: I was working as a call boy at ATV around 1962, doing overture and beginners stuff. Alan had just come over from Canada and he was an assistant floor manager, a wonderful one at that, very calm, very efficient, very smart. We worked together on a series called *All That Jazz* and we became quite pally. I remember him as very dapper then: he wore button-down shirts, quite trendy and neat, and he seemed rather North American. I point this out because when I next met him, at Associated Rediffusion five years later, I didn't recognize him. He'd become very scruffy in the nicest possible way – big tough boots, fourteen layers of jumpers. And he suddenly seemed to be a very broad Scouser. So he'd become the Alan Clarke that everybody now remembers.

JANE HARRIS: Around 1962 Alan started directing studio productions at the Questors Theatre in Ealing. It was a very good amateur theatre, well-regarded, just a touch away from being professional. When he first applied, he was given a show to do as a sort of test, to see if he really could direct. It was Beckett's *Krapp's Last Tape*. Peter Whelan played the lead, in the days before he became a playwright. Then he was asked to do Jean Anouilh's *Traveller Without Luggage*, rather obscure – not one he'd have chosen. But he went on to do O'Neill's *Long Day's Journey Into Night* – he was very fond of that play.

The studio at the Questors was solid brick, no windows, and Alan really liked working there because he could choose whether to do it in the round or as proscenium – it was just a long rectangular room and you set your own seating. And he liked the starkness of the place; he was never very fussed about sets. It used to irritate him when he'd go to the theatre and people would say, 'Oh well, the sets were very lovely.' He'd go, 'The sets? What have the fucking sets got to do with anything?' The Beckett and the O'Neill had little in the way of sets – just props, a bit of furniture and costume really. I would go along and be the assistant stage manager. Alan was always very good with actors. He would never demonstrate how he wanted something done, even though he was quite a good actor himself. He'd just talk with them about the character and the situation, and he'd ask them to find out how to do it for themselves. I remember an actress once asking him to tell her exactly how he wanted her to do something, and he got rather annoyed. In the end he said, in his usual charming way, 'How the fuck do I know? I'm only the director.' But he did an awful lot of background work on the script, huge amounts, so he knew what he wanted.

Robin Brewer was in London with his girlfriend Mary, and the four of us used to do a lot together. It was just a succession of rooms – Mary and I had a room, then Alan and I. I went off to Greece for a bit, Alan was in Europe for a bit. But he went up north after Europe. John Arden and his wife Margaretta d'Arcy lived up in Kirkby Moorside in Yorkshire, and one summer they just invited a bunch of people who they thought might be interested in making little films and pieces of work. Alan went up with a couple of guys for about six weeks. I was in Earl's Court, heavily pregnant.

SUSANNA CAPON: It was July/August 1963. I had just left school, I was nineteen, and I answered an ad in *Encore* which John Arden and Margaretta d'Arcy had placed. They were running an arts festival in their house, and it turned into a rather extraordinary, anarchic event. Fire-eaters turned up. I remember John Arden did *Krapp's Last Tape* in his living room. I got on the train to York, arrived late at night, and I was met off the train by this scruffy, wild-looking man, who said he'd come to fetch me. I asked him what he was doing, expecting him to say he was 'just the driver' or something. And he said, 'I'm a film director.' It was a long journey from York, and during that hour's conversation I found him to be this extraordinary man. He'd just come out of a Canadian college and he had this huge self-conviction. And his story was kind of true – he was making a film there, about the event itself, though I'm not sure it was ever finished. But we became friends, and later I would visit him and Jane in Earl's Court while I was at university in London.

JANE HARRIS: Alan came back from Yorkshire and we took yet another room in Earl's Court. Then our son Gabriel was born and we needed somewhere bigger.

ROY MINTON: Al was fanatical for Everton, of course, so he called his lad after Jimmy Gabriel the Everton centre-half. Not long after that, Gabriel was sold to Southampton, the git. But it's nice that his son ended up going into football reporting. It was always around when he was growing up, for sure.

JANE HARRIS: So around 1964 we moved to Ranelagh Road in Ealing. By this time Alan had moved over from ATV to Associated Rediffusion, still as an assistant floor manager. So it was an incredibly hectic time for him.

SUSANNA CAPON: I think the move to Ealing enabled Alan to get more closely involved with the Questors, which was such an important stage in his development. But at the same time I got the feeling he was having a tough time getting ahead in what he really wanted to do, which was television.

CHRISTOPHER MORAHAN: They were exciting, vivid times to be in television. I was at ITV then for the same reason as Alan, I expect. It was like the Wild West, a gold rush moment; if you showed any kind of nerve you could get ahead. I had been at the BBC for three or four months, but they paid me so badly I had to leave. So I started as Assistant Floor Manager at ATV, and I made the leap to directing fairly quickly – because they were looking around and asking, 'Can you direct? Or you?' I wasn't trained, I don't know if Alan was. So of course there were many charlatans about. We all swam – one or two sank.

DAVID YALLOP: I met Alan at Rediffusion round about 1963, where I was an assistant floor manager. Alan was in the same job and one got to know him over a period of time. I was very struck with his wit, that was the first thing – his lovely turns of phrase. And his life style quite appealed to me. The procedure was for AFMs to put out a series of three calls: 'Artists and staff in five minutes', 'General call for artists and staff' and then an 'Artists and staff, immediately' – as in 'We're not fucking around, get here *now*.' Now that's part of the AFM's job, and of course it does help if you're actually in the building to do it. Alan frequently wasn't and so would be calling up from Neasden or wherever else he'd spent the night, asking, 'Would you put out a five-minute call for me?' while he himself was probably a quarter of an hour away from the studio.

GRENVILLE MIDDLETON: I was a trainee cameraman at Rediffusion when Alan joined as an AFM, and in that same bunch was old Dave Yallop. As a professional at his job, on the floor, Al was very good at communicating with the director through his cans, and relaying it to the actors in front of the camera – really excellent at that. So you felt great relief if he was scheduled on the same show as you.

I wanted to get to know Alan much more; if you're drawn to someone you try and associate yourself with them. And at Rediffusion, if you were after something alternative or exciting then you'd hang out with Clarke and Yallop and that crowd – if they would let you in. The condition of entry was that you had to be able to perform. Your behaviour on the first night out with them was important: you had to get pissed, act ridiculous, and generally just keep the wit and the fun going around the whole group. You couldn't just be a heavy dude in the corner, you'd soon get the elbow. But Alan always gave everyone a chance to shine. He was such a character. At the same time, it was obvious that he knew so much about drama.

JANE HARRIS: Once a year the Questors would very deliberately put

'A professional at his job, on the floor': Clarke as an AFM at Associated Rediffusion

on a festival of new plays, and Alan did a double bill of these in 1964, *No Quarter* by Barry Blancmange and *Neighbours* by James Sanders. Questors arranged for Alan to take them over to the Berliner Ensemble – and they were quite successful.

SUSANNA CAPON: He was very into Brecht. And I'd spent some of my teenage years in Berlin and had a big connection with the Berliner Ensemble, so I'd often go back there. On one of these visits I bumped into Alan – he was at the box office, having a huge argument. In East Berlin they didn't speak English and he hardly spoke German. I asked him what he was doing and he said, 'I've come all this way and they won't sell me a ticket.' I thought perhaps I could intercede and I asked him what he was trying to see. He pointed at the sign: KEINE VORSTELLUNG – meaning 'No Performance'. He said, 'Yeah, I wanna see that. Don't tell me I can't.' I told him his mistake but, being Alan, he just went on and on.

JANE HARRIS: He did Derek Marlowe's *How I Assumed the Role of the Popular Dandy* at the Questors in June 1965. I have a quote from *The Stage and Television Today*: 'Alan Clarke's direction on an apron stage is conceived and carried out with a beautiful tautness.' And a guy wrote, in one of the Sundays I think: 'Certain merits survive, but only two are provided by the playwright and both owe something to Alan Clarke's vivid production.' One was a bit where the guards are ranged along the lighting gangway shouting, and the second was a dinner where the guests are all horribly-masked ghouls. Alan was always fairly intrigued by masks. In the same period he had done *The Maids*. He always liked the strangeness of Genet.

SUSANNA CAPON: His staging of Genet's *The Maids* was fantastic, full of ideas. I think it was that production which was seen by David Jones, who then invited Alan to work at the Royal Shakespeare Company.

DAVID JONES: Alan came to my attention; I knew he was at Rediffusion but that he was interested in the RSC. I went out to see this production of *The Maids*, and it was astonishing. Alan had an all-male cast – as, of course, Genet had always rather hoped it would be done, and instead had been bored to tears by seeing a stream of rather hysterical ladies in the roles. But it made such complete sense with the men, it was disturbing and very funny, it was very down and dirty. Shortly after that I saw the Derek Marlowe play, and this was a much more epic piece of theatre. It had a flavour of late 1920s Futurism about it. I was just really startled by the inventiveness and the use of space, the way he brought in the lighting catwalk. But there was nothing earnest or pretentious about Alan or his work, it had an extraordinary gutsy liveliness about it.

From around 1966 through to the mid-1970s I was in charge of finding the assistant directors for the RSC both in Stratford and London; I would shortlist and select interviewees for an annual board. So obviously Alan came very strongly recommended that year, and I think it was literally at the point where we sat to compose the letter of invitation to join the RSC when he got his leg up at Associated Rediffusion. I was heartbroken in a sense, but I think it was absolutely the right way for him to go. Alan was definitely meant to work with cameras and that level of reality as his way of getting to the truth of the universe. He had an extraordinary ability with actors and a very interestingly subversive attitude to the classics, but I don't necessarily think he would have been very happy for long in the RSC. I've a feeling he would have started to break the furniture at a certain stage.

SUSANNA CAPON: Alan was working in this rather lowly capacity at Rediffusion, but they had given him a certain amount of leave to work at the RSC. I think they then effectively promised that if he came back to them full-time, they would promote him on to the director's training course. So he went back – and they reneged. But his burning desire was to be a television director, so he carried on. It was the kind of situation that would have reduced many people to despair, but Alan didn't seem to care, he just maintained that he would get there somehow.

JANE HARRIS: People didn't always appreciate him at first glance, because he didn't fit the uniform in a way. He wasn't a company man. Early on he could have done what some directors did and come in via commercials. But he couldn't bear all the crap that went with it. You just can't imagine Alan looking at a packet of fish fingers and saying, 'This is how I see it.' Or going to the cocktail parties, as you had to do. He'd much rather go to the pub with the crew.

DAVID YALLOP: He was one of the scruffiest bastards you've ever seen – I mean, he was known as 'Scruff' to many people. When he was still an AFM, he went to be interviewed by Peter Hall for a job. We were working on outside broadcast at the Wimbledon tennis championships; Clarkey came to ask me if I'd cover for him while he was away and I said, 'That's no trouble.' Now he was wearing an army greatcoat and a blue beret, two days' growth on his cheeks. The director of that OB came out of the box while I was talking to Alan and said, 'Look, David, I don't mind you chatting up tramps and derelicts in your own time, but will you get *him* off of the site?' And this was how he looked before going to see Peter Hall. Later on, I asked him how he'd got on and he said, 'Well, I

The young theatre director at work

obviously had the wrong address. I went to Chelsea, knocked on this door, stood and waited – no answer. So I kept knocking, and after twenty minutes I thought "Fuck this" and I went home.' Now I think part of him was playing a game there with the situation. Part of him didn't want the interview. He had a chance there to become a theatre director, but he didn't. Instead he became a trainee TV director, and then a full-blooded director.

JANE HARRIS: Our daughter Molly was born at home in 1966. It was a Sunday, the day after Everton had won the cup, so Alan took Gabriel, who was three and a half then, to watch the replay of the match on television. They came home and Gabe's baby sister was there.

3

'Stella's Boys': The making of a television director (1967–1969)

DAVID YALLOP: Rediffusion ran a system at that time whereby once a year they would 'board' for a couple of directorial jobs. And we all felt that if there was any justice in this world Alan would get one of these; it was a measure, I think, of the enormous affection and respect in which he was held. Now we're entering the period with Stella Richman and the *Half Hour Story* – Stella called us 'her boys.' Clarkey was one, I became one when I took up writing full-time. Roy Minton was one of her boys, so was Paul Knight.

STELLA RICHMAN: I was appointed Head of Scripted Series at Rediffusion, and I had all these prima donna writers on hand like Edna O'Brien and Doris Lessing. I needed an assistant and within Rediffusion there was nobody. Paul Knight had started at ATV in the post room, he'd been an AFM on a series I produced there called *Love Story*. So I called him and said, 'Listen, I think I could get you in here as my Associate Producer.'

PAUL KNIGHT: That was my Big Break. Stella was a power in the land then, she was the most dynamic person working in television. She was very much a writer's producer, knew a lot of them through her past work as a story editor, and she could get scripts out of established writers. Then she matched these with new directors, and the most important new director she was keen to use was Alan Clarke.

STELLA RICHMAN: As soon as I got this job, I started being lobbied by a lot of the studio people. One after the other the Head of Lighting, Head of Cameras, would come to me and say, 'What are you going to do about Alan Clarke?' And my response was, 'Who's

Alan Clarke?' It transpired that he was a floor manager with tremendous talent. A lot of the chaps had been out to see his productions at the Questors.

So I asked to see Alan and in came this lovely, scruffy chap in a sweater down to his knees with great holes. And he said, 'I'm doing a little production at the Questors at the moment, would you come and see it?' I said, 'Yes, what is it?' He said, '*Macbeth*.' I thought, 'Oh Christ.' But I said 'OK' and I went.

JANE HARRIS: He did *Macbeth* on the proscenium stage; there were three high flats, like columns, at the back. And the lighting was powerful because it cast deep shadows. I remember the Lady Macbeth Alan cast; he deliberated over it for a while because physically she wasn't the sinewy type who's usually in that role. But she had a wonderful voice. One guy at the Questors was very distrustful of Alan, called it a very left-wing production. Alan was never overtly political, certainly he had more left-wing views than right-wing ones – part of that was his background. But I think he just saw the play as being about the continual overthrow of the Man At The Top by someone who becomes a tyrant in his place.

STUART GRIFFITHS: I remember Alan describing aspects of that *Macbeth* to me many years later. As he had staged it, after the murder of Duncan, Macbeth reels out of the chamber and he is so convulsed and sickened by what he has done that he is, in fact, physically sick – somehow they worked this effect. And it's entirely right in the context of the scene – one can't imagine a more visceral rendering of Macbeth's immediate remorse.

STELLA RICHMAN: It was stunning – I mean, I've seen a lot of *Macbeths* in my time and a lot of Shakespeare generally. Clearly Alan had wanted to do something different, and it was stark and thrilling; I was glued to my seat. But then the heads of departments at Rediffusion told me, 'Look, he'll never get through a selection board. He's been up for two and turned down both times.' The trainee directors of that time had almost all come from university, and that was what the blockage was. If you were going to get on and be officer class, you had to have a 'good accent'. Which Alan clearly did not.

PAUL KNIGHT: There was a strong element of the old school tie at Rediffusion, it seemed to be run by the navy: Captain Brownlow was the managing director, Commander Everett was another highly-placed chap. But I was under Stella's protection, and she cut through them like a knife through butter. And Cyril Bennett was the Controller of Programmes in those days, a young one at that. He would have encouraged Stella.

STELLA RICHMAN: So what we did was we fixed it. All the heads at the studio and I jointly signed a recommendation to the board – we said, 'We have amongst our number a most brilliant potential director.' I pointed out that I'd seen *Macbeth*; I also claimed to have seen a lot of his other productions, which I hadn't. But we all felt that if we hadn't called attention to his outstanding talent this way, he never would have got past the shortlist. And I mean, by then there would have been a studio revolt if he hadn't.

JANE HARRIS: The first things he did at Rediffusion were the Epilogues – he did those for six or seven months. You couldn't go straight into directing plays; you had to serve your time first – like writing the obits on a newspaper. But Alan played around with them; he would say, 'It's just clergymen talking, let's go in really tight,' so he'd have these big nostril shots of various vicars.

STELLA RICHMAN: And then by an act of absolute and wonderful coincidence Cyril Bennett said to me, 'I've got a half-hour to fill, nine o'clock – it's a bugger, I don't know what to do with it.' So I suggested half-hour plays. I said, 'We can get major writers to write them. Everybody's got a good half-hour in them somewhere, even people who've never written for television.' And this was *Half Hour Story*. Alan went straight on to it as a director. And a lot of top management were rather cross about this, but they couldn't interfere with me. They'd say, 'Why not get so-and-so to direct? He's been here twenty years,' and I'd say, 'Well, that's the problem.'

PAUL KNIGHT: The first *Half Hour Story* Alan directed, though it wasn't the first one broadcast, was *A Man Inside* by Pauline Macauley, Donald McWhinnie's wife, with Freddie Jones sitting in an office obsessed by a young girl in a short skirt.

DAVID YALLOP: For this purpose Alan invented the Cunt Shot. This girl was moving about the office in very provocative gear, a mini I suspect – after all, we are talking 1967. And Alan trained his camera from Freddie's point of view, so that as she was walking around you had this tight shot, following her crotch. And I can remember Stella Richman standing behind him and quietly remonstrating, 'I think that's enough cunt for the moment, Alan.' So he went from strength to strength.

STELLA RICHMAN: Then he did *Shelter* by Alun Owen with Wendy Craig and Colin Blakely. Alun Owen was from Wales, the first notable television writer of the commercial wave – he'd made his name on *Armchair Theatre* under Sydney Newman. And he wrote plays about ordinary people. 'Kitchen sink drama' was always an over-simplified term – he wrote plays about you, me, the man next door, the girl passing in the street. And he had really hit on the idea of the two-handed TV play – two people in a crisis moment. It was perfect television. *Shelter* was shot in the Orangery at Holland Park; the scenario was, two people had run in from the rain to sit by themselves, for different reasons. One was running away from a marriage, the other from some emotional crisis. They started talking in the forced way that people do. And then they formed an alliance across a wooden table for half an hour, and then they parted. But each made the other realize that they weren't the only one.

NORMA MCMINN: The first *Half Hour Story* that went out in 1967, *Shelter* – all the family got round and watched it. If Uncle Al's stuff was on telly you had to be there, and you had to stay there until the credits came up – that was big-time stuff. We were proud, he'd done well.

PAUL KNIGHT: There were two remarkable things about *Shelter*: the

Clarke with Wendy Craig, the female lead in his directorial début for television, *Shelter* (1967)

first, that it went to number one in the ratings, extraordinary for a midweek half hour. And the second, that Alan shot it mainly in big close-ups with very fast cutting between them. It had a signature.

GRAHAM BENSON: Paul Knight and I were sharing a flat in Highgate

Clarke confers with Siân Philips on the set of *Thief* (1968)

at the time, so I knew about Alan. I knew he was one of Stella's boys. And I saw *Thief* by Alun Owen, a *Half Hour Story* about a burglar, with Siân Phillips and the late Alan Lake, and I was incredibly impressed – also surprised and excited by the technique, which was the beginning of noticing how different and original Alan was. He'd set up a scene with an establishing shot but thereafter he didn't worry, he just went in tight – because he was interested in people and what they had to say and how they looked up close. It was filmic, it might have been imitated by others but it was Alan's style.

STELLA RICHMAN: I handpicked Alan's writers for him, like William Trevor, who hadn't written for television before. They did *The Fifty-Seventh Saturday* with Ronnie Fraser. Alan directed several more of Alun Owen's – *Stella*, *George's Room*. The two of them hit it off, they shared a few drinking binges. But really you could put

Alan with anybody. He started doing Edna O'Brien's two-handers. She couldn't stop writing these; every time Edna had an incident in her life it became a script, and Alan directed them all. *Nothing's Ever Over* was about her divorce, with Eileen Atkins and Michael Craig, all set in the High Court. Glenda Jackson played Edna in *Which of These Two Ladies is He Married to?* And Edna would always say to me, 'Will Alan do my next play?' He was exactly what she'd have gone for at that time.

We did fifty-two *Half Hours* in all, believe it or not. There was something called a budget, but we weren't made too aware of it. If a writer and a director came to me with a sheet of paper, and I knew that they'd talked it through and put a lot into it, I'd say, 'OK, let's go into rehearsal.' Sometimes you took a fall, of course. But there was so much material going out of this calibre that one error – well, you'd think, 'Oh my God, I wish Monday night was over,' but there was always next Monday.

Around 1967 Alan had formed a friendship with a writer called Roy Minton, and at that time he tried to push Roy into getting himself noticed. They went around together a lot, and he introduced Roy to me. I thought Roy was a brilliant writing talent, but very like the young Tony Garnett – on principle he was going to argue with you. He'd outline his story, and before you could say, 'That's interesting', he'd say, 'Now listen, I know you're not gonna like this.' Alan supported him all through that – to his own detriment a bit.

PAUL KNIGHT: I met Roy Minton through Stella; he submitted a play which Stella left me to work on with Roy and Alan, *The Gentleman Caller*. Roy had a great effect on a suburban lad like myself who was interested in drama; he was sort of a conscience, if you like, because of his background. He was a miner's son and he was hard left in those days. There was this firm anti-Establishment feeling about what he and Clarkey did – they were working-class boys together.

ROY MINTON: We had the same background – working class, him Liverpool and me Nottingham – and we were of the same age, and had kids of similar ages. And we'd both got under the net into grammar school. I actually met Alan because my agent had sent a stage play of mine to the Questors, where Alan was working. But he'd just got his director's ticket at Rediffusion, telly was available and he wanted to get on with that. So I sent a little half-hour script to him, knocking about for a bit of telly, said, 'Is there anything doing?' and he said, 'Yeah, anything you've got.' *The Gentleman Caller* was the first thing we did together. It was a little piece about two layabouts, Mike Pratt and Tony Selby. One was living with a woman in a little flat, had his motorbike in the sitting room, and then he got his brother in on the scene. Then they got a visit from the DHSS man, played by George Cole. That was all it was, just a simple confrontation with authority – we had fun doing it. Then we did *Goodnight Albert* in 1968 – again very simple: Victor Henry as a lad who's down the mines, lives with his gran, and she worries because she wants to see him set up in a factory job.

PAUL KNIGHT: I became involved with them a lot socially. Roy was a big influence on Alan, and I think they egged each other on to excesses. Once, we were at the Globe Tavern in Drury Lane having a drink, and they got into an argument with the barman for some reason. He then asked them to leave – which they did – but Alan and Roy then threw their glasses through the window, shattered it, and a big crowd of people were showered with glass, including a well-known casting director. And the three of us legged it up Drury Lane and managed to get into a taxi and make our escape; we hid at Rediffusion while the heat died down – like naughty little boys.

GRENVILLE MIDDLETON: Alan and Roy would get high and pissed and wind each other up and then, lo and behold, there'd be trouble. There was a play on at the Duke of York in the West End, *Abelard and Heloise*; they got into the theatre one afternoon when no one was there and had a crap in the aisle. It's funny, but some poor bastard had to clean that up. But they were always up to something. They had a pair of World War Two gas masks with long snouts and big glass eyes, and their fun would be to get on the tube wearing these masks and just sit there, freaking out the other passengers. And if they wanted a fag, it would be masks up, take a drag, masks down. Terrible blokes, man.

STELLA RICHMAN: In 1968 I did a series of six plays, called *Company of Five*, to open London Weekend, and Alan directed two of them – *Gareth* by Alun Owen and *Stand by Your Screens* by Roy Minton. Roy's play was based on his own family, and it used the technique of overlapping dialogue. They would argue sometimes, Alan and Roy – good, healthy rows. Roy was an impossible person to help, really, and I think Alan knew as much.

But one of Alan's great talents was that he knew the writer was necessary to him, and so it was up to him to make life accommodating and pleasant for that writer. And Roy was an exception – he was Alan's friend and someone Alan believed in, and had to nurse in some way. Alan would often call in at my house at Goldhurst Terrace, with Roy usually in tow. Roy loved my whole family and he ate with us, as did Alan. We sort of adopted them – certainly we fed them. They were always hungry. They'd come round for supper with the kids, and I'd make huge catering-size dishes of shepherd's pie and rice pudding. And the lot would go, seconds and thirds. Roy, in particular, was starving. Alan had work but Roy didn't – though he may have been starving on principle, and Alan probably allied himself to that out of solidarity. Once they were sitting in our kitchen, comparing their childhoods. Roy said, 'Did you have dancing lessons?' and Alan replied, 'Oh Christ, yes – granny gave me sixpence to go to the bloody ballroom classes.' Turned out they both remembered having pairs of pumps hanging on their kitchen doors. We were in hysterics. Then just to cap it, they both got up and waltzed each other round the kitchen: 'One-two-three, one-two-three, step-step-pause.'

Alan and Roy would go around together in these great long plastic macs that came down to their ankles. Terrible things, they wore them whether it was raining or not, and always buttoned up to the neck – wanking macs, that's all I can call them. I was running the White Elephant restaurant then, so clearly they thought, 'Well, Stella's all right for grub.' But the one time I took them to my restaurant, damn me if they didn't turn up in their wanking macs. I said, 'You'll have to leave those at the door,' and Roy said, 'I can't, I haven't got a shirt on.' 'Oh, for Christ's sake.' So they sat through dinner in their wanking macs, all these smart people around them, and my staff looked at me as if I'd taken leave of my senses.

Of course Alan and Paul Knight must have had many a drinking bout too – and David Yallop, quite a few lost weekends in there, I'd say. And I heard that Alan went through women like the proverbial dose of salts, and that they were all crazy about him. But I was kept away from that side of his life. And I never knew a director who did his homework so unostentatiously and so brilliantly as Alan. So the persona just made us laugh. It's a great pity that television doesn't provide the opportunity for people as talented as Alan to become directors today, other than on film. Having learned production from the floor up he was a master of tape, a master of cameras, he knew it all from years of experience.

JANE HARRIS: When Alan first started directing at Rediffusion, he'd be up very late at night working on his camera plans. Everything was on the studio floor with the big cameras and you had to plot everything so that your cameras and cables weren't crossing over each other. He always did that immaculately, and the cameramen loved it; they always knew exactly what they had to do, whether it was long shot, medium or close-up. He was extremely good at seeing it in his mind, and I know that when we went to the cinema or watched television later on, it wasn't really the play he was watching, it was the shots, studying how they did that. Now technically he was absolutely useless, he couldn't put a light bulb in. But that may be another reason why cameramen liked him. He'd just say, 'Can you do this and that?' and they'd darn well do it because they wanted to.

STELLA RICHMAN: In 1968 at Rediffusion we initiated a series by Julian Bond called *Man of Our Times*, in thirteen parts; it was all about the life of a middle-class manager played by George Cole, and Alan did several episodes. So that's what started him off: *Half Hour Story* followed by *Man of Our Times*, which was the closing show for Rediffusion – end of licence. I suppose that was my claim to fame in his career. I do feel proud that I produced so many of his plays, because it's rare that you're lucky enough to work with such talent. After that start he could go anywhere. And then he was taken on by Judy Scott-Fox.

DAVINA BELLING: It always seemed rather wonderfully incongruous to me, the fact that Alan had Judy Scott-Fox as an agent – Judy was such a grand duchess, the last kind of agent you'd expect to be dealing with Clarkey. But then he was always surrounded by strong women.

STELLA RICHMAN: Judy was at London Management, they had smart offices in Mayfair, and she was very keen on Alan getting ahead. She was great with Alan, they adored each other; she was a very forthright woman, she knew when to say, 'Alan, that won't do.' And naturally his wardrobe became an issue. Sometimes very talented people look around at the men in grey suits and ladies like me in tweeds, and they think, 'I'm not having any of that.' That was Alan. If he ever bought a new sweater, then I'm sure he made holes in it straight away. It was a real case of inverted snobbery, I felt. But he was such a genuine person, it became part of that – you couldn't fault him for it.

Judy Scott-Fox called him up one day and said, 'Alan, it's time you went to the BBC. I can get you a job directing a pair of plays. Come up to the office.' That was wonderful, the logical step for Alan. But he turned up in his usual gear, and Judy said, 'Alan, there's one problem. I can't take you to the BBC dressed like that. You'll have to have some new gear.' Suits were regulation at the BBC then, albeit not of the Armani variety. Alan protested, but Judy proceeded to take his measurements, then she said, 'Stay here!' and she ran out to Marks & Spencer in Marble Arch and spent her own money on trousers, a shirt, a blazer – she even bought underwear. Then she came back, presented all of this to Alan and told him, 'Now go to the gents and put these on. And as for what you're wearing, throw it away.' Alan did so, under duress – and as Judy told me later, 'His underwear was *unspeakable*.' So finally he was togged up in his M&S separates, and he joined the BBC.

4
Kicking down doors at the BBC (1969–1970)

VERITY LAMBERT: It was a fantastic era at the BBC, really hard to talk about without seeming backward-looking. I started there in 1963 while Sydney Newman was Head of Drama. You were encouraged to be innovative, it wasn't quite as important to win the ratings all the time. So the artists were braver and I think the decision-makers were too; they could afford to be. It was a golden age.

MARK SHIVAS: Golden age? Well, it depends on what you consider to be golden. A lot of terrible stuff was done in the 1970s too, bad studio plays; I know, I did some of them myself. The golden age is always the one before last – and I don't remember who said this, but in any golden age there's always somebody sitting around saying, 'Don't you think it's a bit too yellow?'

MIKE LEIGH: The following things are for fact, as far as I understand it, but I'm sure it's entirely accurate. We were all brought up on something called television drama that was done in a studio and which was dead from the neck up. Sydney Newman had the inspired idea when BBC2 started to get young people running drama. Tony Garnett got together with Ken Loach and they had an idea. They said, 'Well, people watch the news on newsreel, and the French are out there with Eclairs on the streets of Paris making these films – why don't we get out there and let people see films made in the same mode as the news or documentaries?' That's what they did, and that gave us *Cathy Come Home* and all the rest of it – that is true.

MICHAEL JACKLEY: BBC drama was still very studio-based, but film was coming in, around the mid-1960s. You'd do these rather clumsy 35 mm inserts – which Clarkey used to say were stupid. Like, 'Why have film of a person getting into a car, driving, getting out and going into a house? What a lot of crap, who wants to see people walking down a road?' Of course he made whole films of that in the end – *Road*, *Christine*. He made an art form out of people doing nothing.

CHRISTOPHER MORAHAN: What Ken and Tony did, I think, they telerecorded in the studio on film so they had raw film stock. And they shot on 16 mm on location because they thought that was the right gauge to mix with the telerecording. And it was done through the back door.

KEN LOACH: The *Wednesday Plays* received a mix of notoriety and the odd good notice, and they became a sort of weekly event. And that was the space Mike Leigh and Alan Clarke and others moved into, which became *Play for Today.*

IRENE SHUBIK: From 1967 Graeme McDonald and I shared the producing – there were fifty-two slots a year which you had to fill, sometimes with something that was less than marvellous. But I think the ratio was pretty good, considering. Of course we more or less had a captive audience, without video or satellite or a fourth or fifth channel. Once I broke my leg and had to go to physiotherapy at Hammersmith Hospital by bus, and I'd hear people talking about the previous night's play. A lot of them were old dears, and even if they thought it was disgusting, they watched it.

I knew Alan Clarke from the corridors of the BBC, and I'd seen some of his work; I liked him and respected him. The first *Wednesday Play* he and I did was *The Last Train through the Harecastle Tunnel* by Peter Terson, in 1969. Terson had written *Zigger Zagger* for the National Youth Theatre; he was from a working-class background, but free of any kind of chip on the shoulder – he was a sort of benevolent satirist. The play was a comedy of manners about a young man, rather innocent and obsessed by trainspotting, who takes a journey through this semi-legendary tunnel which is due for closure. And he has all sorts of encounters with people who are

The Last Train through the Harecastle Tunnel (1969): Richard O'Callaghan as Fowler, the innocent and obsessive trainspotter

Sovereign's Company (1970): antagonisms arise between Sandhurst cadets Sender (Oliver Cotton), Cantfield (Gareth Forwood) and Dexter (Clive Francis)

strangely drawn to confide in him. I thought Alan had the right sense of humour, the right skills with actors, and I knew he'd get on with Terson very easily. We did the play in the studio, with a small amount of film.

Then Alan and I did *Sovereign's Company* by Don Shaw. Shaw had been a cadet at Sandhurst, but he left without graduating. The story was about a young cadet with pacifist leanings who didn't really want to be there, but was following in his father's footsteps. And he was so terrified of being thought a coward that he ended up giving some hapless man a dreadful beating in front of the other cadets. A play about Sandhurst seemed hardly Alan's territory, but I thought he'd be bloody good at it. He was fairly macho, and naturally so, not affectedly so. Occasionally, I was scared of what he might do.

VERITY LAMBERT: Philip Saville and Diana Rigg had a house in Ibiza, at one end of the island, quite isolated. Irene and I went on holiday there, it was shortly after the Charles Manson murders in 1969. And Irene became rather paranoid, because Ibiza was a very hippie-ish place at the time. So I invited Alan out to spend a few days with us, and Irene was fairly relieved that there'd be somebody else around. I went to the airport to meet him and he turned up with his arm in plaster. I asked him what happened and he said, 'Oh, Roy Minton and I went to an Indian restaurant, and we told them we didn't like the food.' 'Yes? And? Alan – nobody comes up and hits you because you complain.' He said, 'Well, we did tip the table over.' A typical Alan story. So he was in no state to defend us.

ROY MINTON: We were in an Indian restaurant in Soho, late afternoon. We were a bit pissed, we'd been in a sort of showbiz drinking club called the Kismet. Clarkey didn't normally eat curry, so I ordered for us, but he wanted to change it, and on top of that he wanted something that wasn't curried to take home for his cat. The waiter got a bit iffy and Clarkey stood up and knocked the table over as he rose. So these fellas rushed out from the kitchen and set about us. We fended them off and backed out on to Gerrard Street. And they came out after us with sticks; we were throwing dustbins at them, Clarkey took a few knocks and there was a lot of blood. Al and I went to hospital and were X-rayed. But we got back to Grenville Middleton's place and raided the fridge 'cos we'd never got our curry. Then two nurses from the hospital showed up. When they were taking down addresses, Clarkey had tipped them a wink. Terrible – I mean, he was like that all the time, spoiled. 'Aftercare', I suppose you'd call it.

TONY GARNETT: The BBC for a good part of those years was relaxed enough and the command structure was devolved enough for that sort of laddish naughtiness to be tolerated, and a blind eye turned to it. I've no reason to doubt that when Alan was actually on the set, he was a very disciplined professional, and if he was hung over he got on with it.

IRENE SHUBIK: After *Sovereign's Company*, I teamed Alan with the writer Douglas Livingstone. Douglas is obsessed by Donald McGill, and the work he did with Alan absolutely had that seaside postcard quality, based in fact around Douglas's family. His mother-in-law ran a pub in Margate – and I was not there, I'm glad to say, when Alan misbehaved very badly while they were staying above the pub.

DOUGLAS LIVINGSTONE: I started writing because I was in the West End doing Peter Shaffer's *The Public Ear and the Public Eye* with Maggie Smith. They were two one-act plays and I was only in the first, so consequently I found, having come from rep, that there was nothing to do all day. And the run was about fifteen months. So I wrote – five television plays, all rejected, but the slips weren't so depressing as to deter me, and eventually I got one commissioned. Stella Richman, of course, was a vital cog in this. Irene put Alan and me together at the BBC and we got on terrifically well. Wasn't good for my liver. But as soon as he started directing, he gave up the drink entirely, wouldn't touch it, which was a surprise to me. I don't know if I'd have been so strong.

I Can't See My Little Willie was the first play we did together. I loved this pub of my mother-in-law's in Margate. Of course my wife – who'd lived there a lot – didn't like it at all. But I was a visitor. At that time Margate was wild with day-trippers coming down in coach parties, and this pub was right on the front. So they'd come in and there was an organist and a drummer, and there'd be singing and dancing and conga lines and people getting pissed out of their minds. It just seemed a wonderful atmosphere to me – not so great if you're behind the bar, obviously. But it was another world, so I decided to use it. The play was about a middle-aged man called Arthur Palmer, played by Nigel Stock, who works for local government in London, in the housing department. His brother Frank and his wife run this pub, and they've had a kid who's about to be christened, so the family gathers for a party. But what isn't obvious until the play develops is that Arthur's having a nervous breakdown. And Frank's about to leave the pub, so Arthur gets the wild notion that he'll take it over – crazy, because he knows nothing about it, and his wife and son would hate it – but for him it starts to look like perfection.

We wanted to capture the excitement of that kind of seaside milieu. So every time we moved back and forth in his story, we used versions of Donald McGill postcards as linking devices, and put voices over, and used jokes that were relevant to the story. I love McGill, the honest vulgarity of it. One family member is Salvation Army, and so in a scene at a meeting we see a McGill image of a big woman leaning over, saying, 'I come to bring you uplift.' And it gave a sense of caricature – that was the way Arthur was seeing Margate rather than the reality.

We had three weeks rehearsal, and Alan loved having writers around. He wanted a week to himself and for the rest I was there all the time. The system was that I never said anything in the room, but we went away and conferred together at lunchtime and after the day's work. The pub was built in the studio, but we did a tiny bit of filming in Margate. In fact, I got Alan to come back down one night to judge a talent competition at the pub; Roy Minton came as well. The next morning some of the commuters who were on their way to catch trains to London called in rather pointedly on my mother-in-law and said, 'There's a man on the balcony of your pub pissing on to the road below.' Guess who.

5

'It's only telly': Upheavals and expulsions (1970–1971)

GRAHAM BENSON: I met Alan in 1970 when we did Colin Welland's *The Hallelujah Handshake*, which Graeme McDonald produced. I had been in rep theatre, then joined the BBC in 1968, an AFM in the Drama Plays department. There was a lot of recruitment then, especially from theatre. I remember Alan being about at the BBC, and of course once you saw him, you knew he was there. He was a phenomenon at the time. I mean, you were talking about two schools of television director: there was the tweed-jacketed, corduroy-trousered, coloured-shirt brigade, and there were quite a lot of those. Then there were the rather trendy, fashionable, cashmere-sweatered, Gucci-shod, cigar-smoking brigade with their soft leather briefcases. Suddenly along came Alan Clarke, unshaven, smoking roll-ups, fairly unkempt, drinking in the bar lunchtime and evening.

The Hallelujah Handshake was an extraordinary, intense piece, nothing that Colin Welland's written since has been quite the same. It concerned a lonely young man, a fantasist and a compulsive thief, who tries to join a succession of church congregations. The whole difficulty of the piece was casting this lead role – a man slightly disturbed, and with a heightened imagination, capable of immense confidence and desperate shyness. Quite surprisingly, Alan suggested somebody he'd auditioned and whom I'd worked with at Dundee in rep, a man called Tony Calvin. And he wanted our opinions here. The norm then was that you served the director and nobody much minded, because if directors didn't know what they wanted then they weren't professionals. Alan knew what he wanted, but he was still prepared to share the decision-making and to be questioned. He made the work a pleasure.

If you became a close colleague of Alan's, then you really saw no division between his professional and private lives, you were part of his whole. You knew about his mum in Liverpool, and that he

'A man of immense confidence and desperate shyness': Tony Calvin (standing) as the eccentric Henry in *The Hallelujah Handshake* (1970)

sent money home to her every week in a BBC envelope, always cash. The first thing I remember that I was surprised about with Alan was that he was no longer living with Jane and his children. He'd quite recently moved out of Ealing. I thought this was strange for a man who had such a bond with human beings. Later on I realized exactly why it wasn't so. At bottom I think it was probably impossible for Alan to live with anybody, because of the ferocity of his imagination and the way he attacked his life and his work at the same time. That's a difficult one to merge with the more necessarily placid moments one needs in a marriage and a home life.

PAUL KNIGHT: It's sad to relate, but I think I was partly responsible for his leaving Jane. I was doing a pilot for an improvisation show with a group called the Theatre Machine, and I asked Alan to direct it. I picked him up at Ealing to take him to see the group perform. And at the party afterwards he met Jehane Markham at my flat, and never went home.

JEHANE MARKHAM: My sister Petra was involved with this clowning improvisation show, at the Royal Court and elsewhere; I came to watch them at the Pentameters in Hampstead, and it so happened that Alan and Paul Knight were there. I asked Alan what he did and he said, 'Nothing.' But Petra told me he was a director. We shared a lift to a party at Paul's. I remember we were looking at each other, and we had a dance. Nothing happened, but I found him very interesting, rather strange and sort of powerful; I hadn't met anyone like him before. Soon afterwards we had a terrible, classic one-night stand at my flat. I had a feeling that he'd walked into my life and was going to have a strong influence on me. And I had the audacity of youth, so the second time we met I said, 'Look, I don't want to be a number in your black book.' I think my saying that sort of impressed him, and he said, 'You won't be.' The next morning he went off and I thought, 'Now we'll see.' And over the next few days he left Jane and their children in Ealing and came to live with me. Which was sad, obviously. It wasn't a good way to start a relationship. But I suppose their relationship had broken down and this was just the catalyst.

I was twenty, he was fourteen years older. And it was partly a father-figure thing; clearly he represented that to me in some way, I do understand that now. I felt a sort of undivided loyalty to him, it was adolescent in a way. I didn't have leeway to really argue with him and state my case, I was just swept away by his influence, if you like. I suppose he fell into a category that I would worship because of my background. You know, the Beatles changed my life, John Lennon was my particular hero – I loved his passion and the way he cut through so much hypocrisy. And the fact that they were working class and from Liverpool added to the fascination, because I was middle class and wanting to experience other things. So when Alan came along, it just so happened that he fulfilled a very romantic image I had in my head. He was from Liverpool, this hallowed place, and he had this wonderful accent and this tremendous humour, which had an openness and a level of honesty about things most people don't want to talk about. He wanted a direct communication with people, he couldn't stand to hear stereotypical things coming out of people's mouths. All this, combined with his talent, was a fairly heady mixture; women did tend to find it irresistible. I think, I *hope* I understood things about him over and above the obvious. But he was politically correct in my terms at the time. Romantically he seemed perfect – of course he wasn't at all.

In those days you could share the most wonderful flats all over London for a fiver a week, and we had a funny series of moves. We went to a house in Islington, an eccentric place full of musicians, which didn't go down well with Alan – they were very straight and it was a terrible strain. In 1970 we found a lovely flat with white walls and pine floor, virtually unfurnished, off the Essex Road. In some way that was our happiest time, that summer there. It was a whirlwind crazy thing, but I just decided to go in for this adventure. He had the potential to be dangerous. He would do outrageous and slightly provocative things, partly to shock people. At that place he threw a television out of the window. He said, 'It's only telly.'

TONY GARNETT: I'd say Alan was a professional at going out for a night's drinking – both the drama and the comedy would escalate as the evening wore on. But he acted it, you know; he was expected to behave like that, so he sort of did – there was a bit of that. It was as if the slightest hint of any person or any institution exercising any authority whatsoever was not just an invitation for Alan to behave anarchically. It was as though he almost felt it was his duty – that he would be remiss if he didn't create some mayhem.

GRAHAM BENSON: The BBC Club was an extraordinary place with a great buzz to it. All the people acting in the studios would be in there, all the design staff, costume, make-up, camera crew, sound. And you'd go in there at the end of the day, five-thirty or six, for a drink. And you'd still be in there at a quarter to ten, not from a desire to get drunk but because by and large you were stimulated, there was fantastic conversation. People would argue and form factions and discuss things with passion. We did get drunk in there, we did misbehave.

DAVID YALLOP: Alan's banning from the BBC Club was part of a normal evening's activity which just sort of 'escalated', as they say. You weren't allowed in unless you were a member, and those of us who weren't staff were not members. You could get a temporary membership if you were working on a production, or someone could sign you in – all of that nonsense went on. But there used to be various gentlemen seated at the front desk, throbbing with power. They didn't like Alan, because Alan was not the kind of person who looked like he should be allowed into the BBC Club anyway. Alan would be more likely to undress for the club than to dress for it. But he'd go there for a drink because it was there. Bizarre place it was, because you could see famous faces, international stars sometimes, cheek by jowl with riggers – all chatting away, you know, Charlton Heston waiting at the bar to get served. On this occasion, I think one barman got a bit wary and obnoxious with Alan, because I turned round and Alan was in the process of taking his clothes off. And the barman was saying, forlornly as it turned out, 'I don't want any more of that in here.' But Alan got on the bar, there was a soda-siphon there, and he gave it to the bloke, all over him. Then he marched up and down saying, 'Now – who wants drinks? Anybody want serving?' The barman legged it and Clarke got down behind the bar and starting serving everybody free, until security showed up. So he was officially banned from the BBC Club, and proud of it.

RICHARD BROKE: Alan was also the only person in history to be banned from the BBC lifts, he was required to use the stairs. One day he'd refused to leave the South Hall lifts, as they were called, and he got bottles of gin and glasses and sat in there with mates going up and down. So once again he was solemnly banned.

MICHAEL JACKLEY: By 1970, when I met Clarkey, I had worked my way up to be a Production Assistant, First AD as it's known now. Then the Head of Department said he wanted me to do a studio production with Alan – Dougie Livingstone's *Everybody Say Cheese*. I was due to meet Alan and I came to Television Centre in a brown knitted suit with paisley lining, quite smart. And I stood at the bar in the Club and I noticed Graham Benson and another guy – tousled hair, big smile, a green sweater with a tree embroidered on it, scruffy trousers, boots. They came down to me and Graham gave me a hug and said, 'Oh, Mike, this is Alan Clarke – you're working together, aren't you?' I said, 'Hello, Alan, nice to meet you.' He said, 'Look, you'll have to do something about the suit, I can't work with a scruffy bugger like you.' I went to Oxfam the next day.

DOUGLAS LIVINGSTONE: *Everybody Say Cheese* was, I suppose, an attempt to follow up *Little Willie*. It was about the dwindling days of a couple of beach photographers at Margate who go around taking snaps, and they're running out of work as more and more people get their own cameras. So for that – obviously, I suppose – we used the device of still-frame photographs as commentary. And we animated them to an extent so their mouths opened and they spoke and so on. Roy Kinnear was the lead, gave a very nice performance. But the play wasn't as good. On *Little Willie* we'd gone quite far down the non-naturalistic path and I'd really enjoyed it. I pushed it a bit on *Everybody Say Cheese*, to the extent of giving the characters pseudo-Restoration names reflecting their personalities. I knew I hadn't pulled it off.

MICHAEL JACKLEY: In the studio Alan tended to stay in the box. He wasn't down on the floor much, but he took everybody into consideration – beforehand he went around touching people, saying hello. Sometimes I'd look up to the gallery and I'd say over the talkback, 'Are you still up there? You haven't said anything for a

Everybody Say Cheese (1971): Esta Charkham (Diane), Roy Kinnear (Henry Hunter), James Hazeldine (George Green), Margaret Brady (Barbara)

bit.' And I'd hear his sniff, and he'd mutter, 'Fook off, Mike.' So I would. He never made you feel you were doing his bidding, though you probably were. His powers of empathy were remarkable. He didn't do a lot of talking to actors, he would suggest things and let them find their way. And he liked to experiment if possible.

As it was about a seaside photographer, we wanted to create these sort of animated postcards. So we went to Margate with a photographer and shot these wonderful sequences of the actors made up like so. Alan was outrageous. When he got to a place, he would sort of take it over.

GRAHAM BENSON: This was a man for whom the whole idea of directing was that it was his life. And part of that was directing artists and choosing shots and having a stab at a disciplined day's work. And another part of that was the social side, which was doing whatever was being done that evening. He never stayed in and watched *Coronation Street*, let's say. Or not that I recall. But I wouldn't say he was naughty on *Everybody Say Cheese*. Was the next thing I did with him *Horace*? Yes, he was naughty on that.

6

'So, Mr Clarke, you've arrived in Halifax, I see': *Horace* (1972)

BARRY HANSON: For a lot of us who were coming into television in that period Alan was a very inspirational figure. I say this in hindsight; you didn't know at the time, when there was such a terrific amount of drama going up, as opposed to today where you spend eighteen months doing a six-part series. But people moved very quickly and in drama they tended to be freelance rather than staff. The good ones were always in work at the BBC – Jack Gold, Christopher Morahan, Philip Saville, Alan Bridges. Directors tended to be committed to one or two writers – Bridges and David Mercer, Alan and Roy Minton – because they shared the same kind of single-minded commitment to a subject, and it would sort of get pushed through under the aegis of a particular producer. It all sounds a bit arty retrospectively, but I suppose it was.

MARGARET MATHESON: Alan was a legend before I met him. And the fact is, it's becoming clear to me now – it was all through Mark Shivas. It was a key development for both of them, this collaboration, and yet two more different men you couldn't expect to meet. But interestingly they both shared a certain privacy, a reservedness about themselves. Alan was absolutely gregarious with a crew, with a cast, in any given situation – but actually all of that was just a front. Behind it was someone who didn't let you share his inner life much at all. But Alan and Mark had a mutual respect for each other, which was really the making of their professional collaboration.

MARK SHIVAS: What I admired about Alan was that he treated everybody exactly the same, from the lowliest runner to the Head of Department. In those days you tended to meet directors on the fifth floor, the centre of operations, and it was collegiate in a way that it absolutely isn't any more. It's now a ruthless, cut-throat, don't-talk-to-me kind of operation. But Alan was extraordinary with people, not just actors and crews.

And I guess somewhere deep down I shared his – resentment? – of people who are well placed and have lots of money and privilege. I'm sitting quite nicely now, but my father taught in the East End of London in a school off the Commercial Road – taught Steven Berkoff, in fact. I was never deprived, but I wasn't the middle-class lad people often took me for. And I thought if the BBC couldn't do the sort of things Alan wanted to do, then the BBC wasn't worth having. The first thing I did with Alan was Roy Minton's *Horace*, all on film – I think he wanted to make things on film generally. Roy and Alan came to me together, being something of a duo, and wanted to do a play about a relationship between this backward chap and this boy.

GRAHAM BENSON: *Horace* was an impressive piece of work, something Roy had dragged up out of his past, his memories of his Northern childhood. It was the story of this young man, diabetic and a bit backward, who has a job making joke-shop novelties and strikes up a friendship with a schoolboy who's a bit of a misfit himself. I was particularly interested in this very sparse writing of Roy's, something you'd really only associated with Pinter or Beckett up to that point, not to say that Minton was Pinteresque or Beckettian.

ROY MINTON: I think all of us, no matter what our background, we've all known a subnormal guy or a backward guy, maybe someone at school who wasn't quite right. And there was this guy from my background in Nottingham, the backstreets. He was mid-twenties, much older than us kids, but mentally he was our age. And he was diabetic, but he used to eat surreptitious ice-creams under his coat. I think I started with that image. That was Horace. But the first draft was focused on the boy, his mate Gordon. Then Al said, 'Why don't you write about the guy, move the emphasis on to Horace?'

Horace (1972): clad in his 'magic cape', Gordon Blackett (Stephen Tantum) visits the private universe which is the garden shed of Horace (Barry Jackson)

MARK SHIVAS: *Horace* was made in August 1971, all film, outside Leeds around the Whitsun holidays when the factories were closed. Those were the days when you could go off to the North with a budget and do something without people interfering much.

GRAHAM BENSON: *Horace* was a very smooth production – apart from the first day.

MICHAEL JACKLEY: We'd done the final rehearsal in Acton studios. We were due to go up on a Friday to start the following Monday, but Alan went up a couple of days earlier and we booked him into the White Swan Hotel. Gradually a story filtered down to London that things weren't going so well. He'd been going around having a rather grand time. And he picked a quarrel with the hotel over something, went into the restaurant and tipped over the grill, causing a terrible scene. A policeman turned up, realized that Alan had

had a lot to drink, and decided to take him to the station. And as they were going down the steps, Alan felt that the policeman was breathing down his neck somewhat, and asked him in not so many words not to stand so close. The policeman said, 'I've arrested you, Mr Clarke.' Alan said, 'If you stick this close to me you're going to regret it.' He did, of course. And Alan ended up in prison. We were due to film in the law courts, and the chief of the courts was a Mr Brown. Alan was up in front of him the next day. He said, 'So, Mr Clarke, you've arrived in Halifax, I see.' Then he said, 'How long had you been in Halifax before this event took place?' 'Three hours.' 'And how long do you expect to be here?' 'Three weeks.' 'I don't think so.'

GRAHAM BENSON: I'm sure I went to court and paid the fine, because I had the float. It was a joke that rumbled on, that first day. But none of this was of any surprise to the crew; they hadn't expected it to start normally.

MICHAEL JACKLEY: I arrived on the Saturday; they'd let him out with a caution and bound him over to keep the peace. And he moved into the Old Cock Hotel.

GRAHAM BENSON: Alan was subsequently thrown out of the Old Cock too and finally I booked him into this place outside town, for twenty-five bob a night. Thrown out of there as well, I think, just for his general boisterousness. I don't know if he would get away with it now.

MICHAEL JACKLEY: Things weren't entirely easy on the shooting. Roy was there a lot of the time, and he had a clear vision of what he wanted, but so did Alan. They were both very strong personalities, they may have been at loggerheads at times. But I think there's a point where the writer has to leave it in the director's hands.

ROY MINTON: Visually, Al wasn't so hot – with camerawork. What he did do for me, he read a script immaculately. What he was good at after that was casting – risky casting. He'd have names shoved at him at the Beeb, but he'd say, 'Fuck off'; he was brave like that, and it generally came off and produced some nice surprises.

TONY GARNETT: Alan was searingly honest. Also, a bit like Ken, he had a good bullshit meter, particularly for performances. I mean, if a performance was as phoney as a nine-bob note, he could tell straightaway. And that's one of the things that marks the work out, and one of the reasons why I expect the films will last, because the performances ring true. I have an unalloyed warm view of him, of course, because I never had to handle the bugger.

MICHAEL JACKLEY: One night near the end of the shoot Alan went into the main Halifax police station late to complain about police brutality. Obviously he'd been done over at the arrest, and then the police had followed him around town by car, which he didn't like. So Alan went and said he was being victimized. He said, 'That's what you coppers are like up here.' It was late, there was nobody else around in the station at the time, and the police sergeant came round the desk to the door and thumped Alan, and he fell all the way down the stairs. He got a massive great cut down his face, needed stitches, and he had the scar for the rest of his life. So the police got their own back. And in a way they were quite justified, though I wish they hadn't done it. But from a production perspective, wearing a BBC hat, I'd say he did do things that he shouldn't have, which weren't in the manual.

MARK SHIVAS: It was heartbreaking, *Horace*. I remember it as a major piece of bleakness and sadness and sweetness – everything Roy and Alan were best at, without pushing in any direction except the absolute truth. It's very funny, and at the same time you can see very early on the awfulness that's going to come, without it being signalled.

ROY MINTON: The trick is, if one's tackling anything that might lean towards the harrowing, then without humour you're at a loss, you're deep into boredom territory. What I learned in theatre was get 'em laughing and then put the knife in.

GRAHAM BENSON: Alan directed Roy Minton's work better than anybody else, and Roy wrote better when Alan Clarke was directing. Roy was, and is, a great writer. He had his moment, his time, some would say it was a short time. But so much of what we understand to be good contemporary drama has its roots in Alan's work, particularly his work with Roy.

7

'Sort of Stygian': The basement, Number Three Almeida Street (1970–1977)

GRENVILLE MIDDLETON: I had left London in 1967 and gone back to South Africa for a few years. But I returned around 1969 and contacted Alan, who was living in Islington with Jehane Markham. My wife Juliet and I had a house nearby in Almeida Street, and I wanted to let out the basement flat. And of course I always loved being around Alan because he was such a sport and such an education – like a walking university for me. He came with Jehane and took the flat, around 1970. And he ended up staying there until around 1977 – it was the most amazing period. Jehane was there for some time but finally she decided she'd go, she couldn't cope any more.

DAVID YALLOP: Alan would always say of the squalor – and this was no designer squalor – that it was the only address in London where the refuse was delivered.

GRENVILLE MIDDLETON: Various people would blow in and out, or he'd arrange for them to come round. Dave Yallop moved in, eventually. Roy Minton would come down for some script meeting or other, talk for hours, and that would be that – that night would be women, drugs, drink, blokes coming in.

JEHANE MARKHAM: I wasn't too keen on the lads, to be honest, not that I had much to do with them. But it was a bit of a nightmare to me. It was old-fashioned, working-class, patriarchal, it wasn't good. And I was a silent woman, a young woman. It made my life with Alan quite separate, and that isn't a good sign. Because if someone is going to be part of your life, you kind of integrate them with your friends and family, and I couldn't. He did love his work, he was a workaholic, maybe too much so. In my dreams of him he was always working and I would think, 'I can't reach him.' When we worked together years later on *Nina*, that was resolved. But I think he knew the balance of his life was wrong. Obviously he was very scared of being trapped and contained and held back by a woman or women, he had to be free and unencumbered, and I think that was a battle within him. I don't know if he regretted that, whether he felt we could have shared a life together while also being independent artists. It's a lovely idea, but it takes a bit more than wishes, and it wasn't to be. One night he came back late; I asked him where he'd been and he said he'd been with a woman. I could literally smell her scent on him. So I left – obviously I was very hurt. But it couldn't be sustained. And after I left it became wild.

GRENVILLE MIDDLETON: I met a stunt man called Bronco McLoughlin on a film in South West Africa and had a good time, so I sent him along to Almeida Street and got him ensconced with Clarke down below. It was just too tough otherwise. Clarke never cleaned the place, just emptied the ashtrays on the floor. But Bronco came along and kept a good house for him.

BRONCO MCLOUGHLIN: We were both coming and going a lot of the time, this job and that. Sometimes I'd go away for a week and while I was gone Clarkey would do a bit of set-dressing, y'know? He'd get things back the way he liked them – overflowing ashtrays, milk bottles lined up against the wall, algae everywhere. I'd get back, I wouldn't say anything. Then he went to work and I'd clean the whole place out. He'd arrive back, wouldn't ever say, 'Ah great, Bronc, thanks, man.' But he was happy if there was a nice stew in the pot, he liked rough and ready food.

GRENVILLE MIDDLETON: Al didn't live permanently with a woman in Almeida after Jehane moved out. He had his lovers – Pam Brighton, Verity Lambert, Jacqui Lyons. He had so many girlfriends, attractive, intelligent women. He was such an intelligent bloke, he needed women who could keep up with him and give him something to bounce off. It would have been hopeless with some dumb woman who couldn't cut it. They were always wonderful, lovely women. They accommodated themselves to Al's ways a bit, there'd be hours of drinking. But no one ever lost their dignity with him.

GRAHAM BENSON: He clearly was a very earthy man, a handsome fella, but it wasn't 'handsome' they went for. And sex was an extraordinarily important part of his life – he had to have it. Of course, I didn't see it at such close quarters because I wasn't living there. Maybe I didn't want to see it.

GRENVILLE MIDDLETON: But he gave everyone who was with him a good time – it was always exciting, nobody could regret that. Clarke was a guy who took you to the limit, a bit like Jack Nicholson in *One Flew Over the Cuckoo's Nest*. The party at the end of that film when Jack's putting alcohol in a guy's drip – that was Alan all over. My introduction to acid was through Alan. I was in bed for three days recovering; he probably went out and did it again. Jesus Christ, I don't know where his head went, but he could take that – his tolerance was astounding.

VERITY LAMBERT: I got to know Alan socially rather than through work, just by generally behaving badly as everybody did at the time. Sometimes it was the BBC Club, sometimes at Almeida Street, which was fairly eccentric. Sort of Stygian really, like someone's lair – you weren't sure there wasn't going to be a wild animal in there. Sometimes there was. But the only aggressive side to Alan was that absolute desire not to conform and be middle-class. He had to overturn all those middle-class values, which he saw as despicable really. Even now I still see him as he was. I remember him as unbelievably scruffy and looking like he absolutely should be put in the bath and left to soak there for six months. But a very attractive, good-looking man. And I think part of his charm was that he was genuinely interested in people – that's always charming. He listened. Once you were there as a friend, that never went.

GRENVILLE MIDDLETON: Verity was very sophisticated, she saw

through him, managed to get out. Sometimes it used to get desperate – he'd charm the hindleg off a donkey, old Clarke, and some of these women would fall in love. Then they'd be crying on the doorstep because he'd be off with the next one. And somehow he was never there, so I'd have to deal with it.

PAM BRIGHTON: I knew Alan on and off from 1971–72. In some areas we were phenomenally similar, very similar backgrounds – mine was working-class Bradford. I'd been vaguely introduced to him, we both used to drink in the King's Head at that time, I lived in Highbury. And I can remember the night he picked me up, he told me that his wife had died very recently and he was terribly depressed and this was where he came to drink. I thought, 'Oh God, this is awful.' Obviously he completely wooed me with it. And then two weeks later he revealed it was all complete flannel. He could be amazingly amoral, Alan, and treated women, me included, appallingly. After we met, we had a relationship for about eighteen months, two years. And then I married a Canadian. That didn't last very long and I'm sure in part it was a reaction, I wanted somebody just unutterably sober and boring. I think the only way I survived in a relationship with Al was because we were mates on another level – because we experienced the world in quite similar ways. So somehow we managed.

JEHANE MARKHAM: After I'd moved, I'd occasionally be impelled back there, we couldn't sever all connections. I didn't have any other relationship in my life and although it screwed me up pretty awfully, at the same time it was worth it. He would ring me drunk and say, 'Come over,' and I knew I shouldn't but I would, I'd stay. And then I'd think, 'How could I have done that?' But I knew I'd rather see him than not. One day I went over and I was angry about something, and I thought 'No' and got in a cab. What changed my life was that I met my present partner Roger, and my life began to develop in a way that was right for me. On one level I think Alan was a bit put out.

PAUL KNIGHT: There was a discipline under Alan's wildness. One wonders how much of it was bravado. There were a lot of sexual conquests, and certainly he seemed to need to be seen to have a lot of women all of the time, and to be living up to this reputation. 'Clarkey' became a legend in his own lunchtime: 'I can drink a bottle of vodka a day', 'I smoke this much dope', 'I have four women a night and one at lunchtime, get 'em in and kick 'em out.'

DAVID YALLOP: Always, one must make the caveat of setting Jane aside from this, as she was the mother of his children, and that was a long-term relationship. He came close to commitment a number of times after that marriage broke up, but it never happened.

GRENVILLE MIDDLETON: He always went to see Molly and Gabriel in Ealing on the weekend. He'd leave Friday night or Saturday morning, back on Sunday night – completely faithful in that respect. I remember a female friend of his saying to him, 'You will never leave your family!'

8
'Somebody will have to swing': *To Encourage the Others* (1972)

MARK SHIVAS: Just after *Horace*, in the winter of 1971, we made *To Encourage the Others* on multi-camera videotape and 35 mm. The piece was brought to me by David Yallop and my script editor Margaret Matheson – then Margaret Hare. The subject appealed to me very much; I'd been at school in Croydon in 1952, at the time when Derek Bentley and Christopher Craig were on the roof of a nearby warehouse. The sixteen-year-old Craig had shot a policeman, and was detained at Her Majesty's Pleasure, and the nineteen-year-old Bentley, who was with Craig and hadn't shot anybody, was hanged. David Yallop had a burning desire to right the wrongs of this case, which were indeed monstrous. So there was a crusading zeal on the part of all of us, we wanted to obtain some sort of posthumous pardon for Derek Bentley.

DAVID YALLOP: By 1969 I was a Floor Manager for London Weekend Television in their first year. But I'd started to write for various comedy shows. And I was working on an idea about scapegoats for a TV series, and a rigger called John Silver suggested the Derek Bentley case to me. He was a South Londoner like I was, and we both remembered the case very vividly, it had reverberations for us. I was born in Balham and brought up in Clapham; I lived only a short bus ride away from where this policeman Sidney Miles died in Croydon. I'm very intrigued by society's need for scapegoats, and Bentley was clearly made one. The question to ask was, 'Why did we do that to that person?' And in Bentley's case, 'to encourage the others' seemed to sum it up in a line. There was a fear afoot in society of teddy boys and juvenile violence – not that it hadn't happened before, but this was the first post-war wave of it. And here was a policeman being shot, and somebody would have to swing for it. The fact that the person who was executed was innocent really didn't matter very much – in fact, I'm sure that certain elements in society thought, 'Even better, that'll strike fear, that'll sort out those working-class fuckers.' In fact it was very bad PR for the hangman, because if you go round hanging innocent people, at the end of the day you don't get a very good press.

The series idea got nowhere – I was basically unknown as a writer, certainly of heavy drama. But I began to see the Bentley case as a full-length play, and to structure it thus. I don't know how far I was on the first draft, but it was Derek's father William Bentley who said, 'Why don't you do a book on this?' So I approached a few firms and was knocked back a few times, but finally I showed the material to W.H. Allen and half an hour later they offered me a deal. So I had a book deal in place before I had the play in place, an interesting departure from what I'd planned. I went and saw Gerald Savory who was then Head of Drama at the BBC, and he said, 'Where's the relevance for today in this play?' And Clarkey was enraged by that question. His response was, 'They took the boy out and murdered him. There's the fucking relevance for today.'

Mark Shivas had tried to get this play on and not succeeded, and then suddenly they lost a play in a slot that he was doing of six plays, and there was a window. And I was walking in with Alan on my arm. I had shared the research with him. I was virtually living with him at this stage. And I can't recall any given moment when Alan said, 'I want to direct this,' but really it was unthinkable that anyone else should.

MARGARET MATHESON: Alan was very respectful of writers, and he enjoyed their company – sort of similar to Stephen Frears in that way. Alan was happy to have a writer around, certainly during his preparation – and certainly with Yallop, because they were wild men together. I guess they were fellow spirits, even though Alan was an Evertonian and David was a complete Cockney. But seeing them together you felt as though they'd grown up together.

DAVID YALLOP: Because Alan and I were contemporaries, I think we both understood a lot about the mores of the time. The 1950s we thought of as a rationed generation, it was a black-and-white generation, there was colour but not much of it. Clothes were still the drab pre-war stuff. Between 1945 and 1952 American influences had got a footing, certainly the teddy boy thing. But we were coming out of austerity, most of the foods were still on ration, sex was on ration, everything – and black and white summed up that world. Of course there is a black and white clip in that production, which is Pathé News period footage of the real Christopher Craig. I had hoped to shoot the whole thing in black and white – Alan was up for that – but Mark said, 'You can't, this is a flagship series.'

MARGARET MATHESON: Alan was absolutely meticulous, he used to write all his production notes in capital letters – not because we were illiterate, but because he wanted to be clearly understood. And it was real script editing, because the script was all over the place and it was way too long. But they were terrific, they'd say, 'Oh, Margaret, just cut it, sort it out.'

DAVID YALLOP: Alan cast Charlie Bolton and Billy Hamon as Bentley and Craig, and I wasn't sure whether they were going to cut it, but they were both extremely good in quite different ways. With Charlie, all Alan had to go on was *Please Sir*, this very funny Larbey and Esmonde comedy starring John Alderton and a cast of young kids. Charlie was playing the class dolt, and that's probably where Alan saw the connection with Bentley's low IQ. Billy was a very powerful young actor, he had to hit it very high from the first frame, which was the shooting on the rooftop – and it came from nowhere.

MARK SHIVAS: Albert Pierrepoint supervised the hanging, causing poor Charlie Bolton to turn absolutely white. Alan was certainly a stickler for getting things done absolutely as they were. They're always different and more horrifying in reality, and the sheer banality of how this was done was particularly nasty.

DAVID YALLOP: It was my idea to get Albert Pierrepoint down to talk to Alan about the techniques of the hanging. Normally on tele-

To Encourage the Others (1972): Christopher Craig (Billy Hamon) and Derek Bentley (Charlie Bolton), up on the roof with nowhere to run

vision you just cut away. But I wanted to show the nation what we'd done to Bentley, and I wanted it to be precise. Pierrepoint's autobiography gives an insight into the man because it's surreal. Basically the thrust is 'Nobody hangs like the British.' And he'd talk to us about the Nuremberg hangings and say, 'Well, of course, the master-sergeant was a nice man, but all he knew about was electricity, he didn't know about rope. He got the drop all wrong. There'd be people still alive, hanging there and calling out. Others had their heads torn off. It's a scientific art, you know.' And for Alan and I, there was a mixture of astonishment and fascination in this. We wanted to pull out more. We had coped with the awfulness of Bentley's fate by engaging in very black humour, so Mr Pierrepoint was a gift from the gods to us.

Pierrepoint was there when we shot the hanging in the studio. Pierrepoint was a bluff Northern 'How y'doin' lad?' type of guy, and the crew were chatting away to him. And there was Charlie Bolton, dressed in Derek Bentley's clothes, his shirt and jacket – he'd wanted to get into the part so he'd borrowed these things from the Bentley family. When we went for the take, obviously we had an actor playing Pierrepoint, and after several goes Pierrepoint muttered to me, 'He's not getting the rope right on him.' Now we were using Pierrepoint's own ropes and straps and everything. And I mentioned this to Alan, and Alan said, 'OK, show him.' And Pierrepoint went down to the actor, took the rope off him and fixed it on Charlie Bolton's neck, just a bit too tight. And Charlie let out a scream because he was so psyched up. After we'd got it in the can, and the figure in the hood was hanging there in the gallows, Pierrepoint went over. And nobody would help him get these things off Charlie. Nobody would look at him and nobody would talk to him. Whereas before they had, quite happily, in that blasé way. But suddenly the reality of it had just hit them very hard, and Albert was someone they wanted to be rid of as fast as possible.

MARK SHIVAS: The piece caused a stir: Reginald Maudling responded publicly after the first broadcast, and we added this to the repeat in 1991. It's a pity that it didn't quite do the business for Derek Bentley, but it did impress and move a lot of people, and still does.

DAVID YALLOP: I remember one review in the nationals: it said, and I'm paraphrasing, 'There was surely some remarkable degree of talent working on this production. How else can one explain the calmness with which this outrageous story unfolds?' That catches beautifully Alan's quality – 'cos that ain't me.

DAVID HARE: I imagine *To Encourage the Others* still looks fantastic, its power and its originality were quite remarkable at the time. Obviously Alan's shooting style was then much simpler and plainer than it would become. But it's this gift that Alan had of never being seen to whoop up the drama – and yet the tension underneath the apparent surface realism remains so intensely dramatic.

9

'This had better be true – Alan's directing it': Diverse works 1972–73

Achilles' Heel (1972)

VERITY LAMBERT: I was at London Weekend in 1972 and I'd been asked to do some single plays. *Achilles' Heel* was one, written by Brian Clark, and I involved Alan from quite an early stage of the writing because I knew he was mad about football.

ROY MINTON: Once I saw a newspaper write-up on a match, the headline was 'Nottingham Forest 3 Everton 2'. And Forest being my team, I clipped it, put it on a postcard and sent it to Alan. He went fucking spare for about two weeks, wouldn't answer my phone calls – it was that bad.

VERITY LAMBERT: *Achilles' Heel* was about a footballer at the top of his game, played by Martin Shaw, whose Achilles' tendon goes, and he has to come to terms – or not – with the fact that his life as a professional is over. In his handling Alan tried a kind of experiment which didn't really come off, which was treating everything as if it was real time – so that when Martin Shaw's character got up in the morning you saw him cleaning his teeth and so forth. But in the end I had to say to Alan, 'Listen, I don't want to compromise your integrity in this matter, but watching someone cleaning their teeth is like watching grass grow.' So we did trim it a bit. I remember one funny moment, there was a love scene, and Martin Shaw was going through a rather po-faced period and wouldn't let us show his bottom. Alan and I had one or two laughs about that; he didn't have much time for that kind of coyness.

'Nothing ever happens in prison': Maurice O'Connell as Johnson in *A Life Is Forever* (1972)

A Life Is Forever (1972)

IRENE SHUBIK: Tony Parker and I discussed his writing a film about life imprisonment around May 1970. I commissioned him and he delivered a final script, *A Life Is Forever*, in May 1972. We started rehearsals on it straight away, and then I became quite ill. So Mark Shivas finished it off.

MARK SHIVAS: Its basic premise was that it was worse to be locked up in jail for life than to be executed – that was the thrust. Not that it was a plea for capital punishment, clearly. But it was just a study of the grinding life of being locked up. Alan cast another unknown in the lead, Maurice O'Connell, a saxophonist who hadn't been acting very long. Again, one could say this was a device of Alan's – to make the audience feel for the reality of a character in a way they might not if he had gone with a name actor.

BRONCO MCLOUGHLIN: I was on *A Life Is Forever*, stood in on the scene where a black guy hangs himself. It was showing prison life, what's it all about. Boring, every day same guys doing the same thing. Clarkey says to me, 'That's what I want to show. Working the machine shop, stitching the mailbags. No drama, every day boring. I wanna bore the fuckin' audience.' I says, 'Ah, you're going the right fuckin' way about it, Clarkey, y'know?' But he was right, though – nothing ever happens in prison.

MICHAEL JACKLEY: For preparation we were allowed to get inside a prison and have a look. But Alan had an ex-con on board as adviser, even though Tony Parker had been a prison visitor and knew plenty himself. The adviser came with us, and we were banged up in cells for a while, which Alan quite loved. And he knocked about in the recreation room for a bit, chucking snooker balls down the table. But once the Home Office found out we had this ex-convict attached, they said, 'In no way can you do any filming anywhere near a prison.' So we did it all in the studio; Richard Henry the designer built virtually an entire wing of a prison. And after broadcast some Home Office body rang up to say, 'Surely you must have got in somewhere?'

Man Above Men (1973)

MARK SHIVAS: David Hare wrote *Man Above Men* for BBC2, and it was done in the studio. I thought it was an interesting piece – a woman appalled by her father's actions as a judge. But I don't remember much about it, and nor will history, because it wasn't published and the BBC have wiped it.

DAVID HARE: It was a very early play of mine, I think it was quite a naïve work. It's about a judge and his daughter, who commits suicide at the end of the play. It concerned what I was then writing about, the hypocrisy of public faces and the private faces behind them. This was about a woman who was bitterly ashamed of her father, ashamed of his ignorance and the way he treated the people who came through his court. Simply put, it was a very naïve attack on the right of middle-class people to sit in judgement on the lives of people about whom they know nothing. It was trying to show the process of the law as a process of mutual ignorance. And so it was, at a political level, appealing to Alan, no question. At a dramaturgical level – I can't say I'm unhappy that the tape has vanished.

Alan did it jolly well, having said that. It was an excellent cast – Alexander Knox and Gwen Watford. Alan was *almost* the most inarticulate director I've ever worked with in terms of what he was able to say, but it was all done with 'Y'know?' and 'Just a gnat's more' and 'Just a gnat's less' – that was his entire directorial repertoire. And actors ate out of his hand, knowing exactly what he wanted all the time. Under Alan's scrutiny, actors auto-censored their falseness because his eye was enough. He watched them and at the end they would say, 'Oh, you probably didn't like that bit where I did such-and-such, so let me do it again another way,' and he would just sit there and say, 'Fine, yeah.' It was like an eye of truth. And I think we all felt that, I felt that as a writer, 'Oh, this had better be true, because Alan's directing it.' He wasn't interested in the ordinary professional expertise, he was interested in the degree to which actors recognizably resembled real human beings.

It was plainly unusual for him to take middle-class material, and I don't know why he liked the sound of my voice, given that he usually felt so strongly about trying to do working-class subjects. But having been drawn to it, his method was one of intense preparation, which prepared him for complete spontaneity. His girlfriend of the time cursed me and said, 'He's up at three o'clock.' I mean, we're all used to professional obsessives and you could say of any film director, any British director, that they have to be. But this was more than that. It wasn't professional obsessiveness in that it was all he could talk about – on the contrary, he didn't talk much about it. But you knew it was the only source of real value in his life – the work. That, and the football.

It was in those days of studio drama, and Alan brought to bear upon it that intense concern for reality that he had. The classic instance was, I think, in *Man Above Men* when an actor had to pay for a drink. Alan stopped it and said, 'Hang on, how long does it take to pay for a drink?' And the actor said, 'Oh, I thought I'd just make it quick,' and he said, 'Oh no, you never have the right change to hand. Do the transaction properly, look for the change, send the barman off.' And it appeared to have no dramatic point at all, but that was typical Clarkey. Now there could be a stubbornness in that, and yet there was also a strength. It did make some of his work unwieldy and oddly unbalanced; often in a Clarkey play you do think, 'Why's he going on about that?' His rhythm isn't like any other director's because of that. But then sometimes it creates this incredible density of realism, which no other director had. So he could both draw you in and push you out.

If you were to say *Man Above Men* was a bourgeois play – well, I can't imagine Alan doing that play five years later. He and I might well have collaborated again very happily, but not on that kind of play. By then he was finished with all of that.

The Love Girl and the Innocent (1973)

CHRISTOPHER MORAHAN: I had met Alan through Mark Shivas, and in 1973 I asked Cedric Messina if he was interested in doing a production of Solzhenitsyn's *The Love Girl and the Innocent*. And I said, 'I think you should get Alan Clarke to do it.' I knew he worked on video as well as film, and I was keen to get video out of the studio, so he fitted the bill. He was an extraordinary stylist, not at all doctrinaire, and he understood the medium totally. So this was a kind of signature piece for the time I took over the job of BBC Head of Plays – a way of saying that the long form, even if it's a stage play, needn't be a studio reproduction of a classic or a West End success.

RICHARD BROKE: Solzhenitsyn made sense for Alan because he was still in Russia and still a hero of the left. His lionization by the right – that lay ahead. At the time it was considered a great coup for the BBC to do it.

MICHAEL JACKLEY: It was big logistics, lugging a great big OB unit, it had to be worked out minutely. We had a helicopter flying over the country looking for sites: there had to be a certain amount of superstructure, we couldn't build it all. One day we drove to Cromer in Norfolk to an ex-RAF camp. As we approached it Alan said, 'Oh, it's got the right fookin' feel.' There were huts as big as barns, and towers, and a Globe cinema, as all the camps had. It was freezing cold, the wind came off the sea, it was ghastly. I've never been to a Russian labour camp, but this seemed to fit the bill.

DAVID LELAND: I had acted in a play in the Theatre Upstairs called *Gaffers*, which Pam Brighton directed. It was so offensive that even the Royal Court took it off before the run was complete. Alan had cast a man as Nemov, the production chief – 'the innocent' who was in fact Solzhenitsyn – it was really a story about his experiences in a labour camp. But then he had to let this man go, and he said to Pam, 'Who the hell am I going to get?' She suggested me, and I went to talk to Alan. That morning I had hair down to my shoulders and in the evening I was bald. That same day I went to

'Trying to find love or comfort in extraordinarily vile situations': Gabrielle Lloyd as Lyuba, David Leland as Nemov in *The Love Girl and the Innocent* (1973)

wardrobe at Television Centre and they had row upon row of these awful mud-grey uniforms. I was in my jeans and I met this fella, a Polish man who had a small part, bespectacled, wearing a tie. And we went round the back to change and came out again at the same time. He took one look at me, and then saw himself in a mirror beyond me, and he looked down at the floor. And then I saw his tears hitting the ground. He wiped his eyes and he said in a thick Polish accent, 'Brings back memories.'

It was very evocative, *The Love Girl*. We got completely submerged in it. It was a story about trying to find love or comfort in extraordinarily vile situations – the hardness of that. Alan was striving to show those simple human relationships.

Traditionally, when BBC drama was studio-based, the writer was allowed to be at the read-through, at the producer's run, and – as long as he didn't say anything – he could sit in the box while it was being recorded. The three most useless times for a writer to be present. Alan blew all of that out of the window later on, as I found when I wrote for him. If he could have had Solzhenitsyn there he would have done. 'Solly Neasden,' he used to call him. 'Let's see what Solly Neasden says.'

Tougher than the rest? Clarke and his peers

CHRISTOPHER MORAHAN: At that time we cared about a tradition of storytelling at the BBC, and I think we felt that this was where the talent was. We had Loach, Clarke, John MacKenzie, Stephen Frears, Mike Leigh, Mike Newell, Michael Apted, Jack Gold. We gave Alan Parker his first film. We just understood that certain talent needed to be recognized. And certain associations were formed which begat more work, as with Frears and Alan Bennett. In fact, I think our major responsibility was to the writing. The major enterprise was not to do with the director's self-expression, it was to be measured by the quality of ideas, which were represented in the form of the script. They weren't producers' films, as in the Hollywood system; they depended on a collaborative atmosphere, the meeting of producer, director and writer.

MIKE LEIGH: Any of us who were around the Beeb doing those films, you'd know each other from the corridor of the drama department on the fifth floor. The joy of the BBC in particular, and later Channel Four to an extent, was that free spirits went in and did it – John MacKenzie, John McGrath, Gavin Millar, Neville Smith. All those people were floating around being creative, and you'd bump into each other and in certain circumstances you'd have the opportunity to get to know them. But I don't think anybody 'came together'. People came to the BBC and did it, but usually with different producers, and there was no sense of togetherness. We're talking about the early 1970s here. We all came out of the 1960s basically, that's the real point. But you look through the lists of directors and writers of *Play for Today* – a substantial number of them had been working for years, they were older than us. Lots of very good stuff was done by them too. Apart from Ken Loach – who is for my money entitled to enjoy some regal privilege in the history of this, he's the daddy really – the rest of us were in there with everybody else. I think it was more fluid, less august – it wasn't such a collection of geniuses. Just because a few of us have gone on, it means you look back at us, but there were other people, some of whom have fallen by the wayside.

STEPHEN FREARS: I don't know where Alan began, how he came up. But we were all down from universities, and I always thought that Alan had come from a different background. And apart from these rather glamorous drinking stories, he seemed to be a much more bread-and-butter director. He did tape as well as film, he did studio productions, which were somehow looked down upon in a rather silly, snobbish way.

MIKE LEIGH: I don't off hand know of another director, certainly not then or particularly now, who came from so overtly or uncompromisingly a working-class background as Alan, and that was unique. And it relates to his earthiness and his in-your-face, upfront directness, which you see in the films. Whereas Ken Loach comes from a lower-middle-class background, and Les Blair's background is similar, and my father was a doctor from Salford – most directors went to university. But I think, with all due respect, the problem is that people always bang on about the class aspect. It's important, but only up to a point. When it comes to the crunch, this man was a film director – he wasn't a car worker or a docker, he was a fucking film-maker, and he worked a film-maker's hours and was paid a film-maker's wages, and he had all the hassles and privileges of a film-maker. And film-making is a middle-class job, full stop. Let nobody get mixed up about it, that's a fact.

STEPHEN FREARS: Ken and Tony Garnett were much cleverer, their work was public in some way that Alan's wasn't. They were sort of nuisances, they always maintained that they could bring the docks out the next morning. I can see that a writer like Alan Bennett had an audience. Dennis Potter, there'd always be petitions coming round about him when he'd been badly treated. But Dennis could look after himself. Alan didn't do any of those things. He didn't pretend to be consistent. His choice was more eccentric – probably why we all loved him. Alan's was private work, private and unacceptable, and rather pensive and aggressive – so in a way he must have been difficult. He didn't make films about public opinions. He defended people who were in a much more complicated position. And people did just adore him. He can't have got good audiences or anything like that. So it's rather an extraordinary story – he went on making these rather difficult films about rather unlikeable people and unlikeable things. It's really only now that you can look and see there was a kind of coherence, a shape to some of it.

DAVID HARE: Alan knew his stuff was tougher than other people's stuff but that didn't worry him. He saw television as an opportunity. And I know that I did hear him make that analogy between Hollywood in the 1930s and 1940s and the BBC. 'This is a place where you can do a lot of work, and because of that you can do a lot of *different* work, you can push your luck.' Which is what he was doing all the time – experimenting.

10

Angels and incubi: BBC Birmingham and *Penda's Fen* (1974)

BARRY HANSON: I first worked with Alan in 1972 on *Thirty Minute Theatre* at BBC Birmingham, after the opening of the Pebble Mill studios. In a way, Pebble Mill was a white elephant, so they'd given David Rose this brief to just do something – whatever.

I should point out that Alan got himself banned from the bar at BBC Birmingham. He started doing rugby tackles on people and ended up dangling out of the window by his fingertips, two storeys up. The club cleared and Security were called in, it was complete and utter chaos, and Alan ripped a telephone off the wall before being removed. They said to me, 'Look, he's your responsibility,' and I decided I had to get him out of there, so we got a taxi to an Indian restaurant. At some point during the car journey I asked Alan what time it was, and he pulled this telephone out from his jacket and said, 'I don't know, let me just . . .'

I wasn't credited, but I set up *Penda's Fen* and got Alan and David Rudkin together. They were chalk and cheese in some respects, but they both had the same sort of intensity and a mutual respect for each other's work. If you're talking about writers who are distinctive, in a way there isn't anyone quite like Rudkin, and Alan appreciated that. And Alan himself had a mind that was rather bleak and elemental. *Penda's Fen* is a play of mystical Olde English, a boy beset by angels and devils, and a pagan king emerging through an earth that held various appalling nuclear secrets. It also had Mary Whitehouse thinly disguised in it, and all sorts of obsessions and fears that were abroad in that early part of the 1970s. You name it, they all cropped up, and Alan was perfectly at home in that environment. I remember a marvellous matte shot where the aisle of a church was rent asunder. You'd never get away with it on the BBC now.

DAVID HARE: We were all working together on the same corridor at BBC Birmingham when Alan was making *Penda's Fen* – Stephen Frears and Mike Leigh, Alan Bleasdale and I, Willy Russell. And there was David Rose just being a wonderful impresario. When I saw *Penda's Fen*, I just couldn't believe it. And that is the whole BBC Birmingham culture right there, which was David Rose letting people do what they wanted and nobody in London knowing what was going on. You know: 'The earth splits open? Oh yeah?' There's just no way a London producer and script editor would have been having that. But my God, that film went out at nine-thirty at night on a majority channel, it's incredible – an hour and a half long. And how bold to do it!

IRENE SHUBIK: I saw David Rudkin's stage play *Afore Night Come* in 1964 and I thought he was an extraordinarily original writer, we did several *Wednesday Plays* together. Originally he had trained as a musician and taught classics. And he came from a very puritanical, evangelical Christian background; since his father was a revivalist pastor who joined the Church of Christ, inevitably there was an influence.

DAVID RUDKIN: I was brought back into drama by David Rose's new outfit at BBC Birmingham. I wrote two experimental half-hour pieces for David at his suggestion, and then I began to conceive a larger piece, which I talked to David about speculatively. I had no story, just certain visual intonations – about the ghost of Edward Elgar, and witches. And bit by bit it began to join forces with a story about a boy at a school who wouldn't cut his hair. My conversation with David was not much more specific than that, but David and Barry Hanson were the kind of people who responded intuitively to those kind of stirrings in a writer. They said, 'Get something on paper, half a page.' So I shook the ideas down a bit, found a configuration, and on the strength of that David commissioned it.

There was a narrative factor which pulled everything into its first focus. My wife was a teacher who went peripatetic to various schools. She came back from Worcestershire one day and said, 'It's very strange, the road was blocked and there was a sign saying "Road Blocked to Pinfin". But it's Pin-vin, somebody's misspelt it.' I was intrigued enough to look it up in a place-name dictionary and discovered that it was an older pronunciation. And that began to gel it, names being like layers of archaeology. This one went back to Pendefen, and then there was Penda's Fen. Given the historical status of King Penda as the last pagan king of England, it began to belong with my first stirrings in a still obscure way.

When David saw the first draft of the script, he said, 'I'd like to talk to you about Alan Clarke.' Now I knew him to be possibly the best director in television at the time, but it seemed a very surprising piece of casting. I had not associated Alan Clarke with that type of what you might loosely call visionary, poetic material. This was realistic and naturalistic but it was not representational drama in the conventional television sense. It had angels and demons in it. But David wasn't given to perverse matchmaking. So the script was sent to Alan and I gathered his first response was that he didn't want to do it, he considered it an intellectual piece. In any case we had a meeting and David said, 'Alan's got a question for you,' and he said something like 'How many books have I gotta read before I do this muck?' I said, 'Only the screenplay.' I asked what was worrying him; he said, 'All this music and Latin and stuff.' I said, 'You don't have to know anything about that, any more than the spectators do. It's the boy's business. The important thing is the emotions – that's what actors play. Let's just get it right between you and me, and then shoot it.' That was the gist and I suppose he must have been convinced. He seemed to be identified with a naturalistic polemic and *Penda's Fen* doesn't seem to come under that rubric. But when the chips are down, *Penda's Fen* is just about somebody who has to kick things over, has to become free, and in the end it was the same story and the same issues which concerned Alan.

Alan was something of an anarchist, though he might not have put the label on himself. We did briefly talk about politics before shooting, just as we were skirting around each other. We talked about anarchism as an ideology, and he understood that spirit of ungovernableness.

The view from the Malvern Hills: Spencer Banks as Stephen in *Penda's Fen* (1974)

An angel briefly appears to Stephen. A lot of people worried about that angel, very literal-minded post-Newtonian people that you deal with. If it had been a Continental film they wouldn't have had a problem, but because it was on British television it wasn't supposed to break the rules in this way. When we came to it Alan said, 'This angel, have you written it in the right order?' 'What do you mean?' 'It says he sits in front of the stream, we look across the stream and there's an angel behind him. And then we see Stephen's point of view of the reflection of the angel in the stream. Shouldn't he see the angel before we do?' I said, 'No, totally different meaning. To present it the other way round is to explain the angel and imply that it's Stephen's hallucination. But the angel is really in the field.' Alan said, 'OK.' It's a beautiful moment, it has a sort of Buñuel-like quality of the apocalyptic, but in the landscape. It's just treated like any old thing in creation that happens to pass by. Now I had a language of reference in this respect because I was a film buff, but if I'd dared to mention someone like Buñuel for the way in which the visionary alternative world is made visible, as in *Belle de Jour* or *Discreet Charm of the Bourgeoisie*, Alan wasn't interested. He knew who Buñuel was, but it didn't assist him to clarify anything. It works with lesser directors, you hear them saying to the lighting cameraman, 'You know that bit in that Hitchcock movie when . . .?'

NORMA MCMINN: *Penda's Fen* – all my kids loved that, my daughter Gill thought it was really scary. That thing on the end of the bed?

DAVID RUDKIN: I don't know if we got the incubus quite right. I had asked for a high shot over the bed because again we needed to show the audience it was really there. And it was a bloke, a small actor wearing this webbed costume. I think that, conceptually, it was right as a way of conveying Stephen's inklings of his homosexuality.

ROY MINTON: *Penda's Fen*, what was the crack with that? I didn't know what the fuck was going on with that piece, as I remember. Nobody on the production seemed to – amazing. I don't know how you could get out of bed and do it without knowing that much. But then much later, 1990, for some reason it was repeated on the Beeb. And I asked Al, 'Do you know any more now? You directed it.' He said, 'I had no idea what I was doing.'

DAVID RUDKIN: The writer doesn't know what he's done either, beyond a certain level. If you visit a past work again, if it has any integrity it will yield new meanings, there will be more than you knew. And if Alan had imposed an aesthetic on what he'd done, he'd have known the beginning, middle and end of it and there'd have been nothing more for him to learn. But he didn't – he saw it for its own integrity as a piece and made that visible. Alan's intelligence as a maker of cinema was a moral intelligence. By that I mean he wasn't a person who made moral or political or ethical statements, but he was exercised by what was truthful, and he wouldn't accept it if it wasn't, and in my book that's moral. Yet for all that, he was not grand, as I have found lesser directors to be. I think the important thing is integrity, and I think that there are many ways to be a person of integrity. It doesn't necessarily mean that you live the life of a Jansenist. I knew there were stories and hints about Alan's private life, but I wasn't interested, even on a gossip level. I'd collaborated with Genet ten years previously, on *Mademoiselle* with Tony Richardson. Genet's inward life, his private universe, he had politicized it and that was his thematic material. Alan didn't politicize his private life, didn't make it into a polemical issue. Nor did he allow it – as far as I can see – to infect his art or spill over into it.

He was in that sense not an *auteur* in the classical, Godardian sense of a director who, as it were, generates his movies regardless of who's written the screenplay. Alan wasn't someone who said, 'I'm going to make a film about this,' and then found someone to service it. I worked with Truffaut briefly and I know what working with an *auteur* is like. At the time I worked with Alan, he was still the man who did his work and didn't get into the light. But he may have had a very strong take on material – towards the end of his career clearly he did, in *Elephant* and the one-word pieces. He went on after *Penda's Fen* to develop a very rigorous language, you would say a style. Except that it almost abolished style, he became a Bresson sort of figure, I think.

Alan was concerned with the core of the moment, how to make it audible and visible, and that is where Bresson is a major figure. Bresson had a way of making a very simple thing look amazingly fraught with meaning – not in the Expressionist manner of Hitchcock or even Buñuel, but in the way that somehow he seems to perceive its importance in the eye of God. One can't really explain it in any other way. He was always very austere, but one thinks of *L'Argent*, which is so compelling, or something so weird as *Lancelot du Lac*. He's so condensed in what you're made to see. Now, of course, Alan would have said 'Bollocks' to a comparison with Bresson. I don't think he had those fantasies of himself as a film-maker, and certainly he didn't go into his work with that Bressonian consciousness. But I think he was on the same search, and I think in the end it does take you in the direction of austerity and apparent simplicity.

11

'Just a story about this girl': *Diane* (1975)

MARK SHIVAS: Alan never liked casting stars much, he knew about the Anna Scher School and such places. He never wanted people to give performances; the acting in his films was as close to naturalism as you could get, and all the more amazing for it. He would discover people I'd never heard of, but I would never query his choices. When we came to make *Diane*, the lead was an incredibly hard part to cast, and he needed somebody rather ordinary-looking.

JANINE DUVITSKI: I went to East 15 drama school, didn't get into any of the others. East 15 was quite good in taking the sort of people who don't look like obvious glamorous types. But for me it was probably just three years of getting older. You come out and you're all ready to go and it's very difficult to get work, particularly for girls. A lot of women in my year didn't continue, and I think I would have been exactly the same, I'd have struggled for a year or two and then packed it in, if it weren't for Alan Clarke. No question in my mind, really. I wouldn't have had a career.

I got a phone call asking would I go for an interview at the BBC. And if you've never been to one of these, you just think, 'Oh, if I just get in the door they'll realize how brilliant I am and offer it me.' Which is utterly wrong, as I learned, but luckily for me . . .

I met Alan and chatted with him, and he gave me the script to take home. I realized it was this wonderful part. He said it was about incest, but he made a joke of it, he said, 'Oh, I wish I was playin' the dad, Janine.' And I immediately thought he was the sexiest person on earth – that's the truth of it. I remember he didn't have any socks on.

I went back for another interview and there were all these Anna Scher people waiting to go in, the real thing as it were, younger London kids. So I went in and read it with Alan, and then he asked

Janine Duvitski as the eponymous heroine of *Diane* (1975)

me to go and meet Mark Shivas. And Mark said, 'Now this character is thirteen and you're twenty-one?' 'Yes.' 'And Diane is from London and you're from Morecambe?' 'I am.' 'And Diane is a working-class girl – what class would you say you are?' 'I'm more middle-class, I suppose.' 'Hmm – well, Alan seems to think you'd be perfect.' And I went home thinking it wasn't very likely, but I got a phone call almost instantly. And it altered everything, I got an agent and so on.

The script was by Jonathan Hales, it was called *All the Saints*, and it was in two parts; I think it was intended for a series of two-part plays. But there was a BBC strike in the midst of production and we missed our deadline for that. So it ended up being condensed; quite a bit more was shot but whole chunks had to come out.

RICHARD BROKE: Jonathan Hales was literary manager of the Royal Court at that time; I had recommended him to Mark, who commissioned the script, and then we brought Alan in. Eventually Jonathan said he didn't like what Alan had done and he wanted to take his name off. And Graeme McDonald said, 'Don't worry, "David Agnew" can write it for you, he's my man in these situations.' Mark and I used him again, actually. We used to laugh about the idea of someone doing a PhD thesis on 'Agnew's' work some years down the line. If you studied his *oeuvre* you'd get into a terrible tangle, he's done some very diverse work.

JANINE DUVITSKI: When I read the script I don't know if I realized all that quickly that it was 'about incest', even in the writing it was quite vague. But I don't think Alan wanted the usual clichés of a 'subject piece', where it's all spelt out, and the victim is just moody and depressed all the time. In life, people who end up killing themselves don't always walk around looking distraught for weeks beforehand. So I think he wanted to show Diane as being quite unpredictable, sometimes just pottering around in the flat with her dad. And the dad wasn't just some nasty thug, so you understood more about the sort of person who would do that, the everydayness of it. Originally there was a vicar who was quite important, and a religious angle: that went out the window a bit, and it became just a story about this girl, so the title changed.

MICHAEL JACKLEY: The realism of it and the horror of it were captured quite keenly and dramatically. It was very like life, the awful domestic dreariness, the ghastliness of it, the actions taken without thought of consequences. There wasn't as much fun going around in the making. A girl having a stillborn baby by her father and placing it in a rubbish bin doesn't tend to inspire that. Alan worked himself hard, and he was physically resilient and his powers of concentration were strong. But there must have been times when that got on top of him.

MARK SHIVAS: I think it was the first time Alan was using film, 16 mm, with a video feed, so he could see what was going on. We shot in some fairly bleak places around West London.

MICHAEL JACKLEY: I got a feeling that there was something else going on that preoccupied Alan during that shoot. I remember one day he had to be elsewhere. He didn't confide in me. But his full concentration wasn't on the job.

JANINE DUVITSKI: In the middle of *Diane*, Alan was arrested. One morning I went in and the PA said, 'Alan's not able to be here this morning.' I think because I was playing a fourteen-year-old they felt they shouldn't tell me why. But he was in court for having been rowdy in the King's Head and taking his clothes off.

DAVID YALLOP: Clarke, Minton and I were in the King's Head. There was a rock group up on the rostrum stage, the lead singer of which was a mate of ours, Mick Khan – very good voice, Alan used him on *Horace* and *Scum*. The band were doing this twelve-bar rock, and we had taken up a chant of this particular line, 'Why fucking not?' which seemed to capture the imagination of everybody in the pub. And when I left they'd been singing it continuously for about twenty minutes. Well, apparently, subsequent to my departure, a chartered accountant joined the throng, he was vaguely known to us. And pretty soon after that he, Clarke and Minton took their clothes off, and they were jumping up and down on the stage stark naked, chanting, 'Why fucking not?'

ROY MINTON: Dan Crawford the landlord had a new manager in and he phoned for the fuzz. So we were kicked into a Black Maria. They used to be evil down here, the fuzz. They banged us in a big holding cell with all the drunks, and of course we had no clothes. Mike Khan got them together and brought them round, but these coppers wouldn't let us have them. Then they got us out and interviewed us across these tables. Clarkey and I were side by side, starkers. And they said 'Right, bail. How much do you make of a year?' And we told them we earned about twenty-five, thirty grand, sort of money we'd never seen – just for mischief, because the average copper's wage was only about five.

Anyway they let us out about four in the morning, gave us our clothes. Monday morning we went to court in Old Street – and Al had a full crew waiting on him, he was shooting that day. He'd got on to Mike Jackley and they'd organized a barrister. We were held in the cells below and there was a murderer here and a rapist over there, it was quite interesting. Then we were in the dock, and the barrister spoke very eloquently about how Mr Clarke had just been having a bit of fun, and that reflected well on all of us. I apologized, said it wasn't really unusual in that pub. I mean, there'd been girls in the pub with their tops off too, Germaine Greer fans and what have you. But the magistrate sent us down again – and by now I thought we were looking at time. Because they charged us under some ancient law from 1814 about obscenity, which sounded awful – it wasn't about drunkenness or stripping, it sounded like child molesting. We were down there for an hour in great anxiety, then he fetched us back up and said the criminal charge was to be dropped and replaced with 'Drunk and disorderly'. Ten pound fine each. But we didn't have any money. Finally it got sorted and Clarkey went off in a cab to work. We'd had a few mates in the gallery, so the rest of us came back to Islington, went into the pub opposite Almeida, and there was a stripper stark naked on stage. I thought, 'Bloody hell.'

RICHARD BROKE: That was one of my favourite moments in television, going into Mark's office to tell him that the director had been arrested for exposing himself. And of course Mark didn't turn a hair.

JANINE DUVITSKI: I didn't know anything about filming, everything was new. There seemed to be a lot of time spent in working out the character, the discussion of it was a luxury, but then I was in just about every scene. Alan just sort of sneaked things in, he'd come up with the odd whisper for you but you didn't notice him directing. The early scene where Paul Copley and I are sitting on Wormwood Scrubs and he tries to woo me – that was mostly all in one take. And so is the scene in the second half, on the bench with Diane and her dad, when he's out of prison and wants her back. Such a luxury, those long takes – I didn't know that films were usually made by doing bits here and there and cutting it all up and chopping around.

MARK SHIVAS: Alan's style was changing on *Diane*. Now he would let the camera sit in front of people for some time, and let people move in and out of frame, and he wouldn't cut. It prefigured his later work in some ways. And it was a seminal piece for him in terms of the bleakness of the style, the paring down and the working within the frame, matched with the bleak subject matter.

JANINE DUVITSKI: Diane has a big speech when she tells the vicar how she's had this stillborn baby by her dad. I had looked at it at home and I thought it was this big emotional speech and I'd probably be crying, so I did a lot of work on it. But I think what Alan didn't want was for me to emote away – which is the way that would have made me feel I was doing it rather well. So he asked if I would just not move at all, and be still, and say the words – he said it was just a camera rehearsal, he wanted to line up. So I did, but then when I finished he said, 'OK, fine, let's go with that.' And I was going, 'Oh no, Alan! I can really do this speech well, please!' 'No, that's fine, I've got it.' 'No!' But he had an effect in mind, and instead of asking me for that or giving me a line reading, he knew a better way to arrive at it. That was completely his talent.

CHRISTOPHER MORAHAN: He was an extraordinary stylist. For ten years or so his camera placement was open to parody, it was very still, rather emblematic – he would hold a frame for a very long time because the life was in the frame, an Ozu kind of style, albeit on a smaller canvas. There was a rigidity and a classicism.

MARK SHIVAS: *Diane* was controversial. I think one of the tabloids helped us immeasurably by splashing the fact that this scandalous incest film was coming to the BBC. But I don't remember any great hooha inside the BBC on that score. It was completely unerotic. It made the predicament understandable from all points of view, without saying, 'You must think this.' With a lot of Alan's work you're left to make up your mind about what you think of these people. It was somewhat like Otto Preminger's in that respect, an odd comparison perhaps. But *Anatomy of a Murder* would have been a perfect Alan Clarke film, great film that it is.

JANINE DUVITSKI: What was Alan like? He was sexy, charismatic, funny, principled. Principled in his workload – he stuck to what he thought was the right thing to do. Most people cop out more than that. But he was committed to television as a medium, where he could reach a lot of people. Funny – he could be wonderfully sarcastic without being cruel. Sexy – for about a year or so after *Diane* I would go round to his flat in Almeida Street. It was a den of iniquity, I suppose; it looked scary. I remember hovering at the top of those steps to the basement, wondering whether to go down. But you sort of knew all that. I thought, 'Oh, I shouldn't go there really,' but I did – you did whatever he suggested. If you describe some of the goings-on, it does sound a bit dark. And if I hadn't enjoyed it so much, it would have been slightly off. But I just loved it. What I wasn't was unwilling. I think he was for people having a good time and I don't think anybody who was frightened or unwilling would have gone down there.

12

'Alan Clarke's never sold out' – 'Who'd want him?': Return trips to Liverpool 1973–1975

NORMA MCMINN: The Beatles gave Liverpool a lot of recognition, but I was bringing my family up by the time they came along. And there was poverty then in Liverpool, and you still see it now. Now they do up the docklands, like in London – they dress up these warehouses and derelict buildings. But we've had dock workers on strike. Factories closed. And if you go to the inner city it's a slum. They've iced the cake, dolled up the edges, but in the city the streets are awash with litter, blocking doorways. They should sort it out.

GRENVILLE MIDDLETON: Alan was a bit like a godfather with his family, Norma and the others – you couldn't get to them, he sort of kept them away from his life. It was a funny blockage. I tried to get them up to Almeida Street many times, but he wouldn't allow it. Eventually one of Norma's kids came to work at the puppet theatre I run. He got away from that Liverpool scene that was so grim, no work, and awful sorts of 'work schemes' instead.

NORMA MCMINN: In 1968 Alan had come back to the scene in Leasowe for a bit. John and I had five children by then, and we'd got a house in Morton. He said to Mum, 'I've got something to tell you, and I'd like it if Norma could come down.' I turned up and she said, 'So what is it?' He said, 'I'd just like to tell you you've got two grandchildren I haven't told you about.' We still weren't on the phone and he hadn't wanted to write, he wanted to tell it to our faces. But after 1968 there was another spell of years when we didn't hear from him. Alan never discussed his ongoing personal, domestic situation. Far as we knew he was living with Jane and his children. Until he changed his address for Almeida Street. Then about 1973 he and Grenville came up. A lot of Guinness got drunk then – my mum liked a Guinness.

GRENVILLE MIDDLETON: I went up there with Al in 1973 and I met Norma. He hadn't been there for years, though he used to write to his mum every week and send her money. The estate in Leasowe was grim, they'd built it around the factories, such as Cadbury's – then the factories closed, and the buses that came into Leasowe stopped running. And everything was shuttered up and behind bars, having been broken into constantly. Graffiti on every inch of wall space. John McMinn was a bit of a petty villain, and Al would tell the most terrible stories about him. Al's mum had her little council house in Leasowe and if she'd gone out for the day, John came in and he sold all of her furniture. I met him a couple of times, he was always funny, full of quips. And John and Norma had five lovely children. But eventually John got really bad.

NORMA MCMINN: By 1973 me and my husband were having a lot of trouble. John was out of work and a bit violent, he knocked me about a bit. Alan heard of all this and he was very protective. I was coping. But Alan wanted to invest his money in something and he bought a house in Westmoreland Road, New Brighton, so me and the children could get away. I had got a legal separation so I could get the giro instead of John, because he would get the money and just disappear. It was a pretty bad time. But I was lucky to have Alan, he really did help me. And we moved in 1975. John'd turn up here begging me to go back to him but it was no good, he'd done too many bad things; I was coping better on my own than with him. I got a divorce in 1979 finally, and John died that year.

Jane and Molly and Gabe helped with the moving here, and they stayed for quite a bit in the first summer, around 1975. Alan stayed for a month, he went back and forth between London. He'd come home odd weekends to see the kids and that, but after the first day he was on edge all the time, to get back to his work, back to London. He couldn't relax much.

GRENVILLE MIDDLETON: Who knows where his talent came from? He just had to get away from Liverpool to realize it. When you come from that sort of background, you've discovered the baseline, haven't you? But if you're from a middle-class background, especially in England, and you're planning on doing drama – then you've got to get yourself down in the gutter, then you can start to understand the motivation people have for what they say and do. But if you're coming out of that environment, then you have it all in the bank. And no one can get at you. He would never put himself in any kind of vulnerable position, Alan. You couldn't get to the bloke behind the surface, there was no softness, no sore point. And I think that's a protection that comes out of the society he was born and brought up in. They were very fashionable in the 1970s, Northern writers and tough Northern dramas and documentaries. But at the same time they were coming south, having a good time, taking our women. Roy and Alan were as left as you could ever get, revolutionary almost. All their film-making was directed towards the overthrow of the ruling class. But of course in order to do that – well, Alan always insisted to me that Lenin had said, 'Sometimes you've got to work from within,' which is really what they were doing. But simultaneously they were having a good time. So you don't know where the hypocrisy starts, or where the political honesty ends – that's what I'm saying.

TONY GARNETT: Alan was on the left just in his gut, wasn't he? Also, almost instinctively, without thinking about it, he had the capacity to reveal on the screen the lives of people whom the world had pissed on one way or the other. And there wasn't a whiff of the patronizing in it. The humour that came from those characters and their predicaments was always through them and with them. He never put a foot wrong. I don't think he was capable of patronizing working people. Also, his anger was untempered by success or his presence in luvviedom and the professional middle classes, which was of course what he was, what we all are. It wasn't diluted at all by that. He just hated the bosses. Alan didn't wear his ideology on his sleeve, and in a way his films are all the more political for that.

JEHANE MARKHAM: There was a terrible bleak side to Alan, which he exaggerated later when he was living on his own in the Grampians at Shepherd's Bush, which I never went to. He was obsessed with a kind of annihilation of domesticity, possibly to do with where he came from. I did go up to his mother's house, to the estate in Leasowe. I felt quite honoured to be invited. And that was quite a revelation. The estate was incredibly bleak and there was hardly anything in that house because they just didn't have the money. When I saw him in the environment in which he was raised, it made a lot more sense. Maybe he was driven to recreate that, to touch base in some ways, to never feel that he'd been taken over by another life.

PAM BRIGHTON: It was sort of a joke – 'Alan Clarke's never sold out.' 'Who'd want him?' But the reason why people like him are so important is that he insisted on doing things absolutely with integrity – because he had it, did Alan. He was never bourgeois – it was his saving grace, really. He never wanted the BMW. He'd have lived on a camp-bed in order to do the work.

13
'A few scrapes' 1975–1976

Funny Farm (1975)

PAUL KNIGHT: I actually went and had Roy Minton committed once, about 1969. Roy was an alcoholic at that point, he had ulcers, he was gambling a lot. His then wife phoned me and I went up to Nottingham. We committed him to the mental home because that was the only course – he was in a terrible state and she'd been in touch with the doctors and so on. We went to this enormous and incredibly grim fortress-like Victorian building and put him in, and left him there after tearful farewells. We went back home and had dinner, and about four in the morning the phone rang; it was Roy and he said, 'Get me the fuck out of here,' and that was that. Most of what he wrote was based on his life, so I suppose there was a bit of that episode in *Funny Farm*.

MICHAEL JACKLEY: Roy had done a lot of research for the script, then Alan did a bit himself by going and working in the hospital for a bit; he got his little white jacket on and did a few stints. I think Tim Preece did too; he was playing the lead, the nurse who has to run all over this ward dealing with these terribly distressed people. Now to be a male nurse, the qualifications aren't so exacting and these people aren't so well thought of in the medical profession. But the piece was about the intolerable burdens of that job, the low pay, the long hours, the stress of coping. We had real patients coming in and out on that shoot. Your blood turned to ice when you went in. Obviously, I don't agree with care in the community now, because it plainly doesn't work, but you could see the arguments for closing places like this – mile-long corridors.

MARK SHIVAS: This was the start of Alan's penchant for people

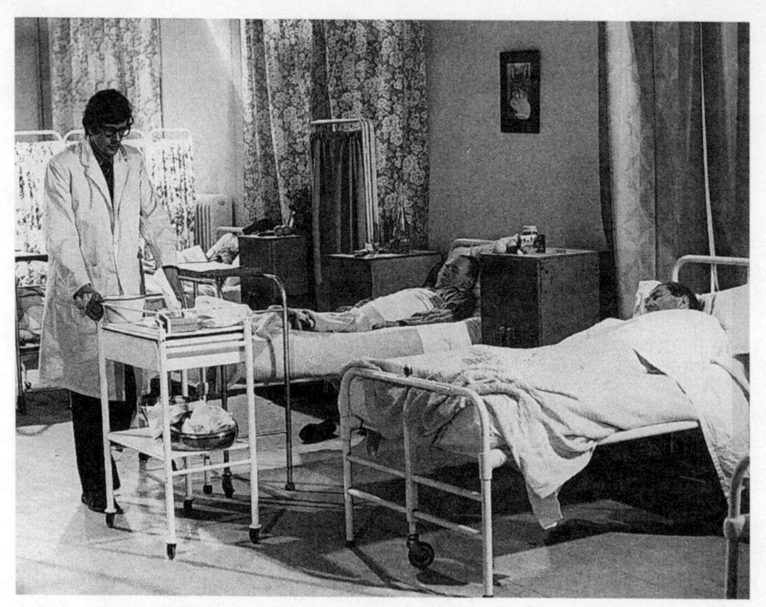

Nurse Alan Welbeck (Tim Preece) goes about his thankless business in *Funny Farm* (1975)

walking down corridors, I think. Very often we saw the Tim Preece character making his lonely way about the building with the camera at his shoulder. This may have been assisted by the newer lightweight cameras, which made Alan a bit more flexible in getting about.

CHRISTOPHER MORAHAN: It was commissioned as a seventy-five-minute play and it came out at one hundred and five. For me this was like working on a newspaper – we were working in fictional journalism if you like – and if you write a thousand words when your editor asked for five hundred, he has to spike half the article. This was during the three-day week, and we had to be off the air by eleven o'clock at night. There was no way it could be broadcast at that length.

MICHAEL JACKLEY: The cutting was bad. Alan thought, 'Just 'cos the news is going on at nine, why should my fookin' film have to finish?' But I think you have to cut your cloth according to your means. There may have been a bit of arrogance in there. Alan had a few scrapes like that.

CHRISTOPHER MORAHAN: Yes, Alan got very angry and petitioned the plays department against me – stood at the gate of the BBC and handed out pamphlets. It got pretty rough, and people said I had been censorious. But it was entirely to do with the length and when we had to be off air. In one sense, however, I did behave in a totally high-handed way, because Alan wanted to have his name taken off and I refused. I said, 'Don't be so silly, it's very good and it's improved for being a bit shorter. It's your work and you should sign it.' His attitude was 'No, it isn't, you've cut it.'

Love for Lydia and *Fast Hands* (1976)

STEPHEN FREARS: I went to London Weekend around 1976 and Clarkey was there. There'd been some mysterious row where he'd been working on some H.E. Bates series, he'd done the first episode and then had left.

DAVID YALLOP: There's no *Brideshead Revisited* in Alan's filmography, he avoided all of that because he knew the area of his expertise. Hence the arguments over *Love for Lydia*, perhaps. There were six episodes planned, I think, and Alan had the idea that he'd begin the first episode on wide shots, hold those right the way through. And as the story progressed, week by week, he'd tighten the shot – so you'd end up with the last episode shot all in close-up. A couple of episodes in, Cyril Bennett came to have a look at a rough cut. And Cyril said, 'Alan, where are my stars?' Alan points at these small figures, says, 'There and there. That's them ice-skating.' And he explained what he wanted to do, this trick of getting closer and closer. Cyril said, 'Alan, by the time you get to the last episode there'll be nobody watching. I've paid serious money for these people, I want to see them.' One totally understood what Cyril was about; equally, one understood Alan. As a strategy for a single play, it certainly would have worked. But over many weeks –

Clarke has a lark on location during his ill-fated work on *Love for Lydia* (1976)

well, Cyril had a point. Alan was fired on that, they brought in someone else and there was reshooting. But it scarred Alan very deeply.

ROY MINTON: Al had a very sound ego, intact most of the time. But his ego took a bit of a bashing over *Love for Lydia*. I said, 'Just tell people you were fired, don't polish it. You'll get a lot more respect'. And he brazened it out. But I think he was so hurt that he said, 'Bollocks to that.' And he became a sort of cynosure over at the Beeb, where he liked working anyway.

BARRY HANSON: He was obsessed by the long shot, the long shot where, in actual fact, nothing much happens. I mean, just as he'd shot Glenda Jackson all in close-up for a *Half Hour Story*, he was perfectly capable of shooting everybody in the longest possible shot. He'd go, 'Eh, it's just a phase I'm going through Barry, like.' There was this perverse side about him. So you'd go, 'Look, we've been on this shot half an hour.' 'Yeah, very interesting, isn't it?' '*I'm* not fucking interested, Alan.' Certainly it wasn't that Alan didn't care if he failed, but he was ready to take that risk. And he didn't fail at all that much.

Plays for Britain was meant to try and force the pace towards certain grittier things which hadn't been done on Thames – it had been a bit middle-class and fancy. Howard Brenton did *Paradise Run*, which Michael Apted directed, Philip Saville did a play about child abuse, and Alan did *Fast Hands*. It was very good, very raw, done in about five days, ten minutes a day. It wasn't possibly among the prime pieces in Roy Minton's oeuvre – Roy would say, 'I've just thrown this together for a bit of cash.'

It was about a boxer suffering a bit of brain damage. And it involved a very realistic fight. We'd seen Bill Buffery in a National Youth Theatre piece about boxing, cast him as the kid and got him a professional trainer for six weeks. Bill took a lot of knocks actually, because the guy he was fighting, who was training him as well, was a middleweight contender. And however hard Bill could hit, with a middleweight contender you bash him anywhere and it doesn't register.

ROY MINTON: It got out of hand, because I quickly realized that this actor was going to be knocked out. They sparred in rehearsal, but when they shot it, the pro boxer was meant to put the guy away in the eighth round – and his attitude seemed to be 'Well, it's gonna hurt a bit but it'll soon be over.' Clarkey was a bit remiss with that one. Maybe because it was such a slender piece, he went to the actuality to try and find a nucleus for it, a gut in the middle of it. But it wasn't necessary. And by then the make-believe had gone.

14

A demonstration to the authorities: *Scum* (1977)

ROY MINTON: When we were shooting *Funny Farm*, I was staying with Al at Almeida, we'd come back there at the end of the day. And on one of those evenings we started chatting about doing a trilogy. What we came up with was police cadets, boys entering the army – and boys in Borstal, the other side of the coin. And once we sparked it off, we got rabbiting. And after shooting one day we fixed to see Chris Morahan at Wood Lane, six-thirty in the evening. He said, 'Sounds good, but I haven't got the money.' We said, 'That's all right, we'll piss off then,' and he said, 'No, let's talk.' And Clarkey and I said, 'What's the point if we haven't got the dough?' The upshot was that next day he came up to location, said he'd been thinking about it and that he would like to commission one of them, whichever one we chose. For us it was quite obvious, it had to be the Borstal idea. He asked if we wanted to do it with Mark and we did. So he commissioned me to write that with Mark as producer.

The research for *Scum* was really harrowing, I did it all at Almeida Street. I got Mark to advertise in the *Guardian* and the *Islington Gazette* – y'know, 'Writer seeks to interview ex-Borstal trainees.' Most of the response came from the *Guardian*, strangely enough. And down in that basement, I tell you, I had guys coming through, sometimes four or five a day, not one of whom gave me their real name, all of them paranoid. I had to arrange the meets so that I got one guy out before the next one arrived. The response was very good, very varied – quite a few guys from showbiz came through, and some successful businessmen, in good suits with handy cars outside. Some people clearly fucked up for ever. And it was a weird three months. Clarke was around some of the time, he met a few of the guys. And what I finished up with was this sack of fucking misery; it was appalling, what had happened to these people's lives. Researching *Funny Farm* was a pleasure by comparison.

When I started, I didn't know what I'd end up with. But one of these men who came to see me was a local villain who'd been a 'daddy'. He became the Carlin character. And that figure was essential, all the drama and the confrontations flowed from that idea of one trainee being the boss inside. And then I did meet a guy who shouldn't have been at Borstal, given his age. He was older, disillusioned, and he decided, 'They've had a piece of me, I'll have a piece of them and I don't care how long I do.' So that steered me towards the character of Archer. It wrote itself quite easily then. I went up to the Lake District and knocked it out, sent a copy to Al and one to Mark. Al phoned me straight after he'd read it, said, 'Brilliant.' I thought, 'That's nice.' Mark turned it down – said it was too biased.

MARK SHIVAS: I don't remember why I turned down *Scum*. I don't think I'd had enough of Roy Minton. Whether they'd had enough of Mark Shivas – it's possible.

ROY MINTON: Then Al and I set about trying to place it as a movie – we both went skint in the process, but we really concentrated on it, went to everybody. I remember Puttnam saying that he liked the piece, but he thought it would be two years before the British film industry was ready for something of this nature. I said, 'That's ideal, let's do it then, it'll take two years and you'll be the first in.' But nobody would go near it, it had to go into abeyance. We were worn out, disillusioned, put it to one side. If you approached the British film industry at that time, your main problem was finding it, you'd be up and down Wardour Street all fucking day.

STELLA RICHMAN: I was running my own production company then, the first of the independents, with David Frost. Alan and Roy needed money for *Scum* but I had to tell them that we weren't in the business of raising money for films, we were in the television business. Alan and Roy went all over London, still in their wanking macs – can you imagine a more unlikely couple?

ROY MINTON: Then Margaret Matheson, who I'd met when she was Mark's script editor, went back to the Beeb as a producer. And I got in touch and we arranged to meet in a pub in Notting Hill. I had three scripts with me in a plastic bag and I gave them her, but I said, 'This one here, *Scum*, that's not for sale' – I still thought it would go as a movie. I went back to Nottingham, and Margaret called me one night – no surprise which one she wanted. And one was skint at the time, so . . .

MARGARET MATHESON: I was as green as it was possible to be. I'd been hired by Jimmy Cellan-Jones, so-called 'Head of Plays', to produce *Play for Today* for a period. I had four films to find and twelve taped plays – I mean, a completely unheard-of luxury now, you were just given these slots, Jimmy signed off and you were away. Naturally, everybody hits the new person with all the stuff that's been previously rejected, and one of the first things I got was the script of *Scum*, which I read quite fast, thought was fantastic, and which I decided to do straight off. It was certainly my ambition to produce drama that was strong meat, drama that was focused on very public subjects of interest. It was a somewhat journalistic ambition, but it fitted very comfortably with what Alan wanted to do. I didn't change a word of Roy's script. What they gave me was what we would shoot. And we found these brilliant kids, awfully young, mostly from the Anna Scher School.

PHIL DANIELS: We must have had an open audition for *Scum* at Anna Scher's. Anna used to go round the empty schools in the summer holidays doing theatre workshops. I was eleven or twelve, and the sister of one of my mates was doing it and we went round to pick her up. We sat at the back, primarily to take the piss. But I quite liked what was going on, and somehow Anna had that knack of getting people involved, and she got us in. Then I found out where she was in Islington and I carried on going. It was complete improvisation, what she did. It would be, 'You, you're home late from school – and you, you're the parent and you wanna know why.' So what you did was act out a lot of the things that really went on in your life. And that's why I think a lot of her people are quite real, that's the sort of style that she taught you. *Winstone*, of course, went to Corona, didn't he? It's a *stage* school, like fee-paying, and you take your ballet shoes and tap shoes. But I suppose he did get chucked out.

RAY WINSTONE: By the time *Scum* came up I'd made up my mind not to be an actor, I was leaving drama school. I'd lasted twelve months, no remission. They tried to get me out a couple of times and they were probably right, to be perfectly honest; I was a bit of a toe-rag. I was told I was a bit of a danger to the other kids 'cos of my accent. So I sabotaged the headmistress's car – I got a lolly stick and put all these tacks through it, put it under her front tyre and when she drove off, bang. But some straight kid turned grass – he lollied me up, as they say – and I was asked to leave the premises. And it was probably the best thing that ever happened to me. They were having a casting and I was only supposed to be there saying good-bye to my mates. I got talking to the receptionist and she said, 'You wanna go in and meet the director?' I said, 'Nah, not really, I'm off for a drink with the boys.' I was flirting with her really, showing off, but I went in and met Clarkey. And I got the job! I didn't have a clue what it was, hadn't seen the script, and I didn't really care. I thought, 'Yeah I'll do it, bit of a laugh.' It was written for a Scotsman originally, he was a Glaswegian in the script, Carlin. But apparently Al gave me the part because he liked the way I walked down a corridor.

In a way I loved Carlin and I didn't. Like it said on the poster of the film, 'Survival rules OK,' and there's always some of that in Clarkey's stuff. He left it open to the audience, didn't shove it down their throat. I think I saw Carlin as a bloke in a situation with his back to the wall. He'd got nicked and banged up. There was a bit of the hero in him – because the system and the way the kids are treated, they're supposed to be educated and rehabilitated, and the point of the film was to show that they weren't. They're actually punished to such a degree that they come out full of hatred. Carlin goes in and doesn't want the violence, but it's inevitable that he's gonna get it. His only way out is to go full in

Scum (1977): Trainee 4737 Carlin (Ray Winstone) faces the Governor

and take charge. He plays the game in the end. In the original he becomes a prison poof, and that's true, that happens in prisons. They're prison poofs when they're inside, outside they're straight as a die – I can't work that one out myself.

ROY MINTON: One of the guys I met during research, a professional villain, he told me that once you're in a dormitory, the public school element prevails. It's not a homosexual thing, he made the point I gave to Carlin, 'I'm no fucking poofter.' But it's not unusual for professional criminals to engage in a bit of that. I thought the gay scene opened all sorts of areas up and said a lot about Carlin, his flexibility – and also the problem about being a pretty boy, which is the same in adult nicks.

MARGARET MATHESON: We rehearsed in the BBC rehearsal rooms in Acton and it was very interesting to me. I'd been to quite sedate rehearsals before, where everything would be blocked out, and there was always a studio approach, whether it was a studio piece

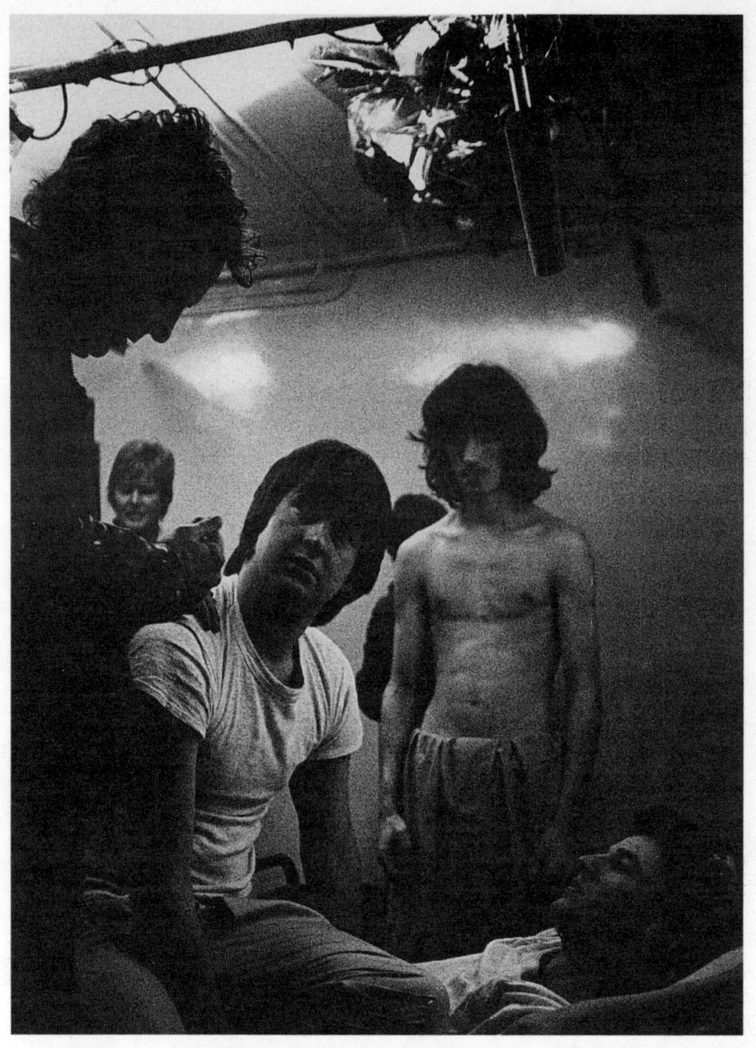

Scum (1977): Clarke directs John Blundell, Phil Daniels and Ray Winstone

or not. But the boys in *Scum* were drilled – partly because of the nature of the piece and partly because Alan just wanted it to be absolutely solid. He'd repeat and repeat the scenes in the rehearsal room so that the boys could just do it on the day. He removed any fear of the action they were going to have to do, or the knowing of the lines. Then we shot it March/April 1977, we had some laughs about it but it was a pretty tough film to make, because what it's really about is very, very distressing. We ended up shooting in a freezing cold ex-old folks home in Redhill.

MICHAEL JACKLEY: Obviously there was a black–white polarization in the script and we had to find a big black guy to play Baldy, the rival daddy. Peter Harris stood out – he was amazing. We found other lads in youth clubs around Redhill. We used to bring everybody to the location on the train from London on special tickets; we couldn't afford to put them up, but British Rail had a deal whereby they could travel for fifty pence a head, so I went around selling tickets to these hundreds of lads.

PHIL DANIELS: There was a little bit of picking-on in the cast, just 'cos we were all still at school age. But he run a very tight ship, Alan, always. Everybody respected him, so there wasn't a lot of liberty taken. We was late when we filmed *Scum* once. And he fuckin' couldn't bear that, lateness – real strict. He gave us a real bollocking in front of everybody, oh yeah. About three days later two of the big sparks were late, spent too long in the pub – Al did exactly the same to them. So you knew. 'Ah! That's fair.' You see? That made him quite popular.

RAY WINSTONE: I got a lot of kudos from *Scum*, which is down to Alan. Technically I didn't have a clue what I was doing, I just used my instincts about how people talk and what violence was and so on, which was a great schooling for me. And that comes from Clarkey. My performance in *Scum* is Clarkey's performance, not mine. If I'd known about acting, I'd have been acting. But what he would do before a take, he'd come over to me and he'd go all Scouse, scratching his arse and picking his ear, and saying, 'Er, Ray, like – how's the family, kid? Is the mum and dad all right, y'know?' I'd say, 'Oh yeah, fine, Alan,' feeling all mellow. And we loved him, y'know? We respected him – as a chap. And then I'd do the scene – and then he'd come up to me and call me a cunt! And it would really wind me up, 'cos someone you like calling you a cunt and meaning it, you'd do the scene and wanna beat the geezer to death. Clarkey was manipulating that all the time, which is what a good director does – he gets you into that mood where you bounce off of it. Directing, he'd get very quiet, and he'd do all this gesticulation with his hands and make these noises and say, 'Give it a bit of . . .' and 'Some of . . .' He'd bring me up and take me down, he could do that. I realized it later, but he ain't here now. I've learnt to use it myself now, but I learned it from him. With Clarkey there's nothing that's impossible. 'My character wouldn't do that.' Bollocks – my character can do anything, 'cos I can, and I'm making him up. You experiment and do things with it and he was for that. 'What do you wanna do, kid? Don't matter what I want, what do you feel about it?' He enjoyed teaching, for his own reasons too. And you can see all the actors he's trained. Forget all those Method books, he was the best teacher from my point of view, he was the geezer. I was lucky to have him. Like when now and then you forget how to act – it happens – I just have to think, 'Oh yeah, Clarkey, that's it; the truth, just the truth.'

PHIL DANIELS: We always wondered like, 'Is he gay?' Because he used to put his arm round you all the time. Me and Ray would be like, 'Is he fuckin' bent or what?' His directing was 'Phil, come 'ere.' Arm round shoulder. 'You're a good boy really, aren't ya?' 'Thanks, Al.' And off he'd go. And you'd think, 'Yeah! I'm a good boy.' So you'd wanna do your best for him. But he knew, y'see – he knew what we were really like, outside all the bravado of it, all of us tryin' to walk round being tough. Well, Ray is a bit tough, isn't he? Good as gold, though. But Clarkey was like our hero when we were doing these films 'cos we all loved it, running around, being in Borstal. We'd heard the stories about him, hanging out of the BBC Club with his trousers down and all that, we liked that. And he seemed much more accessible, directors in those days were sort of university bods. And he was a Liverpudlian and he was a fucking tramp, wasn't he? That's what I used to like. I had this leather jacket, sort of German and ripped to bits, and he loved it, Clarkey. I used to let him wear it.

MARGARET MATHESON: The 'murderball' scene was very drilled, so that everybody knew what was going to happen. Of course, he was constantly encouraging them to go for it. But they would never have done anything except what he wanted.

PHIL DANIELS: Murderball is two teams in a gym, a medicine ball in the middle, and one team has to get the ball up at their end. Now Al got this youth club in from Leytonstone to come and play against all us actors, didn't he? That was the opposition. But we were a rough lot ourselves, not exactly wimpy.

RAY WINSTONE: There was a lot of tension, he wanted that, he was a stickler for reality. He'd go down before the murderball scene and say to the black guys, 'Now look, guys, there's a rumour going round, the white guys are gonna steam into ya. I don't want no trouble, but be ready, OK?' And, of course, all these black kids from Leytonstone are gonna go, 'Bollocks – if it's going off, it's going off.' Then he'd come down to the white kids and say, 'Look, the black kids are a fuckin' bit tasty.' And we were a bunch of herberts from South London, East London. We thought, 'Alright!'

PHIL DANIELS: And then Alan stood up on the tower above it all, like he was in charge of a garrison. They had two or three cameras running that day, 'cos obviously there'd only be one shot at it. I got whacked and I said, 'What's happenin', Al?' He just said, 'Get in dere, my son.' And that's all we did, we got stuck in. And I think we held our own.

RAY WINSTONE: There was one bit where Phil Daniels actually saved me from getting a beating. It went right off in the corner, this fella and I were having a row and he got me pinned down by the legs and these three geezers were bearing down on me, but Phil steamed in and pulled them off. It was mayhem, but Clarkey got it all on film and that was his thing. You lived it, you were in there.

PHIL DANIELS: It was dodgy, I suppose, murderball – but not dodgy enough for him not to do it. All the kicks and the hitting, he was very keen on it to be true. All the slaps were real slaps, and all that kicking between the bollocks – after about fifteen takes it really started hurting. But that's why the film's brutal, it's about brutality and you can't pull too many punches, I suppose.

MICHAEL JACKLEY: I took most of the lads to hospital during the making of *Scum*, they were maimed. And I picked up a chest infection that felt like a heart attack, so I was carted off too.

RAY WINSTONE: I said to Clarkey at one point, 'I retired from boxing to become an actor so I didn't get hit, what's going on?' There was one of the screws who was a bit heavy-handed in a scene, and so the word went round that in the big riot scene where it all went off, he was gonna get it. But I think someone bottled it and told him – 'cos he moved very quick. That was just the atmosphere that was created. He was probably a nice guy – but if we'd got hold of him, he'd have been in trouble.

PHIL DANIELS: Yeah, all that with Ray and John Judd – but it was good, y'see. Clarkey said, 'Y'know, fookin' give 'im a bit o' stick.' And then Ray had that – didn't like him, see? Didn't like that actor, thought it was too much. So whatever methods Alan used, he got results, but sometimes they were slightly out of order.

RAY WINSTONE: Ray Jewers was co-ordinator of the fights. There was one scene where Baldy and I have our head-to-head in the boiler room. The way it was planned, I hit him with an iron bar, he gets up and chins me, and I do him. I'm thinking, 'Bollocks.' If I hit him with an iron bar and he gets up, I'm fucking off, I'm heading for the long grass here, y'know? No, if I hit him with an iron bar then he's gonna stay down. And I said this to Clarkey and he said, 'OK, do it.' So that's how it was: 'Where's your tool?' 'What fucking tool?' 'This fucking tool' – bosh, smash, crunch, kick the fuck out of him and goodnight. I hate fights in films where they're hitting each other all day, that's just not the way it is. And I'm not for censorship but to me that's the violence that should be banned if it comes to it.

MICHAEL JACKLEY: The riot scene is where the boys smash up the dining room after one of their mates has been driven to suicide. It was something of a climax, and you could only do it once. We had cameras mounted up on towers to shoot from one or two angles. They started banging the trays and chanting 'Dead!', and Carlin threw his tray at the wall – and they just ran amok. And they ended up demolishing the room, breaking the windows and indeed the frames. And without it being choreographed, this pyramid of broken tables was piled up in the middle of the room and they paced around it. One of the girls on the crew was weeping, it was so real. And it was frightening, they wouldn't stop. I got a broomstick and walked in and shouted, 'Stop, cut, cut!' Clarkey gave them a lot to work with, but it developed a life of its own, and it was almost inevitable that the devastation would take on that kind of ferocity.

It brought into sharp relief how these young people were forced to be – vilified by society, deprived of parental care, all the things that bring people to these situations. It was rebellion against an unreasonable regime, whatever they'd done to end up there. It was the man in Alan that drew out the human qualities of the piece, he had great sympathy with the trainees, he knew some of them had never had a chance. And there was sensitivity in those people, whatever you say about it. The film has moments of great tenderness; they played funny little domestic scenes, like David Threlfall as Archer reading a letter for an illiterate boy.

MARGARET MATHESON: I had anticipated a storm over *Scum* at the outset, but once we'd actually made it I thought we were through the danger. And I was very careful. I was absolutely determined to behave like this was any old piece of drama. You sent out what was called an Early Warning Synopsis, which I wrote for *Scum*. And I was very scrupulous in listing what happened, in absolutely bald, cold language, without adjectives. It just read 'So-and-so commits suicide' etcetera, and it listed everything, because I didn't want them to say, 'You didn't tell us!' further down the line. So anyway it went sailing through. The then-Controller of BBC1 was Brian Cowgill, and this Early Warning Synopsis was copied to him and a number of other people, and was unremarked upon. Then in July 1977, after production but before it was scheduled, Cowgill went off to be Head of Thames, and Billy Cotton took over as Controller of BBC1. So that meant he had a licence to say, 'The past doesn't count.' And the programme copy had gone to the *Radio Times*, such were the deadlines in those days. But then Billy Cotton wanted a postponement of the broadcast. Then suddenly we got a call about wanting cuts. Specifically I think they wanted the rape of Davis in the greenhouse to be shorter. They also wanted to cut one of the two suicides. And they wanted to cut the moment of impact when Carlin hits Richards across the face with the snooker balls in a sock. We were allowed to show the build-up but not the actual strike.

RAY WINSTONE: To cut the impact of the balls, that would have killed it. 'Cos you see that swipe and feel the weight of it, and the noise when it hits him, and the noise Phil makes himself, like a whimper. And because you don't see the cut, it hurts.

MARGARET MATHESON: Needless to say, we bridled at all of these suggestions and we made a fuss about it. Alan used to charge up to the fifth floor in his Doctor Martens, whereas I was a proper producer who dressed for the occasion. Michael Swann was the Chairman of the BBC – charming man, dead now. I rang him up from a phone box outside Broadcasting House and said, 'Look, I need to see you.' He said, 'Fine, jolly good, up you come.' I was straight into his office, and he was very understanding. So we dug our heels in, and got involved with the Managing Director, Alasdair Milne, who would offer us large glasses of whisky while we sat having these arguments.

ROY MINTON: James Cellan-Jones phoned me up and said, 'I'm getting a group of Home Office people in, screws, governors, a good cross-section of the bureaucracy, can I have your permission to show them *Scum*?' I said, 'Do you need it?' He said he did, so I said, 'No, you can't. If they can see it the public can see it, they paid for it.' But they saw it anyway, and the only criticism they could make was that it couldn't all have happened in a fortnight. There's nothing in the script to suggest it's a fortnight, it could have been three months, three years. But that was their only objection. It seemed to me that on those grounds you should show it. But instead there was this farce.

MARGARET MATHESON: Milne showed the film to a couple of people, notably David Rose, the Head of Drama in Birmingham, and to Tom Mangold, who was a *Panorama* reporter then doing something about prisons, and very in with the Home Office. David Rose didn't think the film should be shown, certainly not in the form it was in. And Tom Mangold said it wasn't true. His line was that it wasn't that any of these things couldn't happen in such an institution, it was just that they couldn't all happen in the space of seventy-five minutes. Well, you think, 'Welcome to dramatic fiction!'

ROY MINTON: I was in Brussels and Margaret called me to say the BBC had banned *Scum* and could I get over? I wrote an article for Margaret to lobby with, 'The Billy Cotton Banned Show'; they had badges made too. My point was, the way BBC drama worked, responsibilities and budgets were delegated down a long line, and somebody somewhere had missed the boat. Either you delegate or you check before they're made, but you don't spend all that licence-payers' money then chuck it in the dustbin. I found out later that Bill Cotton was a magistrate, he had a vested interest – that would have been another pellet in the gun. It was an abnegation of responsibility, the freedom you enjoyed at the BBC was out the window. Cotton had his own reason for banning it, and Milne just decided to back his guvnor, simple as that. And how awful and ironic that Alan has to die before the fuckers finally showed it, eh?

TONY GARNETT: I would suppose that Alan would almost temperamentally have to test the limits of tolerance at the BBC, and then push it further. Because to be banned by the BBC, I'm sure he would wear that like a medal.

PHIL DANIELS: We were disappointed it never got saw, y'know. It did feel like a political nobbling. And that was quite good, we quite liked that – big lefties.

DAVID HARE: Alan was free to get on uninterrupted at the BBC until *Scum*. And I believe *Scum* is – well, I would stand by what I said at Alan's memorial service. 'Along the fault line created by the banning of *Scum* flowed all the lousy decisions and abject behaviour which left the BBC ten years later having to fight to justify its very existence to government.' Meaning that the decision about *Scum* was particularly craven, it was a pure political decision dressed up as an artistic decision. And there wasn't any real justification for it, except sheer fear of government. And once you had the simple equation – the Home Office licenses the BBC, therefore you cannot make films which are critical of Home Office institutions – then the BBC's credibility was destroyed. The government looked Alasdair Milne in the eye, and he blinked, he simply said, 'I'll destroy our own work.' To not back your own creative people when they haven't done anything wrong and everybody knew they hadn't done anything wrong was a very grim moment in the history of the BBC.

We campaigned. I went to a writers' party which was given at the BBC, by Alasdair Milne actually. Brian Clark and I went round the party with a petition to get *Scum* shown, and the people running the BBC were incensed, because it was their party and they said it was an abuse of their hospitality. And nobody who worked at the BBC would dare sign the thing, you know? But the feeling got incredibly bitter. And it made Alan angry, he was determined that it wouldn't be the event he became hung up on for the rest of his life. But to me – his work quite clearly heads toward *Scum* and then heads away from *Scum*You know, as Alan said himself, there were an awful lot of television directors called Alan, and a lot of people didn't know whose work was whose – Alan Bridges, Alan Cooke, they all got mixed up, and it wasn't entirely unfair. I mean, up to *Scum*, Alan Clarke is a very, very good – you know, the best – television director. After *Scum* he becomes something more. There's a deepening in him. And it undoubtedly did deepen his work and gave it a sort of wildness that it didn't have before. He's quite a controlled artist up until then. Then basically anarchy breaks out and his attitude is, 'I'm going to smash the toys in the shop, and I'll just do what I can get away with.' As in that thing of throwing out the script of *Elephant* and so forth. There was a 'So fuck you' about him after that incident – incident's underplaying it, after that *event* – which I understand.

BARRY HANSON: Alan was unleashed after *Scum*, but there was also a maturing, a bit like when a director in the theatre stops singing to the sets and gets back to bare boards and a passion. It's got a similar quality, the journey he took with it. And in a way, more difficult to do in television because it's not built for that, that isn't appreciated – stripping it down to an essential level. That can be a lonely thing, and he did manage it.

15

Darkness visible: *Danton's Death* (1978)

DAVID YALLOP: I think the thin end of the wedge for Alan at Almeida Street came after Gren Middleton sold it. Alan was a sitting tenant, but the new people were a little difficult; they couldn't appreciate Alan's life style and they wanted him out. So he returned the compliment and came to stay with my wife Anna and I, until our son Fletcher was due to make his appearance in June 1977. Alan was then under an extraordinary pressure of work, this was the time of *Danton's Death*.

STUART GRIFFITHS: I had been directing and editing drama at BBC Radio when James Cellan-Jones appointed me script editor of *Classic Plays* for television in the summer of 1977. David Jones asked me to contact Alan with a view to doing a production in the first series. Alan was at Ealing, a hard man to track down at the time. He was under some strain, editing a documentary about a Russian dissident and having difficulty in getting it on air. But I kept ringing and persistence was rewarded. We met and discussed several possibilities, and Alan was particularly keen on Büchner's *Woyzeck*.

PAM BRIGHTON: I'll never forget finding a copy of *Woyzeck* on Alan's bookshelf, and it was all annotated perfectly by hand, masses of notes in it. I mean, it was the only thumbed thing on that shelf. Mao and Marx? Untouched, I'm sure. But I found this Büchner and thought, 'God!' I was amazed.

DAVID JONES: At some point he came across Werner Herzog's movie of *Woyzeck*, and I think he felt that had done it in the way he'd had in mind. So Stuart and I began to urge him towards *Danton's Death*. Alan was always a very political creature, he had this very humanist left-wing attitude. And the play is about this great revolutionary tragedy – why did Danton go under and Robespierre survive? And though Alan was full of very positive life force, I do think his view of human nature and human history got increasingly black and pessimistic. So he took an awful relish in the idea that a guy like Robespierre should come out on top in this kind of revolutionary tumult.

STUART GRIFFITHS: Yes, Alan might have identified with Danton – this rich love of life and women and carousing. At the same time Danton was possessed by a kind of fatalism – he had the chance to escape, but he was so confident he wouldn't be executed that he returned to Paris. His fatalism came out in lines like, 'What do we do in life? We just walk – we put one foot in front of another.' The sense of life as boring monotony. That has a sort of dark existential connotation which I think appealed to Alan. Another speech he particularly liked was Camille's condemnation of the theatre, as something inferior to life as it's actually lived. The painter David was included in this condemnation – David, of course, painted the dying tortured prisoners of the September massacres, and turned that reality into art. I think Alan had some sympathy with Camille's views.

DAVID JONES: Alan was like this Liverpool roaring boy and Stuart was like an Oxford don, and they were absolutely inseparable. Alan was enormously amused by Stuart, and very impressed by his intellectual background. And Stuart loved letting his hair down and going a bit wild with Alan, so it was one of those hugely unlikely partnerships. I just let them get on with it.

STUART GRIFFITHS: Alan and I read as many as twelve translations of the play. And basically we decided that none of them were satisfactory, and that the best course would be for us to do our own version. So over three weeks or so, we carved out the structure together, we cut it and reshaped it. And Alan and I shared the credit for the adaptation. We were determined to keep the suspense going for as long as possible. In Büchner, the great speeches attacking

Danton occur in the middle, and you know then that he's doomed. We split these up and, in particular, we put Saint-Just's great tirade against Danton near the climax. So that when Danton was giving these tremendous speeches in the Convention, you felt he might actually turn the tide his way. We reduced the level of metaphysical discussion in the piece but kept some of the fine phrases. And we did things that would certainly have offended the purists. We inserted speeches from *Woyzeck*. I came across a speech of Robespierre's to the Convention, in praise of 'our lovely revolution', an almost sensuous way of addressing it, as though it were a woman. And I inserted that in the script. It suggests a romantic obsession on Robespierre's part – and we made the point that Robespierre was utterly puritanical and totally uninterested in sex. Whereas Danton was certainly an enthusiast.

We didn't want the drama to be held up by too much information. We wanted to sweep it on and simplify it as a Robespierre–Danton conflict – which may have been against Büchner's original intentions.

Of course David Jones's contact with the RSC enabled us to cast very well, and we bagged all our first choices – Ian Richardson as Robespierre, Michael Pennington as Saint-Just and Norman Rodway as Danton. I'd say the actors really enjoyed coming to work each day. And Alan treated me as he tended always to treat writers – if they were willing to be there from the start of the process, he gave them enormous say. He'd give his notes and then invite me to speak up.

DAVID JONES: Alan had a low boredom threshold – something I can understand – and both in approaching the text before shooting and afterwards in the editing, he kept throwing bits out, he pared it down to a minimalist presentation.

MICHAEL JACKLEY: It had terrific scope and design possibilities. Alan was after a kind of tableau effect at times. And Stuart Walker's design was very impressive.

STUART WALKER: I joined the BBC from the Royal Academy School, having been a painter, and in a way the BBC was like an extension of art school. It felt like an apprenticeship. I was an assistant designer to various very experienced designers who taught me what they knew – you were gradually brought along until they felt you were ready for the bigger things.

I knew of Alan's renown as a hell-raiser when I was allocated to him for *Danton's Death*, and we met and had a few long talks, kicking it around. There was no fixed point when Alan said, 'I want it to look like this or that.' But I think he reckoned this as a production that a designer could get his teeth into. One issue that came up almost straight away was how he was going to shoot the piece. He was then into his long lenses, and he was the first television director who'd raised the topic with me. It's common enough in film, but in television you've got zoom lenses and it's all close-ups, mid-shots, one-shots.

DAVID JONES: Alan was hugely interested in technical possibilities without necessarily wanting to spell out their theoretical implications. He decided to shoot all of *Danton's Death* on narrow lenses, so that in the studio the cameras were never closer to the actors than about fifteen yards. It was impossible to see what he was shooting unless you were looking at monitors. He got a very cool, detached feel to it. What you get with those lenses is enormous emphasis on close-up, with the background much more nebulous.

STUART WALKER: We were in TC1, the biggest studio in the BBC, about 160 feet by 100. And sure enough we ended up with the cameras right on the perimeter of the studio, shooting close-ups of actors right at the other end, so you had to be unusually careful that people didn't walk across the shot. And shooting that way lends a very different feel than moving in tight and doing the same close-up on a wider lens. The reason was that we looked at pictures of the period, eighteenth-century paintings and engravings of French society, and we discussed them. A lot of those pictures present tiny figures in big rooms and surroundings, and in order to convey the sense of scale, instead of flats and building I used frames of tubular steel with material stretched across, which were fairly expensive. And into those frames were spaces for windows and doors and architectural features, which we popped in. The sets were quite large, probably thirty feet long across a flat wall and twenty feet high. I know it caused a bit of trouble while I was doing it, because the scene crews hadn't experienced this before and took exception, but I'd say the effect repaid the effort.

STUART GRIFFITHS: The idea of the revolution devouring its own children – that interested Alan. He and I talked about the Russian Revolution, the transfer of power from Lenin to Stalin. This was all very alive in his mind, I suppose, having just made his documentary about the Russian dissident, Bukovsky.

Danton's Death (1978): Danton (Norman Rodway) savors the salon life while he can, in the company of Julie (Katherine Fahy)

Nina (1978)

MARGARET MATHESON: As a producer I resist fact-based drama, I don't like doing it because it's very restricting to have to adhere to people's actual lives, which can never be represented in the way they remember them. I prefer not to have that responsibility, and I like to think Alan would agree with me – that it's better to take a distance and use fictionalization to make a point. *Nina* was closely based on certain Russian dissidents, but it didn't purport to be biographical. From my perspective *Nina* was pure fiction, just influenced by a few surrounding circumstances.

JEHANE MARKHAM: My father David Markham had got involved with this Russian writer Vladimir Bukovsky, and Alan and Grenville Middleton did a documentary about Bukovsky when he came out of the Soviet Union in 1976. Bukovsky had been kept in prisons and psychiatric wards for years. And the point of the documentary was to show up the hypocrisy of the British government. They had shown no interest for years and years while my father kept up what had started as a rather pathetic little vigil, wearing a placard, and which had grown and grown and carried other people with it. Of course, my father's vigil wasn't the only reason why Bukovsky was released, they did a swap with another guy. But it had become an embarrassment and the government wanted it to quieten down. I was rather entranced by Bukovsky, we all were, and it was very exciting – this Russian guy comes out of a Russian prison and straight to our house. Alan's concern was with having a go at the system and exposing a truth, he wanted to help. He was also very concerned, obsessed even, with people in prison and being restricted – which goes back to the strange image I have sometimes when I think of Alan, of someone being confined in a very bleak, blank space. There's no doubt about it, he was interested in how people survive in the prison system – and in dissidents, and causing a fuss, and showing the underside of events. So the treatment of Russian writers by putting them into mental hospitals was something he just was naturally drawn to.

I thought his documentary had a terrific rawness to it, and Bukovsky at that time had an incredible beauty to him, having survived this experience, and being incredibly articulate about it. But I was very sad that it could all wash off him. I mean, sometimes prison can bring out the very best in a person, it can even bring out wonderful writing and poetry. So maybe it was something similar with Bukovsky. But when he came out, there was something disillusioning. It doesn't happen to everyone, it did to him. So I was sorry for my father. What happened to Bukovsky later was awfully sad – settling in and becoming a Tory and not fulfilling my father's dreams.

GRENVILLE MIDDLETON: Bukovsky went the other way, which Markham never cottoned on to until he got him out. Then he realized how right-wing the guy was. But then no one here realized how right-wing these communists were, their awful treatment of people, except intellectuals like Bukovsky and Marina Voikhanskaya and people like that.

JULIET MIDDLETON: Marina was a hospital doctor in the Soviet Union who found herself being required to dispense drugs to patients who clearly had no need of them – it was to shut them up. She couldn't agree with that, and she managed to get out of Russia, but she had to leave her son Misha behind. There was an understanding with the authorities that he would be allowed to follow her, but they then prevented that, so we organized various demonstrations. Marina got work here, though she had to resit all her doctor's exams to get reciprocal qualifications – amazing woman, she learned English very quickly. And in time Misha did get out.

JEHANE MARKHAM: Marina is an extraordinarily brave, admirable woman, and she helped me enormously with the script of the play. I plundered her life pretty mercilessly, but I hope I didn't do her any disservice, I think she liked what I did. Alan had said, 'There's a play knocking about here somewhere, why don't you have a go at writing it?' And part of me thought, 'God, this is too close to home.' But I suppose I had as good a chance as anyone of getting the stories from these two people. It was horribly hard work putting it together, but Margaret Matheson was terrific, almost daunting in how good she was.

MARGARET MATHESON: In Plays we didn't work things out in

advance, so the way I commissioned the two years' worth of stuff I did there was by backing writers or directors or subjects. I'm sure Alan just said to me, 'This is Jehane, this is what she wants to write about and this is what I think we should do next.'

JEHANE MARKHAM: I couldn't write a completely political piece because that's not what really interested me. I was interested in it as a love story that goes wrong. 'Yuri', the writer, was based on a wonderful bloke Marina was involved with. But she found him simply impossible to live with, it couldn't be sustained. She wanted to integrate into society and get a job and get her son over, and he was still playing the passionate dissident and getting into terrible havoc by not turning up at meetings and getting terribly drunk and losing a lot of money. I wanted to show the difficult passage for them in London, how different their culture was and how it isn't always easy to be given freedom.

MICHAEL JACKLEY: Alan cast one actress as Nina who then fell out. But Eleanor Bron came in and she was very impressive.

ELEANOR BRON: It must have been February 1978. What had happened was that they had been working for a week, Alan and Jack Shepherd and another actress who'd been cast as Nina. I think they came to a mutual agreement that they were all unhappy and she dropped out. So they were pretty desperate. I didn't know much about Alan except that he was very highly thought of. I went to meet him and pick up the script, expecting a long conversation. He just gave me the script and said, 'Now can you get back to us as soon as possible?' Just absolutely straight, which was how he was. I learned later that when my name had come up, he was not at all in favour of having me because he felt I had the wrong sort of image. But I had been doing some workshops that Jack Shepherd and Richard Wilson used to run, improvisational workshops of a high order, and Alan became aware of that and that made him slightly think again. And of course, he was up against it. It was a wonderful script. My one reservation was that Nina had to bare her breasts at one point, not something I was very keen on doing. It

The main players of *Nina* (1978): Margaret Matheson, Jehane Markham, Eleanor Bron, Alan Clarke and Jack Shepherd

did seem justified here, but I wanted to discuss it. So I phoned Alan. He said, 'So what do you think, do you like it?' I said, 'Well, I think it's wonderful, but –' 'Great, see you tomorrow at nine-thirty.'

The great quality that Alan had as a director, which is so rare, was to make himself as vulnerable as the actors. Very often directors want to play their role as directors and be seen to be in charge – maybe it's a fear of losing authority. But Alan placed himself on the same level as everybody else, whether in rehearsal or on location. There are certain directors who don't seem to intervene, but they know how to ask good questions. By asking the question they're not suggesting an answer, just inviting you to share what's on their mind, which comes in the form of a question – it's the dialectical approach, I suppose. You never felt Alan was pushing you. We weren't told to do something, we came to a conclusion together. He had a very tough image but really I think he was the reverse of that, and this was one of the guiding things about him. He was extremely sensitive – sensitive to other people's pain, which most of his work bears witness to.

MICHAEL JACKLEY: There was a whole preamble in *Nina*, featuring her child, which was shot and not used. They decided they didn't need it. The way the couple destroy each other is its main thrust: heartache and the breakdown of a relationship. It got very heavy. It was down to a difficult domestic relationship, set in the context of dissidents coming to another country, and how a sophisticated woman dealt with that situation. We did the final scene in a smart hotel and, of course, it winds up in fighting and devastation.

ELEANOR BRON: The last scenes, the break-up and the fight, they did require a lot from us. I had been alarmed at the thought of doing them and yet I found them rather wonderful because they seemed true, and they felt as heartbreaking as they must have been. There was one point where we were having the fight and Jack cracked my rib, I heard it crack. But again Alan maintained this atmosphere of good humour and concentration. We didn't do it too many times, you know, we just went for it.

I was surprised that Alan and I got on as we did, because he had a very brutal honesty. But it was a kind of honesty that I felt ill at ease with because I'm so horribly – not 'horribly' – but I am middle-class. And there is an awful middle-class tendency to smooth things over, and to enter into the world with a lot of half-truths and false politeness and not saying exactly what you mean. And that was very at odds with Alan's style.

MICHAEL JACKLEY: Eleanor and Alan lived together for a while in her place on Harley Street. I saw them there a couple of times, but it didn't last. I thought it would have been quite lovely if it had happened, but I wonder if Alan was really able to stay in a relationship. In the way that he divested himself of so many trappings, I'm not sure if people didn't become like possessions in his mind.

SUSANNA CAPON: That was a very strange part of his life, because with Eleanor Bron it seemed to be the most serious attachment of his life, after Jane. And for a time he was a totally reformed character; she was the person with whom he really tried. I lived around the corner from the place they were sharing in Harley Street and I remember seeing Alan in the launderette! Nicely dressed, as well. A very unlikely relationship – nobody could quite believe it. And I think the failure of that relationship was very difficult for him. I think the fact that he was unable to create a lasting relationship after his relationship with Jane, who was a kind of saint – I think that was a sadness to him. There was a sense of 'I'm no good at relationships, I'm not going to try any more.' He's not the only person I've met who's taken that view.

16

Recidivist tendencies: *Scum* – the Feature Film (1979)

CLIVE PARSONS: When the *Scum* controversy was going on at the BBC, my partner Davina Belling and I read a piece by Stephen Gilbert in the *Observer* about the ban. And I remember a sentence which sparked my curiosity, likening *Scum* to a James Cagney Warner Brothers movie. There was this whole notion whereby a guy enters a prison situation, sees the injustice going on, does nothing, and then decides to take control. And it did seem like a terrific theme for a commercial movie.

RAY WINSTONE: James Cagney was my man. I believed every word he said. He could have played that part in *Scum*, played it well. Watching Cagney – that's where I learned how to play violence on the screen.

CLIVE PARSONS: Immediately I got in touch with Margaret Matheson and said I'd like to see the film, and in fact it so happened there was a screening the next day in a little theatre on Wardour Street. I went to see it, and I was blown away by it. Alan was there, and Roy Minton. Afterwards, I remember crossing the street to a pub and meeting them. And funnily enough the hard thing was to persuade Roy Minton that we should do it as a movie. I said, 'This has got to be seen, it's got to be done.' So we talked about totally reshooting it, and upgrading it from 16 mm and seventy minutes to a 35 mm feature. And from that conversation with Alan and Roy, we decided we'd do it.

Then there was this odd period for us when, naturally, the people who had been involved in the TV version were very keen to persuade the BBC to broadcast it. And we were the opposite, because we saw it could be a terrific movie. If the BBC changed its mind and screened it, we would lose the right to do the film. The BBC had a very odd contract with writers at that point; basically Roy Minton's contract said, 'OK, we're paying you for the script, whatever's the going rate. But if we have not made it and *transmitted* it by a certain date, the rights return to you, the author, despite the fact that we've spent hundreds of thousands of pounds making it.' So we were keeping our fingers crossed desperately that they would not transmit it by that date, and indeed they didn't. There was a print around and we managed to commandeer it for a while. So instead of going to people and saying, 'Here's a script, read it, and give us the money to make this movie,' Davina and I would say, 'Come and see this movie.' Don Boyd then had a fund for financing low-budget movies and he gave us the money to make it. The preparation was fascinating because we could look at the TV play and say, 'This is fabulous – this we should maybe change.' It's extremely rare that a director has the chance to reshoot a movie in the way that he wants to do it. The irony was that when we came to make it, it all went very well, but inevitably there was at least one scene we had to reshoot, and so that was a third pass that Alan made at it.

RAY WINSTONE: The BBC ban didn't bother me so much because I'd retired from acting for a couple of years, retired from life really, and I was just ducking and diving when I got a call from Davina Belling about the film. I didn't have an agent, but I knew it would be a laugh. Got eighteen hundred pounds.

PHIL DANIELS: I'd done a couple of films by then, I knew a bit more about the camera and things. On the first *Scum* one I was just mental. I nearly didn't do it the second time, just 'cos I'd done it, but Alan sort of talked us into it really. Hundred and fifty pound a week. I said to him. 'Well, 'ow much we gettin' this time?' He says, 'We're all doin' it for pork pies.' 'Oh yeah?'

RAY WINSTONE: I could have seen the point of him recasting it more than he did – I'm glad they never did, from my point of view. But there were a few changes, Mick Ford took over as Archer. I don't think David Threlfall wanted to do it again, to be honest. But I liked them both in their own ways. I thought David's Archer was harder, but that Micky Ford's was probably more intelligent, and maybe a bit lighter.

SEAN CHAPMAN: I got a call from my agent asking me to meet Alan for the film. The first impression I had of Alan, which never altered afterwards, was of his directness. I remember him looking me straight in the eye and saying, 'Now, Sean, there's a big scene in the movie where a guy gets it right up the arse.' 'Yes, Mr Clarke.' 'He's not a poof, this character, but men in these extreme situations, their emotions get very high, they get frustrated. And it has to be real, and it's a cold day and it's gonna be horrible. Now can you do that?' 'Yes, I think I could,' I say, very keen and young. He said, 'Good, 'cos you strike me as the right man for the job.'

RAY WINSTONE: I remember Clarkey got hold of me and said, 'Look, it's more difficult to do it a second time, just 'cos you'll want to improve it, but you don't need to. You've learned a bit more now, but I want you to do it exactly as you did it before.' Which was a great note – it wasn't broke, didn't need fixing.

CLIVE PARSONS: Obviously it was a crucial thing to find that main location, we went to masses of places. In the end we found this vaguely disused mental hospital, partly in use but not properly, so if we needed a kitchen or a boiler room we could use it. We shot it so quickly, thirty days. The film was made in the winter of 1979 – bodies unburied, rubbish uncollected, buses not running – and it was snowing, which was wonderful because we were able to use it in some scenes. Somehow everybody clubbed together, crew and cast, despite these dreadful conditions.

SEAN CHAPMAN: The atmosphere that *Scum* was shot in is tangible, it comes off the screen in waves – this bleak, blue English winter light. Compounded by the fact that the way we shot it was brutally simplistic. Posses of young blokes would turn up at Charing Cross Station at six in the morning, leading characters, featured characters, extras. You'd get on a big minibus that would ferry you to the location. And it was very unpoliced, so if you didn't turn up, the bus left without you and you got there under your own steam.

PHIL DANIELS: We nicked the bus once as well, drove round and round, picking up passengers. But Alan encouraged all that, didn't he?

RAY WINSTONE: We were all young guys, getting picked up six in the morning and working till eleven at night; we were all knackered, cast and crew. And Clive and Davina would come down on the set and faff around a bit. Eventually Alan gave them his viewfinder, said, 'You fucking do it, I'm off.' They went, 'Oh no, no, no!' And that night about six o'clock he said, 'Right, that's a wrap, we're going home.' And the producers went white, 'Oh my God.' But it was a smart move; the next day everyone was fresh, everyone respected Alan ten times more, and from then on we all worked till eleven without a moan.

CLIVE PARSONS: I think it was Martin Campbell's idea to get Phil Meheux in as lighting cameraman, they had worked together previously. I think it was Phil's second feature. And he did all the handheld stuff, as in that famous scene with the snooker balls in the sock. There was no Steadicam then and Phil did it all in one shot; it's one of the scenes that everybody remembers.

RAY WINSTONE: It starts with me walking down the stairs, follows me into the snooker room, I put the balls in the sock: 'Carry on.' Now there's a geezer lying on the floor, under the frame line – we swap the balls, out of shot but same shot, Phil turns round to me and before he's even looked at me, I smash him in the head. Then I back out, dump the snooker balls back on the table; I'm up the stairs, look into one room but there's just a fella there, into the bathroom and there's Banks – bosh, do the business, 'I'm the daddy now,' and I'm gone. That's one take, there was an insert or two put in, but it was basically one take. Now that's Clarkey. In a second you've done someone, and that's the reality of violence.

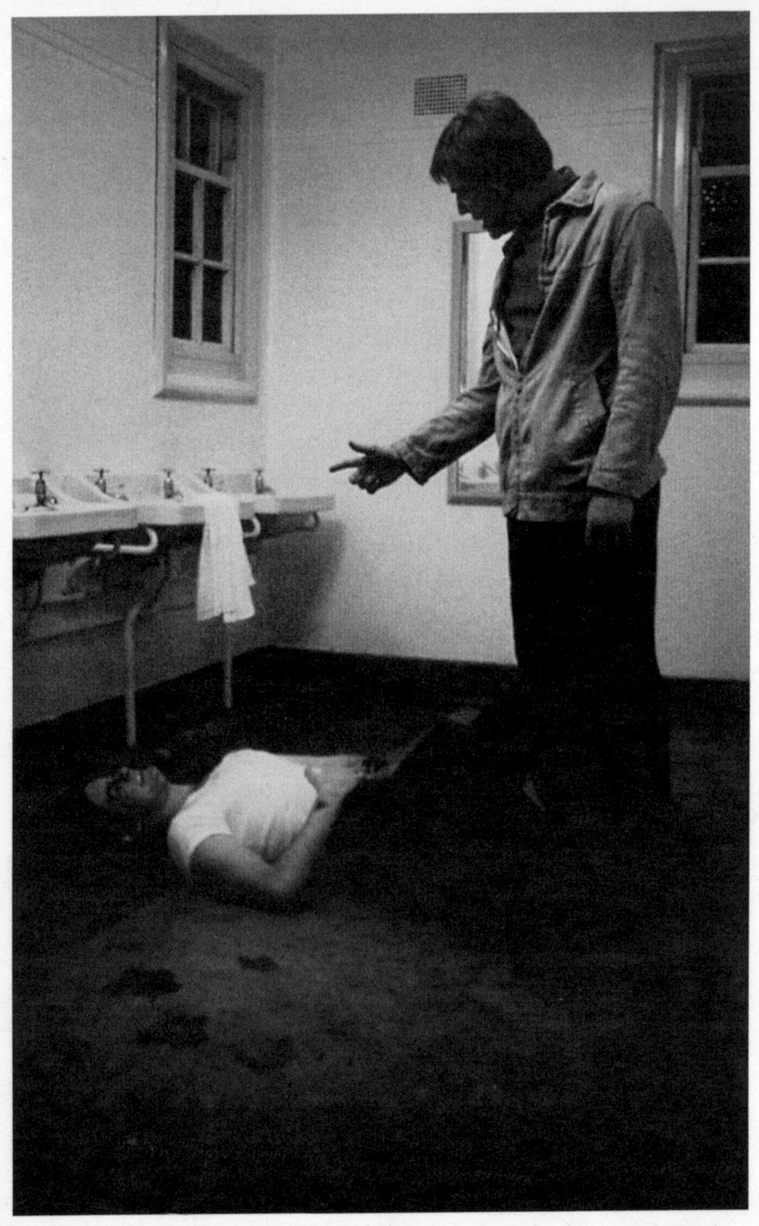

'I'm the daddy now': Carlin (Ray Winstone) usurps the authority of Banks (John Blundell) in *Scum* (1979)

PHIL DANIELS: It was different doing it over again, that rawness wasn't there. And because it was a movie they threw it all in, all the suicides, all the buggerings.

ROY MINTON: In the feature I found the rape scene in the greenhouse gratuitous, the three-on-one. I had a word with Clarkey on that one, I said, 'C'mon, what are you doing here?'

SEAN CHAPMAN: Alan asked me how I thought the rape should play. The location was a huge greenhouse with a steel walkway leading to where Julian Firth's character was potting plants. I said I thought it should have urgency. Time was short to get it done. He said, 'Yeah, it needs that feeling all the time someone might come in and then you'll cop it – it's something you want to get out of the way, like a wank.' But he took Julian aside and said, 'When he's got you over the table, put up a fookin' fight 'cos this would be agony, right?' And once we were rolling, Julian was kicking away beneath me with his industrial boots, a bit close to the groin, and I began to find it a bit irritating. So between takes I had a word with him, but he just said, 'You're not gonna get me, you're not.' He was so wound-up. Next take, his boots came up again, and I thought, 'I'm not having this,' I whacked him in the ribs. Then he gave it some more and I whacked him again. And we finished that take and Alan said, 'Yeah, we're getting somewhere now.' It was pushed to the edge of the envelope. Ray came in that day to watch, stood on the edge of the shot, ready for a good laugh. But after a couple of these takes he came up to me, and his whole expression had changed, he was pensive. And he said, 'Yeah, – it's looking fuckin' good, that. It's a bit tasty, that. S'horrible.' Then we knew we'd nailed it. Afterwards, Alan told me he was very proud of the scene. He said, 'It's not gratuitous, you don't see anyone's cock, anyone's arse, but you don't want to see anything you're not seeing.' It was a moment of real connection for us, I think – what symbolism there is in that I don't know.

DAVINA BELLING: I remember that an edict was issued before the riot scene that nobody was to have any weapons concealed about

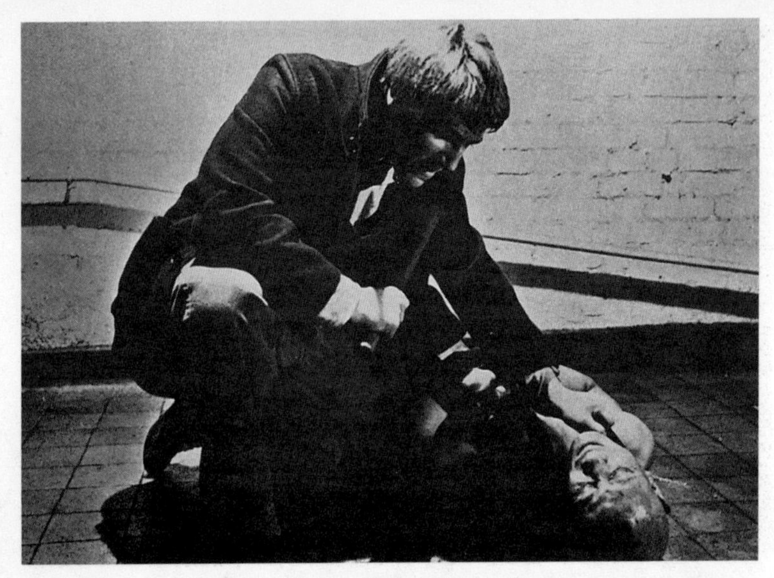

'What fuckin' tool?' 'This fuckin' tool!': Carlin puts one over on Baldy (Peter Harris) in *Scum* (1979)

their person; that it was found necessary to issue that in the first place tells you everything about our cast. And just before shooting, Martin Campbell said to Alan, 'You cannot break any of the windows, we just don't have the money.'

And of course the windows were indeed smashed. And Alan was literally afraid to see Martin in the pub afterwards – he came in hiding behind Clive and I. I mean, ordinarily it's the director and the producers who are at each other's throats, and the idea of Clarkey hiding in itself is so hilarious. But he was just so afraid that Martin was literally going to kill him. It was about three thousand pounds worth of damage, which is a lot for a film budgeted at two hundred and fifty thousand.

RAY WINSTONE: I really liked the original, because we were younger, there was something about that that made it seem more violent, more terrifying. We were vulnerable kids, being abused by men and then abusing each other – in every way, violently, mentally, sexually, the lot, in a fucking Victorian building. We were

Scum (1979): the climactic riot of the trainees

kids in the feature film but in two years we grew up, we weren't so vulnerable any more.

ROY MINTON: The stuff between Carlin and his 'missus', the pretty boy, it's not in the film and it's a sad loss – one of the reasons why the BBC version is far superior to the movie.

RAY WINSTONE: Alan said to me, 'About the scene with the missus, where he's wanking you off, how do you feel about it?' And it was totally my fault, I was probably feeling a bit macho at the time and I said, 'Al, I think you lose a bit of feeling for the character there' – which was total bollocks, that wasn't what the film was about. And he took that on board and left it out of the film and it was my decision in a way, and I was wrong. I missed the point, I thought it was too much, and I was being a bit of a geezer – didn't want to be wanked off by a geezer in a film. So I think there was a scene shot but not used, where we had a cuddle and I made his hand slip down my strides. Might just be my imagination, or wishful thinking.

DAVINA BELLING: I don't know whether we were all naïve at the time but when the film came out we were all very shocked at the reaction, that we were so vilified for making a film that, certainly in the public's eyes at that point, actually promoted and incited violence.

PHIL DANIELS: I think we were like the geezers from down the road acting,[136] and that's why *Scum* became a bit cultish, because kids went, 'God, he's just like that bloke at school.' But it was macho too, the whole thing with *Scum*. Women hated it, my missus wouldn't see it. Just too violent. But for all the lads, it was like those kung fu films where you came out doing kicks. When you left the cinema after *Scum* you'd be walking round going, 'I'm the daddy now.'

NORMA MCMINN: Alan didn't really talk too much about *Scum* to my mum, 'cos it wasn't very nice. He made an episode of *Love For Lydia* and she liked that, it was flowery and romantic and all. She'd say, 'Why d'ya only make *one* episode?' Then in 1979 this film loomed on the horizon, *Scum*. She'd say, 'You've actually made a film, amazing, that!' He said, 'You won't like it, Mum. It's not gonna be on telly. It's not nice, it's about horrible things.' But being me mum – it was playing at the Tatler cinema on Lime Street, Liverpool. She goes over there one cold evening – old-age pensioner in her fur hat with her shopping bag, going to the picture house. And the man on the door says, 'Why're ya goin' in to see this? You're not gonna like it, y'know.' He's quite concerned. Of course she says, 'I'm not going in for what it is, the fact of the matter is my son directed it.' He says, 'Ah yeah? And I'm Napoleon's grandson.' He wouldn't let her in, he convinced her. Alan was glad of that. But when he heard the story he couldn't stop laughing.

17

'In bed with murderers': Clarke at Fox and *Assassination on Embassy Row*

STEPHEN FREARS: And then he went to America, Sandy Lieberson took him. Sandy was running Fox then, he thought very highly of Alan and you know – like they all do, they want to turn us into American film-makers – Sandy just said, 'Come out and be there.'

SANDY LIEBERSON: I went to work for Twentieth Century Fox in 1977, and I instituted a programme for bringing newer directors from all over, including Australia but Europe mainly, to Los Angeles for a six-month period. It was designed to give them an opportunity to see what it was like working within the Hollywood system – exposing them to the United States as well. So they could do anything they wanted during the six months, but at the end of it they had to come up with a number of ideas for films, and at least one short treatment which we could or could not make, depending on what we thought of it. Fred Schepisi came, Franc Roddam, Gillian Armstrong. So I invited Alan to do it and he agreed.

Knowing Alan, I put him up at a very small and modest hotel in Beverly Hills, I think called Clark's, it was on Clark Drive just off Burton Way. I saw him when he arrived, made sure he got to the hotel safely and checked in, said that I would see him the next day. And that was it – he disappeared, we couldn't find him. Nobody at the hotel knew where he'd gone. And about a week later he called in to say that he'd moved out – which I'd gathered – and he was now living on Hollywood Boulevard. He hadn't liked the hotel, so he'd moved to this seedy part of the Boulevard, it was a transient hotel used by prostitutes and drug addicts, and he decided that was where he felt most comfortable.

I invited Alan to come out to the studio so we could have lunch and talk, and then we met any number of times. We showed *Scum* to people. He was quite bemused by the whole thing, and as always

Englishmen abroad: Alan Clarke and Stephen Frears in a photo-booth somewhere on Hollywood Boulevard, 1979

felt very much an outsider, and it was one of the things I loved about him. He felt outside of society, felt no need to be part of the mainstream in terms of his personal life. But I think he felt more comfortable in the United States. Quite often that happens, you're much more self-conscious in England amongst your peers than in the States, where people are so much more direct and accessible and easy. So I'd say he felt at home – amongst the drug addicts and prostitutes and street people.

We agreed that for the remainder of his time in the States, he was free to have an office at Fox and to meet people there. But he decided to forego all that because what he really wanted to do was to travel across the United States. And that was the last I saw of him until the very end, about five months later. He ended up meeting Hubert Selby Junior and deciding he was going to make a film of one of his novels, about a mother and her drug-addicted son. Anyway, it was totally inappropriate for Twentieth Century Fox to make it. But he'd enjoyed himself and I was pleased to have given him the experience.

STEPHEN FREARS: Alan wasn't at all fazed by Hollywood. He said to me once, 'You don't realize, we're the best trained people in the world.' Meaning we can deal with this because we've been so well trained at the BBC.

DAVID HARE: I recall Michael Apted was thought to have completely saved *Coalminer's Daughter* in 1980. He said, 'I've directed fifteen *Plays for Today* and what I did to that script is only what I've done to every script – just organize it logically and move a few scenes round, and it worked.' And yet in Hollywood, that was regarded as an almost mystical expertise.

STEPHEN FREARS: Then he got involved in a project about the killing of the Chilean ambassador Letelier, and he was working with a woman called Ros Heller. But he ran away. I think that's the story.

ROSILYN HELLER: I had been a V-P at Columbia Pictures all through the 1970s, and then when everybody was gone I moved to Fox as a producer around 1979. I remember the day I went to look at my offices was the day that Alan Ladd quit, but Sandy Lieberson was still there for a time. I was starting to look for a director for *Assassination on Embassy Row*, because I had managed to get CBS Theatrical Films interested in acquiring it for me. And I remember Lucy Fisher, who was a creative executive at the time, telling me about Alan Clarke and a movie called *Scum*, which I then managed to see. Then I went after Alan.

Assassination on Embassy Row was a non-fiction book written by Saul Landau and John Dinges, who were colleagues of Orlando Letelier's at the Institute for Policy Studies. Orlando had been the Chilean ambassador to the United States all through the 1960s, then he was a cabinet minister in Allende's Popular Unity government. After Pinochet's coup in 1973 he spent some time in prison, and then was released because of a big fuss made by the international community. So he went into exile and came to Washington DC and was here for a couple of years, working with the IPS and organizing opposition to the Pinochet regime. And then in September 1976 he was blown up in a car bomb with two young colleagues, Ronni and Michael Moffit, a newly-married couple who by extraordinarily cruel circumstances were using his car. The investigation afterwards took years because, of course, it was Pinochet behind the whole thing and the US government, having backed Pinochet for years, were not about to accuse him. But after two years of investigation, 1978–79, they finally arrested Michael Townley, who was the assassin. He was an American who had been living in Chile and was recruited by DINA, the secret police. He came to the US and he had ties to a number of Cubans, terrorists, who were part of the Cuban national movement. And Townley recruited them for this murder.

Alan was very interested, which seemed to be quite a coup, given that he'd turned everything else down in this country. He was obviously fussy about material. But this was a great political thriller, this story, similar to some of the work Costa-Gavras has done, and happening right here in America. This hadn't been touched on before that time. I kept saying, 'This is about how the US gets into bed with the most godawful people as long as they oppose our enemies.' Like we did with Saddam Hussein, and we're still paying for that. Throughout our politics we've always been in bed with murderers – and then we're surprised when murder comes to our doorstep?

So anyway, I showed *Scum* to CBS Theatrical and got them very excited, and we brought Alan back over. He spent a lot of time with my family and I in Nichols Canyon; he didn't become very friendly with a lot of people in this town. We had a beach house, he was there a lot. We hired Abraham Polonsky to do the script, and we got a very interesting, very clever first draft. The main character of the piece that Abe wrote was a kind of composite FBI man, whom Abe very cleverly brought in right at the beginning, even though the investigation didn't start until after the murder. CBS brought us all in for a meeting on the script. Donald Marsh was the Head of Production at the time and the first thing that came out of his mouth was, 'Well, who do you think we should get to play this FBI guy? Robert Redford?' And I remember looking at Alan, knowing what his response would be to such an idea. He never said a word, but he did blanch. And I gave him a look as if to say,

'Let's be calm, we'll discuss it outside.' I told CBS that wasn't what we had in mind, that with Alan doing it we had more of a *Battle of Algiers* idea in mind, we didn't want known people in it and certainly not movie stars. Now I think I did feel at the time that if we could get somebody like, say, Dustin Hoffman, who would be acceptable to them, then Alan and I could talk privately about whether it was acceptable to us. But I saw his expression.

Anyway, we took Alan back to his hotel and that evening I get a call from a friend saying, 'Oh, do you know where Alan is? We were supposed to have dinner together and he never called.' And as soon as she said that, I knew Alan was gone. Apparently, he checked straight out of the hotel and went to the airport without saying goodbye to anybody. Personally I was quite upset about that; he'd become quite a good pal of the family by that point. I suppose I kept thinking that he would call or at least say something. But we never heard anything more. And quite quickly after that Donald Marsh lost his job, and other people came in and it was very clear they weren't interested in doing a political story like this – it was way, way too tough. So they gave me the project back in turnaround, and that dropped Alan out of it. For the moment.

18

Broaching the enemy's camp: *Beloved Enemy* (1980) and *Psy-Warriors* (1981)

DAVID LELAND: I came back into touch with Alan after I'd gone to the Crucible Theatre in Sheffield as an actor and director. I tried to get Ron Hutchinson, who'd written for us, to do a play about psychologists and the use of interrogation in the army. I had become intrigued by a book on the subject, *War on the Mind*. But Peter James who ran the theatre said, 'You could write it.' And I did, in a couple of weeks, the first thing I'd written – this was *Psy-Warriors*. Then I went to the Royal Court and we did it there, and I wrote to Alan and asked him to come and see it. Eventually I got this reply on lined notepad paper, in capital letters, saying, 'Sorry I couldn't get to see it, but I'd like to read it.' So I sent it to him.

At this time Alan was in California with Sandy Lieberson at Fox. A month later my acting agent told me Alan wanted to see me, and I thought, 'Great – he's going to offer me a part.' He was living in Harley Street with Eleanor Bron. We met and he said, 'I just want to tell you what I've been doing.' He told me about California, and how he'd met this man Charles Levinson, who'd taken him to a golf course to spy on Richard Nixon playing golf with the Mafia. Now I thought Alan was telling me this out of auld lang syne – he'd read *Psy-Warriors* and thought I'd be interested. We talked for a whole morning. And then he said, 'Well, there's two things, I'm going to do this documentary at ATV with a researcher called Nicholas Claxton. And I've got a *Play for Today* slot at the BBC, all film' – and that was gold dust. I said, 'Al, fantastic!' He said, 'Yeah, and I want you to write it.' And I was floored – it hadn't occurred to me.

So the research began. I worked in parallel with Al's and Nick's work on the documentary, *Vodka Cola*, and that fed into the script. We spent time in Geneva talking to Levinson, the author of *Vodka Cola*, the real voice behind *Beloved Enemy*. The book was called *Vodka Cola* because Nixon's 1968 presidential campaign was largely paid for by Pepsi Cola, so once he was in office this rampant, aggressive anti-Communist suddenly declared détente. He went to Moscow and had those famous confrontations with Khrushchev. But what he did while he was there was negotiate a barter deal with the Russians to market vodka in America in exchange for Pepsi Cola. And immediately after that, Pepsi built its first factories in Russia. There were some very overt symbols of the collusion. You know, Chase Manhattan was so right-wing, anti-Communist Republican, and the address of the Chase Manhattan Bank in Moscow was One Karl Marx Square.

We had many stories we could have told, but we chose the scenario of a British-based multinational locating a tyre factory in the Soviet Union – the Russians wanting the laser technology used in the vulcanizing process and the West wanting a source of cheap docile labour. The technological scenario behind those lasers was Star Wars, which people didn't know of at the time. Clive James wrote an utterly damning review in the *Observer* saying it was Dan Dare stuff, laser beams coming out of space, these guys haven't done their research. He clearly wasn't reading the trade journals of the armaments industry at that time. We knew it was fact, that Reagan had made a huge commitment to multinationals to develop Star Wars. From the very beginning there was a collaboration, through these trade delegations, between the USA and the USSR. They developed these weapons by positing each other as the threat, and the arms industry thrived on that. As it says in the film – you have to have an enemy, thank God we've got a good one.

Right in the middle of this, Solidarity and the free trade union movement got going in Poland. And you were confronted by the hypocrisy of Reagan, a union-basher all his life, suddenly supporting free trade unions – as long as they weren't in America. So there was talk about whether the material was valid any more, people wondered whether there was a revolution afoot. Levinson said, 'No, it just raises the stakes.' The man was revelatory, everything he said he had documented evidence to back it up and what he said was mind-blowing. For Alan, certainly for me, I have read the newspapers through Levinson's eyes ever since. They just looked different from then on, you saw what corporate power was doing and is doing.

All the time we were talking, Alan would be obsessing over how we could show this story. He decided it was in the nature of the deal, of how people do the business deal – that was what the play should be about. I wrote the screenplay and Keith Williams said, 'You can't just have people sitting at a table discussing deals.' They wouldn't green-light it. So I wrote another version, which told a personal story about the head of this multinational, a conflict with his daughter who had a liberal conscience and so forth. And this version was passed, and a celebratory lunch was held in Keith's office. Alan, myself and Charles came along. But the night before, Alan called me and said, 'I've been lookin' at the first draft, David, it's all in there, we don't need all this bollocks.' He'd done a cut and paste job on the first draft, which I then used, and the stuff I'd put in, which was the basis of the green light, came out. And that was the film we made. But he had to go through that loop, and that took enormous guile and strength of will. Not many of us can pull that kind of scam.

All of *Beloved Enemy* was shot on really long lenses, 'the long bottle'. It gave a sense of standing back from it, a certain element of spying. As if the story and these characters were something we could all view vaguely from a distance, but with the right lens you could be very close to it. A visceral thing, that choice.

STEVEN BERKOFF: I think Alan cast me in *Beloved Enemy* because he saw me as kind of an ally. Being a tribal sort of person, he would seek out people who were mates, not just hired actors but team members – the boys, people he could be free with. I didn't have a big role and I used to come in late, I didn't have that much passion for the piece. Now directors will normally say, 'Do you mind not coming in late? You are holding everybody up!' and Alan said, 'Steve, next time you do that, you and me are gonna be wrestlin' on the fookin' floor.' He didn't work in the officious language of the Boss, he brought it down to street language, which was his way of saying, 'Pull your socks up.' One day I got in earlier, and they told me they weren't opening until ten, which was the start of our rehearsal. So I gave them a right bollocking. The manager came up to where we were working and said, 'This actor was behaving atrociously,' and Alan had a good laugh with me. 'I hear you called the canteen manager a cunt.'

The conspiratorial Cold Warriors of *Beloved Enemy* (1980): Tony Doyle (Blake), Steven Berkoff (Koslov), Graham Crowden (Sir Peter), Oscar Quitak (Edward Whitaker MP)

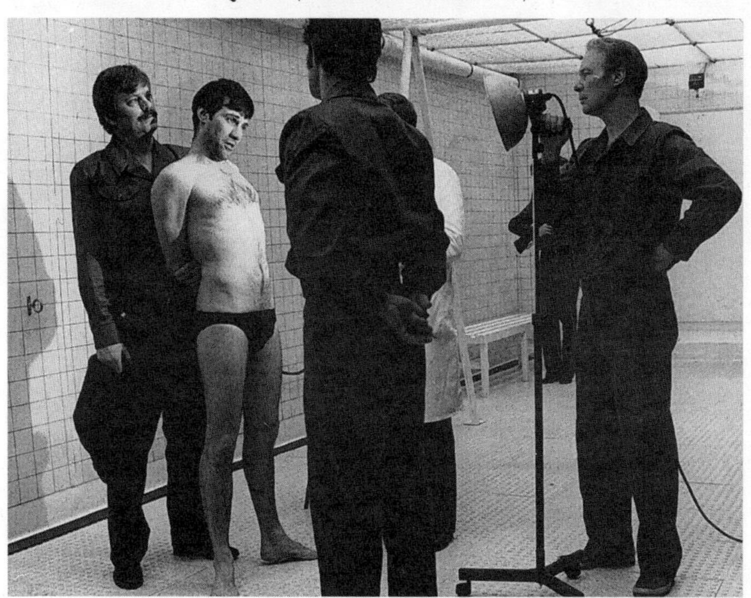

Psy-Warriors (1981): Captain Stone (John Duttine) gets more than he volunteered for from his army training course

DAVID LELAND: After *Beloved Enemy* Alan would walk down the corridors, they all knew him and would give him scripts to read. He would give them back my *Psy-Warriors* script and say, 'This is what I want to do.' And he'd call the next day and bark at them, 'Did ya read David's script?' and he'd get a lot of tooth-sucking in response; they all passed. They didn't want to do a play about army interrogation related to Ireland, it was too hot to handle. But that was his common experience, every time he went out he had to fight for the space, as if he hadn't made anything before. We only got it done because June Roberts had a slot and the money and the bottle to do it; everybody else bottled out.

I thought the actors found it hard to come to terms with the piece, they fought what it was about. They were clearly intensely uncomfortable with the subject. It rubbed them the wrong way, they didn't want to engage in the dialogue. But Colin Blakely was fantastic as the main officer, he had no problems. He had the big climactic speech in defence of the refugee Palestinian guerillas, how they 'kill to breathe'.

GRENVILLE MIDDLETON: I saw *Psy-Warriors* and I said to Alan, 'That's a right-wing film, as far as I can see. You're softening us up as a public. You're not exposing anything, you're just making it OK for them to do it. We were being educated to accept this, not to fight it.' I don't think he agreed with me. But he didn't say anything – funny bloke, quite sensitive in some ways.

DAVID LELAND: I think the ending of *Psy-Warriors* is wrong. The young officer is invited to join this 'anti-terrorism unit', or assassination squad. And he says, effectively, 'I can't go through with it.' In reality they don't say that, though – they *do go* through with it. So it was too much of a statement, we should have avoided it. But if you went away thinking he *was* going to join up – fine. The intention was to show that this training produced monsters. And I'd rather it fell into the enemy's camp than into the liberal camp. I think Alan would feel the same. We wanted it to be dangerous. It happened to go out on the night that Bobby Sands died, and the switchboards were jammed, saying, 'This is IRA propaganda.' So it did its stuff.

David Bowie in *Baal* (1982)

BARRY HANSON: Alan was obsessed by Brecht. Generally, Brecht was a very strong influence when I was at the Royal Court, and I'm not entirely sure why. But if you look at what follows, end of the 1960s into the 1970s – David Hare, Tony Bicat, Howard Brenton, 'the university wits' as Lindsay Anderson called them – that stuff has got that influence, the theatre of alienation and the ideological base. It struck me that the only people who could play Brecht were the Germans, you needed that kind of high definition so it all came as a make-up of technology plus spirit. Whereas in England it always looked a bit wet. But its influence was incredibly strong, and it possibly peters out around the late 1970s, with the onset of Thatcher and the fall of this and that. It doesn't seem to be in the air now, there's been a swing back to the theatre of entertainment, which this clearly wasn't.

JOHN WILLETT: *Baal* was Brecht's first play, not the first to be staged but the first to be written, and so it really reflects the sort of life and interests he had as a young man in Augsburg, even before he went to Munich University. There's a book by his friend Hans-Otto Münsterer that describes the atmosphere of Augsburg in those days, and this gang of young chaps who went driving round the town reading poems to each other, eating and drinking. *Baal* is impregnated with Expressionism.

In 1981 I was contacted by Alan Clarke and Louis Marks; they wanted to know if I'd be interested in telling them more about the later 1926 version of *Baal* called *Lebenslauf des Mannen Baal* – 'The Life and Times of a Man called Baal'. Clarke was interested in that, not least because he thought it would fit with the kind of imagery of *Neue Sachlichkeit*, the hard-edged imagery of 1920s painting and so on, and of course that wasn't especially so. Admittedly, Baal is sleeping in a garage rather than a garret in that version, and there are references to the industrialization of the German landscape. But nonetheless it's still Bavarian society before the First World War, the kind of atmosphere which Baal goes crashing into and breaks up. And so it turned out a bit differently from what Alan was expecting when he came to look at the material. We cut it down a great deal from the final German version, which is fairly long and straggly.

There was a lot of shifting and excising of various elements in the preparation of the script. Alan and I were jointly credited with the adaptation, which is not exactly accurate. We discussed things, but I think I suggested virtually everything, just because he didn't know the alternative material – but that's OK, I didn't mind. Alan had in mind Steven Berkoff for the role. I thought it was a mistake, because Berkoff is a fairly class-conscious actor and performer, and I don't think the peculiar class system of this country can be transplanted anywhere else, certainly not to Bavaria in 1912; it would have anglicized the whole framework, I felt. In the end, I claim it was me who thought of David Bowie, I knew he'd been playing in *The Elephant Man* in New York and I knew that he was interested in the Expressionist painters of the 1920s. Louis went to see him in Switzerland and that was it, we had him.

Bowie's drawback was that he couldn't play the guitar or any other instrument. He'd been given this beautiful art nouveau banjo which would be used in the publicity photographs, but Dominic Muldowney had to teach him how to play 'plonk, plonk, plonk' so he could accompany himself. I was there for a lot of the rehearsal at Acton. The name of the production was never up on the board and it wasn't supposed to be known what was going on, and all because of John Lennon's assassination, which had a number of people concerned for themselves. Bowie had these two guardians always sitting there, one or the other, perfectly pleasant. But he was very unassuming and amusing, and I thought he was awfully good. He sang very well, and everything he did was interesting. But he tended to give a different performance in each rehearsal, which was a bit unusual.

The concrete framework of the production was already determined, because they'd decided to record in BBC Studio One with sets along each of the four long walls, covered with gauzes. And the externals would all take place in a sort of tunnel of gauze which could be used repetitively to give an impression of considerable depth when the characters are walking through southern Germany.

STUART GRIFFITHS: Baal's dialogues with his friend Eckhart in the forest were mainly done on the march, with a landscape drawing

'He deserves our vote but equally he deserves everything that's coming to him': David Bowie as Brecht's earliest anti-hero *Baal* (1982)

on one side of the screen and Bowie and Jonathan Kent pacing through the studio on the other. I think Alan was fascinated by that idea of movement. Of course he went on to explore that to greater effect not long afterwards.

DAVID JONES: An odd choice for Alan? Well, it is and isn't. Baal is a character Alan would identify with – profoundly, you know? I watched little bits of the recording of *Baal* from the control room, and I wasn't sure of what I was seeing, what was going on didn't immediately appeal to me. Again, I had this feeling about Alan that some of his fun and sparkle and natural comedy became a little outweighed by a certain pessimism as he got on. And sometimes that made his work a little more aggressively bleak than it needed to be. *Baal* is a very young play – a subversive comedy, basically – whereas I got the feeling Bowie's Baal was being pressed into a kind of martyrdom. I don't think Baal's a martyr, he's a drop-out and he deserves our vote, but equally he deserves everything he has coming to him.

NORMA MCMINN: My daughter Gill was twenty when Alan was doing *Baal*, she asked Alan if he could get David Bowie's autograph for her. But he didn't want to ask.

19

The *Oi!* Man of the Year: *Made in Britain* (1983)

DAVID LELAND: Alan and I had talked about doing a lot of other projects. We wanted to do a piece about the whole politics of famine, how aid is tied to diplomatic shenanigans. He went and discussed it with Margaret Matheson, who was taking over as Head of Drama at the newly-created Central Television, and she didn't warm to it. What she wanted to do was education. And Alan said, 'You should talk to David, he keeps going on at me about that – wants to make a film about people who educate their children at home.'

MARGARET MATHESON: I would meet with David Leland and we'd discuss what sort of things he wanted to write about that I would be interested in. We were both subject-oriented. Apart from education, the only subject of the moment seemed to be sex, but education seemed more pressing to us at the time because we were both facing the imminent prospect of educating our respective children.

DAVID LELAND: Margaret said, 'You're on – how many do you want to do?' I said I needed to do more research, which she then very sensibly paid me to do. And she gave me licence to come up with the form, and finally I came back and said I wanted to do four separate stories, of which *Made in Britain* was one. I asked Margaret, 'What do I do about writing truthfully? Kids eff and blind.' She said, 'It's your job to write it, it's my job to get it on.'

Alan was very reluctant to work on *Made in Britain*. People may think we sat down to do it together as if it were a natural progression for us. But he was trying then to do *Contact*; his mind was elsewhere. And he was single-minded because of that constant fight he had on anything he wanted to make. It was only because we were friends, we could meet and talk about *Made in Britain*. We had an office in Soho Square, and he'd ask me, 'But how would you do it?' Stephen Frears was cutting *Walter* and Alan went down to see that, and that's where he first saw Steadicam.

STEPHEN FREARS: Chris Menges was such a huge influence. I think he suggested that we shoot *Walter* on the Steadicam because he was technically interested in the possibilities. And then Alan used to come to the cutting room and look over my shoulder and say, 'How did you do that shot?' *Made in Britain* was written very powerfully, and it had these rather long sequences which posed certain technical problems, which Alan had to solve – and if you do it conventionally it's rather boring. So he found a piece of equipment that liberated him from that.

DAVID LELAND: My starting point for writing had been this skinhead, Trevor, delivering a tirade straight to camera, which is in fact the middle section of the film. I had the notion of a camera screwed to the ground and this figure stalking in and out of the space, locked in a room, and talking to the camera. Alan said, 'Yeah, but he does all this moving around, what if he's always on the move? He's got this energy, it's no good shooting off a static camera and picking him up and panning with him. We want to take him all the way down the street, through there, into the dark, out into the light. We've got this fast film, we can push the stock. And we can get this guy Chris Menges.' That's how it evolved. He thought about it until it came alive in his head as a piece of film-making, and then the subject matter came alive for him too.

STEPHEN FREARS: And then he sort of went bananas with it. Alan was always a much more extreme person than me, so he embraced it fully. Steadicam removes the line between actors and their performances in some way; they have to be very, very real. But it's also theatrical in a sense because there's no montage. It lends itself to a certain kind of writing, a certain kind of performance. And Alan had the imagination to cast Tim. He found him, didn't he?

SEAN CHAPMAN: By the time I came to *Made in Britain* I was surprised that there were no people from *Scum* around, none of those

Made in Britain (1983): Trevor (Tim Roth), caught in the act of Taking and Driving Away with his 'friend' Errol (Terry Richards)

lads I later termed the Tribe. Just older actors like Bill Stewart and Geoff Hutchings – and this young unknown guy.

TIM ROTH: *Scum* was probably one of the films that made me want to be an actor more than anything. I went to see it about ten times, and I was just considering acting then, even though I was in art school at the time. But looking at people like that, films like that, you thought, 'If they can be actors, then I can.' 'Cos you think of actors as the toffs, you know? They've studied, they've done their Shakespeare and all that. And then suddenly someone like Alan comes along and shows you that it's not about that, it's really very different – and everything's possible. And that frees you up as a human being. That's kind of what Alan did for me, even before I met him really.

I decided to leave art school, sign on the dole and call myself an actor, otherwise I'd never do it. And, of course, as an actor you end up doing shit jobs, so I was selling advertising space in dodgy magazines up in town. And one day I got a flat tyre on my bike as I was passing a youth theatre that I'd worked at, at the Oval House in South London. I went in there to ask for a pump and they said, 'Nah, sorry. But we do have these auditions that are going on for this TV film. You have to shave your head, mind.' But I'd already done that for a production of *Othello* I'd done there, so they said, 'Why don't you go up for the job?' So I met with Alan, and I liked him. And then he said, 'Well, here's the script, fuck off and read it.' I read it, thought, 'Ah God, this is amazing.' He got me back in, I met David Leland, that was the next stage, and then he said, 'OK, we're gonna get you back again for the producers.' And I thought, 'Oh shit, this is very serious, this is the money.' It was Margaret Matheson and Patrick Cassavetti. I remember getting there early, and Sean Chapman was waiting outside. I knocked on the door, they said, 'Do you mind coming back?' It was in Soho Square, so I said, 'Well, I'll just go wait in the park.' And I fucking *knew* they'd be watching me out of the window. And so I got into character a bit. And luckily enough a guy that I knew came along – guy with a big peacock punk haircut, he was in a weird band called King Kurt that was knocking around Brixton, mad fucking guy. We were just talking and then the police pitched up, and he got moved on; this copper told me, 'Careful, son – I'm watchin' you.' And all this time I knew – that was the audition. I went up, read, got the job. And later when we were filming, Alan said, 'Oh, we were watching you, out the window.' I said, 'Fuckin' knew you were.' He said, 'Well, I fucking knew that *you* knew that we were.' That was how I got to be Trevor.

SEAN CHAPMAN: I think Alan was a massive crusader for the working-class voice. And he often cast against type, cast intelligent voices where people didn't expect them to be. It was a way of saying, 'You think because I live here and look like this that I'm scum or I'm shit. But hear this.'

TIM ROTH: What I liked about David's script was that he's smart, Trevor. And I think that's what Alan latched on to – 'Make him speak. Make him really fucking speak.' Skinheads had always been portrayed as marauding idiots, and that's a very stupid way to go. It was important at that time, politically as well, to say, 'This guy's fucking bright.' But his intelligence had taken him in that dark, actively racist direction. I went to a couple of meetings, National Front, when I was looking into this. The most scary people weren't the storm troopers, the Trevors. It was the ones who were wearing the suits, the teachers and the lawyers. You can see the other fuckers coming. You can't see your baby-sitter or your teacher or your headmaster. How would you know? They're wearing grey suits. But what's going on in their minds can be exactly the same. And that wasn't what *Made in Britain* was concerned with, but making him smart was a smart move. 'Cos you give him a different haircut and take the tattoos off, put him in a suit and he might be running your business.

DAVID LELAND: In fact, I was later asked if I would write *Made in Britain* 2 – what happened to Trevor. At the height of the Thatcher period I thought he might be working in the City, one of these guys opening Cristal in a bar 'cos he'd made a killing.

TIM ROTH: I got the shit kicked out of me at school, on a regular basis, by racist bastards like Trevor. I spent a lot of time hiding at school, I was just a weakling. I wasn't a bully, I was the bullied – always. So that when it came to playing somebody like Trevor, I knew it 'cos I could smell it, y'know? As somebody who runs away, you develop a kind of instinct for it, you can read it, and I was able to use that in the portrayal of him. I knew how to be, I knew how to look. And it's served me well since. But I brought what I knew to Alan and he shaped it in rehearsal. I had the coldness, I had the lack of compassion, the hatred, I could invent those, and Alan cultivated those kind of emotions and put them into certain areas.

MARGARET MATHESON: I thought Trevor was fantastic, great. I loved his arguments, I understood his feelings. I think I am Trevor, you know? And I mean, as portrayed by Tim and directed by Alan – I should be so lucky. As regards Trevor's more repugnant qualities, well, you've got to say there are a lot of kids like this out there. And by showing it, you do more in asking people why they think that than by not. Obviously, it's the articulate, challenging side of Trevor that's most memorable to me. And his racist remarks and his brick-throwing are what make him true, actually. And anyway, we were in the business of making trouble, so the idea that it might annoy people was the best possible reason for doing it.

TIM ROTH: Alan kept out of judgements. Politically he probably hated Trevor, and so did I. I come from a socialist background and we weren't having any of that.

DAVID LELAND: Alan questioned all the while what was there, but he never changed any of it, he saw his job to make what I'd written.

TIM ROTH: We did two weeks solid of heavy, heavy blocking rehearsals. We rehearsed every single scene, full-on acting, and very heavy discussions. But always laughing our arses off, which was the wonderful thing, probably the thing I remember most about being on his set – the cracking up was ridiculous. And mainly at him – he was a funny man. The actors we had were Geoff Hutchings, Bill Stewart, Sean Chapman, Eric Richard who ended up in *The Bill*.

'Tacky jobs, in't they?': Trevor (Tim Roth) goes down the Job Centre in *Made In Britain* (1983)

Alan and Chris made me think about what the camera does, about how to get through the lens and on to the celluloid and into the audience. I think the most important thing that they taught me – both of them together, because they were a very good team – was, 'Don't be scared, this is the lens and this is your eye to the world. Use it, perform to it – or ignore it. But it's this floating eye, and it's yours, you own it.' And it was a very important lesson for me, that – it took me through my life as an actor. The first shot is a very tight close-up on the Steadicam of me walking into court. Now that became a typical Alan move. You know – 'This is your man, go with him.' And the Exploited are playing over the top of it – that was a great choice. And then Trevor's up in front of the judge for throwing a brick through a Pakistani guy's window. 'You don't invite leniency, do you?' 'No.' I mean, that's Trevor all over. But that's Alan too, that's his sense of humour. But bleeding into it was this sense of political sadness. I mean, Trevor was a Nazi and Trevor was a fascist, but Trevor was a kid. And it was painful, his act was so much 'for the world'. That was the sadness, that the world produces people like him. He's a product of his society, he's Made in Britain – that doesn't excuse him, but that's what I think Alan was trying to say.

We would be shooting whatever was in the mag, ten-minute sequences and so on, all on the move. So it would be upstairs, along the corridor, down some stairs, another set of stairs, into a room, dialogue in there, some more dialogue there, and then out through the fucking door, y'know? And the way that Chris would light it was for source light. So you could really move, it allowed the actors to go for it. Chris hardly ever took the fucking Steadicam off, he wore that thing a lot and he didn't take very many breaks. And he's built, Chris, but he's quite a small guy. It's real work, physical work, as well as trying to compose a frame and enhance the scene and watch the frame lines for the boom and all that.

I did have a problem, because I had to get on the tube at Brixton during filming and they ended up having to give me a car 'cos I still had the make-up and the skinhead and all that, and I was getting a *lot* of fucking shit. And I'm not a fighter. But, of course, you get into that kind of character and you start arguing with people.

Came very close to getting a pasting. And that's when I went in and said, 'Can I get someone to take me to work? Anybody?'

DAVID LELAND: I think it was a really formative experience for Tim. He kept asking if there was a real Trevor and if he was coming to the set. I'd say, 'Yeah, tomorrow.' It became like *Waiting for Godot.*

TIM ROTH: *Made in Britain* has a second act, a twenty-minute scene that all happens in one room in this juvenile assessment centre. They come in and tell him what his life is. And Trevor has his moment, he speaks his mind. 'I'm more British than you'll ever be. I'm not your problem. We're all fucking great. You ain't taking bugger all from us, we hate you.' 'I'm a star.' All of that was important to say and show. All Steadicam, that scene – long, long runs.

SEAN CHAPMAN: We worked on that in a very controlled way. And this young lad Tim was under the cosh. It was a twenty-three page scene, twenty minutes of screen time. Geoff Hutchings was off on Day One as the inspector doing his blackboard routine, and Bill and myself just had to chip in, so it became like an interrogation scene. It becomes clear in the scene – there was nothing you could do overtly for this guy there and then. So there's a sort of impatience that builds, and it became tangible as we shot it – 'You can't be helped.' And Trevor's subliminal suggestion is 'Do you want some? 'Cos I'm gonna fucking paste you.' It's a beautifully crafted scene.

DAVID LELAND: Someone had drawn it out for me in the course of my research – the process of how they get caught into it, from home to school to truancy to petty crime, court, and so forth. But not in the way it's filmed. On the first day Alan rehearsed, Geoffrey Hutchings walked in and drew it all up on the blackboard. As a piece of acting, it's extraordinary, a *tour de force.*

TIM ROTH: Alan was a very funny man. I think he knew the humour he'd find in the piece, but it wasn't in David Leland's script. The potential was there, and that's what I think good scripts are. You're not told how to think, it's not all in the stage directions. You know

– gimme the lean shit and then we'll build it. So the humour was Alan's humour, we were all infected by him and so we went off and did it. I mean, me and the black kid Errol shouting, 'You Paki bastards,' throwing bricks through people's windows and running away, is disgusting. But there's something funny about it, odd about it, in the way he filmed it – it was the stupidity of the evil.

I remember thinking sometimes, 'Christ, this is a good shot. I'm in a good shot! Terrific!' Like the tunnel scene near the end – it was fun, and Alan knew it was. First of all we got raided by the police while we were down there, in Rotherhithe. We were shooting and someone had driven through and then reported us, said, 'There's a band of skinheads down there.' It was only me. It's probably the best image in the film, that shot, it's kind of indelible – this skinny little fucking twenty-year-old striding down a tunnel, shouting at the cars. I think I was on T-shirts, I was *Oi!* Man of the Year at one point. But you get that character right there, and that's a sexy shot. You're always looking for a sexy shot. It's just like 'Aaargh!' – that energy. Then we all went to a pub right at the end of the tunnel and we had a lock-in, I think it might have been the last night. And I had the character behind me.

DAVID LELAND: *Made in Britain* has a twin star in *Rhino,* about a very passive young black girl who's a truant and whose life is more meaningful outside of school than in, looking after her brother's kid. She becomes a victim through her passivity. Then take Trevor, who fights every inch of the way in the process of becoming a victim of the same system. He's determined not to, but he does. He winds up in that cell with a policeman leaning over him –'We've got ya now.' And that knock on the knee he gets from the truncheon is so vicious – I still grab my knee and wince when I see it.

MARGARET MATHESON: *Made in Britain* and the other plays in the series were nurtured by a woman called Claire Mulholland. The ITC had offices in each region that had a franchise and she was the officer in the Midlands. I was introduced to her early on and she was an incredibly nice, interesting, bright woman. I decided to take the line, 'This is what we're going to do, so let's find out how we get it on.'

She took the view that *Made in Britain* should be transmitted after *News at Ten*, and on the basis that it be shown late she supported it, and no questions were asked. And my fellow controllers of drama couldn't believe that 'the proprietor' gave us such freedom.

DAVID LELAND: *Made in Britain* is absolutely characteristic of Alan's film-making, it was alien enough to make people want to go round the back of the set to see if it was plugged in properly; in other words, 'How did this get on our screens?' What you work towards is a way of articulating something so as to make people jump – as they did when they saw *Made in Britain*.

MARK SHIVAS: *Made in Britain* was such an extraordinary view, I don't think anything like that had been seen on television before – this laughing jackass, extraordinarily vibrant human being who went about breaking things. You did understand what was going on in his head, and some of why he did it, and why people found him intolerable.

CHRISTOPHER MORAHAN: Alan was the first person I felt in the UK to dynamically use Steadicam – so that you thought, 'Jesus Christ!' It changed him, a kind of stylistic energy had been released, Steadicam was a trigger for his creativity. I don't know if he had been encouraged by influences, Scorsese let's say; he wasn't a person to encourage that kind of conversation.

GRAHAM BENSON: *Made in Britain* is *GoodFellas* to me, that's the film you want to walk out of after five minutes, but if you stay for six minutes . . . There's not one film Alan made that was offensive, some of them are better than others but none of them offend. And yet he was thought of by some people as 'Urgh! Filthy! Alan Clarke?' In his personal habits, sometimes. Not in his work.

MARGARET MATHESON: I remember the ITV meeting to which we'd all go along with our little films and they'd decide which one would represent ITV at the Prix Italia. They were all nice guys, but in the main producing very boring programmes. But with great generosity they decided *Made in Britain* was the one they should send because it stood out. And this was vindicated by it winning. There was a dinner, as they do at these things – really nice dinners for big fat people, at which they're really grateful to us, the artists, while we eat and drink. But Alan got unbelievably drunk before the ceremony, he was in a very melancholy mood at the time. And he had a tiff with someone at this dinner. I went looking for him the next morning and discovered he'd checked out, got on a plane and left. Partly because it wasn't his thing – partly because he must have had the mother and father of all hangovers.

20
Intruders in South Armagh: *Contact* (1984)

SEAN CHAPMAN: Alan was respectful of writers and writing. He wasn't one for letting actors change whatever line they liked. He chose his projects with care, on the strength of what he met on the page, and unless he saw something developing through rehearsal and so on, then he wanted what was on the page. There was no 'make it up as you go' feel, ever. But the time I saw him remake a script was *Contact*.

CORIN CAMPBELL HILL: I remember meeting Alan across a tea-trolley in the BBC in 1984. I had been there for two years, I was a first assistant production manager. He was just finishing a studio piece called *Stars of the Roller State Disco* and Alan and Terry Coles

'If you were an officer in the Paras in South Armagh, how would you handle it?': Sean Chapman as the Platoon Commander in *Contact* (1984)

asked me to work on *Contact*, then called *Midnight Blues*. A.F.N. Clarke, Tony Clarke, had been a captain in the Paras and had decided to write about his experiences.

SEAN CHAPMAN: Tony had served in Northern Ireland and all of this got to him to the extent that he had to leave after his last tour of duty, he was invalided out with terrible ulcers. And two or three years later he was sitting in his parents' garden somewhere in the Home Counties and suddenly had this complete and massive breakdown. He had to write about it to get it in focus. He doesn't talk about the breakdown in the book, but I knew through meeting him that the man on whom this story was based had gone through this nightmarish *Heart of Darkness* experience as a young officer in charge of much younger men in South Armagh. The script of *Contact* doesn't delineate that story at all – it gives you a set of sequences, describing army operations.

TIM ROTH: Alan offered me the lead in *Contact* and I was about to be a father. They were planning to shoot around August 1984, when the baby was due. Alan called and said, 'I've got this great part for you, it's all night shoots; we're gonna do infra-red night vision, handheld camera.' And he sent me the script and the book, and I called and said, 'Look, I'm there, I really wanna do this. But the baby's gonna be born towards the end of the film, I need a couple of days either side.' He said, 'OK, that's no problem.' And then he thought about it again and he said, 'No, you can't, you've gotta be with your kid, you've gotta be with the mother.' And then our son was born after they wrapped. Just one of those things.

SEAN CHAPMAN: I was due to play the Corporal, with Tim as the Platoon Commander. Then the phone rang, and I was told I had the lead if I wanted it. And I jumped around the room. We were on location in the Welsh hills, billeted in an adventure centre with an assault course, and in the hands of a stuntman called Terry Forrestal, who'd been in the Forces. We had lessons from the armourer on handling the guns, we had map-reading lectures, we did river-crossings. Little by little we became a unit. What I got from those long physical days, and long talks with Tony Clarke, was a sense of tremendous camaraderie, but also an acute sense of aloneness. You're always in the company of men, yet you feel yourself becoming more and more withdrawn. I began to use that. I thought if you had these long days in the field, eight or nine day ops, you'd come back to the base and just close the door. And pray to get through the thing and out the other side.

But I was also aware that I kept falling into clichés about playing an officer. I was bogged down in my research, really. And I remember so clearly one evening after rehearsal. I was tired, and Alan came to me and said, 'Look, Sean, you're a terrible fookin' actor. But if you let me in, we can make something of this. You see, I don't want this to be a film about the army, alright?' I say, 'Ah. Right!?' He said, 'No, I'm not fookin' interested in the army, it's full of idiots. I want *you* to be this officer in this situation, Seany. If you were leading the Paras in South Armagh, how would you handle it? You've got the kit on, it's a real river you're wading through, it's really night-time. Don't do anything. Just let me find how you're feeling.' I got to work the next morning, and suddenly the shorthand started to emerge, and we were in a new place. We knew how to be spontaneous. And we started to lose scenes left, right and centre, and take lines out.

CORIN CAMPBELL HILL: Tony Clarke was on the set pretty well throughout, which was unusual itself, at least on the films I did with Alan. But I don't remember any brooding discussions about 'Have we got this shot?' or 'Did we do that line?' There were none. It was 'Is the essence of that scene there?' And I suspect we did let the script sit to one side at times.

SEAN CHAPMAN: In *Contact* there's a couple of key scenes between the Platoon Commander and the Corporal, John Blundell. He comes into my room, where I'm quietly falling apart after one of the men has been killed, blown up. And he says, 'Don't get involved, Boss. It's bad for the brain.' There's a tenderness to it that is purely masculine, and can't be explored by those men in that situation. When I did my research with the Paras and the Marines, I saw that all the time. The buddy-buddy system that the Army runs is dependent upon a great emotional empathy. And I think Alan was desperately interested in that. He could get inside the heads of these characters and I never saw him do that with an actress. His empathy with men was total.

Almost all of *Contact* was shot on these incredibly long lenses. For a lot of the time I didn't know where the camera crew were, and that was Alan's buzz. So I wasn't really aware that Alan was starting to concentrate on the close-ups of my face, blissfully unaware in fact. I just knew I had the freedom to hold a look for as long as I wanted to, or as briefly. But a close-up that's as introspective as that is usually interesting. Alan's gift was he knew that film was about the moment of the head you're watching in the frame. The camera can be staring at the face but it's filming the brain, the mind of the character in shot. And if that's in place, if it's real, you can talk about anything, you can make a scene out of nothing and it will be charged. You could be polishing a fucking car and you could make a two-hour film of it.

There's a scene where we've tracked these men down to a farmhouse, they lie prostrate and I put my gun barrel in this guy's mouth. Neither Alan or I knew what came next in the scene. We knew this was a position of complete power for my character, complete revenge and potentially a complete release of this tension. And I said to him, 'I can hold this look with him for ever, I'm getting off on being in charge here.' He said, 'So hold it.' The tension comes from showing as little as you need to, and a killing would have released that tension. People think Alan's films are brutal. But in the context of the themes he's dealing with, he actually holds back from extreme moments. And with Alan you always know – however well a character makes his point, it's cost something. When Trevor pisses on his files – he's lost something of himself by doing it, he's been forced into a corner and made to take a line that's below him in some way. And it's the same with the Platoon Commander's violence. When he puts that barrel in that man's mouth – he's broken the procedure, now he has to make his own rules, and at a cost to himself. That's the moral crux – it costs you to be there and take such action, even when you think you've succeeded.

The climactic sequence is the Platoon Commander walking down to inspect an abandoned car in a lane, that may or may not have a bomb in it. We spent some time working out the walk, all from one camera vantage, to see in the first instance what we could or couldn't catch. I think Alan wanted to take an establishing shot and then come down to the car to do close-ups. But then he said, 'I tell you what, Sean – when you go down there, I've got it all from here. And I tell you what I'm really lovin', have a look.' He showed me the shot with a second AD in my place. He said, 'I can read everything in your body. You've got this fookin' car here that might go up, might not. I don't need to go close – I've got it. Do you agree?' I said, 'Fine.' And then we shot.

Now some people said, 'No British army officer would do a vehicle check like that.' Throwing the doors open, kicking them shut, turning on the radio – it's not Army procedure at all. That's the point – he's lost the plot. There's a petrol can beside the car – I kick it into the hedge. It's like a moment in *Platoon* where the grunts have spent so long in this foxhole that they break out and go crazy. You literally can't stand any more, you'd rather be dead than for it to go on. You want the hurt to stop, and you want to hurt something – even if it's a car. It was about becoming extremely emotionally and physically tired, thinking, 'Fuck it, I'd rather be taken out than carry on with this level of fear.' That was the story of *Contact*. It seems more and more pointless, the more vehicle checks you do, the more silly gunfights in a field, where nobody seems to win anything. In that sense it's an anti-war film without ever talking about the pointlessness of its project, it's interwoven in the shot choices and so on.

STUART GRIFFITHS: I watched Alan at work on the editing of *Contact* and, of course, he liked to pare things down to an absolute minimum. At the climax you have the marvellously-held shot of the Commander and the car in the lane, that car looking deeply dangerous and sinister. Then the Commander passes onward through the gate – and there in the editing, I recall Alan removing certain shots which would probably have extended the suspense more overtly. So then what happens very abruptly is that the young soldier following the Commander through the gate is blown up – a terrible blast and then a blackout.

SEAN CHAPMAN: On *Contact* I was twenty-two, Alan was fifty, the point being that I can only recall the empathy we had. Whereas, and he never made you aware of this, there must have come a point at the end of the working day when he'd had enough of my company. I never had enough of his. For me he became a father figure in a way that was incredibly intense. I loved Alan, really loved him. I learned more from him than anyone else I've ever met.

His working process looks very immediate and organic, but it was meticulously rehearsed, which is how you achieve that, as in the theatre. He ground his actors down in the sense that he'd take away your acting instinct. He'd let you use your tricks up, and then there'd be what was left – this incredibly free thing that doesn't care how it's judged or read, which is the antithesis of the English acting process.

Another of his phrases was 'Let's let the pig out.' 'Let's let out the thing no one wants to see, and let it walk about and squeal a bit, so we know what fucking colour it is. Then we'll shoot the pig.' Alan was always about taking away and taking away, but getting somewhere that was incredibly multi-layered. But he managed to do it in this incredibly unassuming and unpretentious way – you just knew you'd been Clarked. And once it had been done to you, you never worked without it. He showed actors how to be the beast that they were – let the pig out, drop the mask, drop any form of performance. Don't come to the lens, don't come to me with your story – be your story, and it's up to me to catch it. Of course 'the pig' turns out to be the thing everybody loves, Carlin, Trevor – because they speak from the place that nobody speaks from. It's the liberation of being exactly what one is.

21

'Let's do a musical!': *Billy the Kid and the Green Baize Vampire* (1985)

GEORGE FENTON: Barry Hanson had got me into writing music for television by asking me to do the series *Out*, which is how I met the writer Trevor Preston. And in talking with Trevor I discovered he wrote lyrics, and we ended up writing songs for *Out*. Then we did another series called *Fox*, which Graham Benson produced, and this time Trevor scripted songs into it, one an episode. After *Fox* he showed me an idea for a musical. Trevor had always liked snooker, both the game and the milieu. And the idea for this piece emanated from the first time that Jimmy White played Ray Reardon. It was conceived as a kind of Western showdown between the old and new orders, but in a context where they were both equally bizarre. I must say Trevor had to drag me to do it, but only because I was very sceptical about whether it would ever get made. But we kind of stumbled into it, and then we had a meeting with Margaret Matheson and it started to become a reality.

MARGARET MATHESON: The whole process now of money-raising both for development and production is so much about articulating what the script is going to be like in advance of writing the script, and what the film is going to be like in advance of making the film. So there really is a tendency to crush the creativity out of the thing. Previously, you just did things for what they were. The way that I and many others worked at the time was much more to say, 'Let's do this subject,' or, 'Let's work with that writer,' or, 'Let's do a musical!'

I put Simon Mallin in as producer. I don't remember who put Alan in – probably me, I'd have thought of Alan for everything. We were playing the levy game. Early Zenith films were subsidized by constructing the deals in a way that enabled us to get levy relief. The ITV companies were taxed on their profits over and above

An incensed Maxwell Randall (Alun Armstrong) sings the operatic tirade 'I Bite Back' in *Billy the Kid and the Green Baize Vampire* (1985)

corporation tax, but there was a certain amount of free income specifically from programme sales overseas. So you could construct deals where you got a handsome chunk of levy-free income; it became quite sophisticated and Central was not the only company using that loophole to help finance programmes. But by definition they had to be saleable overseas. Quite how that worked with *Billy the Kid* I don't know, since it was unsaleable here, let alone abroad. Probably we attributed the ITC contribution to overseas sales. We took it to Bernie Kingham, and George Fenton even then was a bit of a star, and I remember sitting there telling him it would be fun, song and dance. And I remember Bernie's horror later when he saw some rushes and said, 'Why's it all so dowdy? Why's it all so underlit?' – all the things you would expect a distributor to say. I don't know why they got themselves into it, and later on they were horrified to find themselves there.

GEORGE FENTON: I don't know what style *Billy the Kid* is in, except to say that it's Brechtian in a way. I suppose the basis of *Billy the Kid* was that somehow the music should be performed by a pit band, that it should be contained in its own world. Everything would emanate from that one little line-up, which meant it would have kind of a sound.

BARRY HANSON: Alan was obsessed by Brecht. *Billy the Kid* was a total homage to Brecht, the tempo of the tunes and so on. It was never going to be successful in the cinema, but it was extraordinary in terms of Alan's vision. It didn't explain the game, it didn't explain its existence really, it explained fuck all.

GEORGE FENTON: In pop music terms, there was something about punk that was like Brecht in theatre. It was kind of monochromatic in its texture, and it was right there, confronting the senses rather than massaging them. Trevor had a book about the Clash that he was very fond of – a photo-journal of them on the road in America, and you could have been looking at pictures of James Dean – black and white shots of cars and gas stations. It's all quite stylish, whatever that means. But Trevor saw the characters and the world of

Billy the Kid as possessing a tremendous amount of style. And I think he imagined that the film would be much more opulent in some ways, that the realism of it would have an intrinsic glamour. It was written and prepared with the idea of going on location. So there would have been cityscapes, rainy streets, urban squalor, faces in car windows – that's Trevor's world. His work is a celebration of the more bizarre, eccentric side of the underworld, which he knows pretty well. And, clearly, when Alan became the director, that was discarded, because Alan decided to shoot it all on a set.

MARGARET MATHESON: *Billy the Kid* was sort of shrouded in the psyches of the people involved – essentially Alan and Trevor, both of whom were quite dark at that time. Trevor suffered from serious depression, and he was quite seriously ill. So he wasn't participating fully in the process, and was quite difficult. And George, who's ever calm and smiling and bubbly and delightful, was somehow not enough to tip the balance.

GEORGE FENTON: It's no secret that Alan and Trevor just didn't see eye to eye over it, and that was a great tragedy. I think Trevor thought that Alan had squandered its richness in some way and that, had it had that richness, it would have been infinitely more successful. But the truth is that if it had taken a different course, it would have been just as likely to come to grief, because it's a hard thing to get right. I'm hard pushed to think of any screen musicals that have really got it just right since the 1950s and 1960s. And this was music theatre in that Brechtian way, on the screen. And that's not exactly a mass-appeal genre anyway, is it? In many ways there couldn't have been a more ideal director than Alan for it, because his work was so gritty and truthful. But I think that the disagreements Trevor and Alan had really stemmed from the fact that Alan saw the realism of Trevor's script and wanted to contain the surrealism so that he could manage the tone of the picture. Whereas Trevor didn't want that under control, he wanted it to be extravagant. Alan's version of realism *is* realism, it's the real thing, one shot where the camera keeps rolling and people do things and the camera follows, and you get these fantastic sequences. Like we all do, Trevor thinks that's brilliant film-making. But I think he saw *Billy the Kid* as more of a jaunt, and that the monochromatic representation of the story on the screen had sucked the blood out of it some way, drained it of its potential.

MARGARET MATHESON: I wasn't a party to much of the discussion between Trevor and Alan. I wasn't mad about the sets. And I had my own concerns about whether there'd be an audience for it, even before it became quite clear there wasn't a buyer for it. We'll never know whether there was an audience for it because they never saw it.

PHIL DANIELS: Alan was famed for not working with people twice. And when *Billy the Kid* came along, I went up for the part of the Kid's manager. But I'd been in bands, I could sing a bit. I played snooker as well, y'see? And I was a bit like Jimmy White. So those were all the requirements really, that's what sort of swung it for me. I did a few auditions, sang a bit for 'em – 'There I was digging a hole', that's what I sing at auditions. Now Alan was a bit different from when we did *Scum*. He ate funny, bits of fish at odd times of the day, and he had to have proteins. And he didn't drink with us on a Friday. He was one of the lads, Al, but he was a bit like the manager of the football team.

GEORGE FENTON: We rehearsed at Fulham Town Hall, we learnt the songs for two or three weeks just with a rehearsal piano. And finally we had a run-through and it seemed absolutely great, like any musical when you suddenly realize there's something there. It was such a positive feeling – everybody was up that day, it was the best day.

PHIL DANIELS: We had a lot of problems on it. Clarkey wasn't having a good time. And Trevor has his dark moods. We had a guy drop down dead on us. We had this scene in a corridor going round and round, and one of the grips had a heart attack. Not good.

GEORGE FENTON: Things about it went wrong because of people's lack of experience more than anything else. My only specific problem was that Alan didn't really choreograph any of the songs. I didn't expect dance routines but, for example, the way the video café scene was written, for the number 'Supersonic Sam's Cosmic Café', it was going to be an orgy of screens and lights and things. Whereas all you see is a line of faces standing over what appear to be glowing screens. So the result of the way Alan shot it – one person singing a four-and-a-half minute song for four-and-a-half minutes – was that there was tremendous pressure on the music to sustain itself for a long time without anything happening. Because of pop videos, people assume subconsciously that when music happens on the screen, somehow images will be compressed and you'll make a journey during the course of the music that you couldn't make without it. Of course, that's what happens in a musical – you get to a point, and someone sings a song and you jump over a fence, because the number expresses something that would have taken another four or five pages of dialogue to wade through. On the other hand, Alan's way was kind of mesmeric as well, so you kind of think, 'Oh, I don't know.'

PHIL DANIELS: There was a scene where I had to sing the line 'What a winkle' and then laugh my head off. And I was really struggling to do the laugh and make it sound real. And Clarkey was standing by the camera, so he started fiddling with his flies and pulling the zipper up and down, up and down, 'Ziiiiip!' and pullin' faces and going, 'Ooh!' And if you watch that scene I'm in absolute hysterics, and it's because I'm looking at Alan Clarke piddling about with his flies trying to make me laugh.

GEORGE FENTON: One day Alan did something that endeared him to me for ever. He'd been shooting too much footage in terms of the ratio they'd agreed. So suddenly on about the fifth or sixth day of shooting, all these blokes in suits turned up on the set. It was completely inappropriate and he was, if not offended, then irritated by their being there. But he wasn't a sulker, he just did things. And they followed him on to the set that day. He said, 'If you think I'm shooting too much and you don't like what I'm shooting, you'd better tell me now, you'd better come see what I'm doing.' So they came trooping in and stood along the back wall of the set, about eight people, accountant types, standing and watching. And Alan set the shot up and then became very sort of urgent and keyed-up, rocking on his heels and going, 'Right! Are we ready? Everybody ready?' as if he was about to spin plates on sticks. And the whole place went quiet, this massive set-up. And he went, 'O-K! Aaaand – Tut!' And everybody looked baffled and stared at Alan. And the cameraman turned to him and said, 'Wh-what's going on?' And Alan said, 'That was "Turnover" and "Cut". I'm using too much footage, you see. OK, let's go again! Ready everyone? Aaaand – Tut!' Well, of course, because he was a maniac, he didn't just do it once or twice, he went on and on. 'OK, we're gonna have a look at a shot over 'ere now. Everybody ready?' Until in the end these suits looked at him pityingly, as if he was some child that they couldn't control – which of course he wasn't. And they just buggered off. And he never heard from them again.

I didn't have any sense of what we'd made until we were in the cutting room. I think what happened there was that Alan probably had reservations about how he was going to resolve the elements, the story, the music, the snooker – of which he had billions of feet – and the surrealism of the story, set against the realism of the characters. I think he was stunned. And so was I, because they were assembling the film without music, just the story. It seemed to me that couldn't be right. I couldn't see how they were going to pace things that happened within the context of the song unless they had the songs. Finally, Alan said, 'Well, you'd better come in and sit and help us put the songs together.' Normally I work on something that's cut, but now I had to go through footage and decide what might be a good way to orchestrate the song in terms of the shots we had.

When I was doing the incidental music score, I said to Alan, 'Don't you want to talk to me about this?' and he said, 'I don't know what to say.' I said, 'Well, where am I going to put the music?' and he said, 'I'm not sure, I've never had any music in my films.' Which was so typical of him. So I just went off into the studio on my own and did what I thought, then took it back again.

And he just nodded and said, 'Yep, yep, yeah.' He was as bewildered as any of us by this stage, thinking, 'How on earth did I get myself into doing this?'

PHIL DANIELS: It was an odd film for Clarkey to make, not the straight-down-the-line reality he normally did. I mean, Eve Ferret on a motorbike with the poodles – and Alun Armstrong *really* being a vampire and me *really* being Billy the Kid, it just had a nice twist to it. I like the vampire's song the best, the one they done as an opera, 'I Bite Back'.

I haven't seen it for years and I know it wasn't the greatest film on earth, but I always thought it was a much better film than it was ever given credit for. They put it out and it had no publicity. And round the same time there was a terrible musical out, *Absolute Beginners*, and I don't think anyone saw either of 'em.

GEORGE FENTON: I know that people who like it – love it. There are four or five nutcases out there who think it's the best thing ever. And currently somebody, theoretically, is going to do a theatre show of it. Let 'em have a go.

22

Walkin' blues: *Christine* (1986)

ARTHUR ELLIS: When I left the National Film School, Alan Clarke was somebody I aimed at, I wanted to work for him, but I couldn't find out who he was repped by or anything. I had a football story about fans going on tour, I wanted it raw and rough and I wanted to get Alan. I didn't know he was a football fan, but I knew he was a violence fan – or not a fan, but that he'd know how to handle it. Because when someone got hit in one of Alan's films you knew it wasn't wallpaper, it was the business.

Alan was doing *Billy the Kid* and I knew Trevor Preston and Simon Mallin. And finally we got in touch. Turned out we lived round the corner from each other in Shepherd's Bush, we had a drink, traded numbers, and that's how we got on together. We'd meet at the Ritz caff for a cup of tea or whatever, end up chatting for four or five hours. I could totally be myself with him, talk about anything without any sense of having to edit myself. He'd made a career out of being himself, and I was intrigued how he'd managed to survive in a business that doesn't encourage that. He was someone I could learn from, everybody I'd met who'd worked with him had learned from him. Nothing happened with the football story. Then I was doing *The Black and Blue Lamp* at the BBC and we'd hang around. And then he asked me if I would do something with him about drugs – drugs and kids. There was a book called *Chasing the Dragon*, written by an addict's mother. Alan had been given it and he was just intrigued by the premise – what addiction is when you're ten or eleven. That was the basis of it, and we decided to set it on a housing estate, which was manageable and economical.

There's two ways you can go with stories about drugs. There's no drama with drugs, you fix and you die. It's not the greatest narrative drive, you know? So you go really boring – or you go really gross. We considered the gross options. We were talking to addicts, asking them what happens when the veins dry up. We heard about one guy who could only inject in his eye, and another only in his dick. So he could only inject with a hard-on. But he was impotent – so what could he do? I mean, that would have been the drama for us, had we gone down that road. But the BBC would never have touched that stuff with a bargepole, and quite rightly – it was fucking revolting.

The theme came for me because I never did heroin, but I used to drink. And there were two ways you could go with a drinking anecdote. One was the kind of 'Then I mounted the pavement, fuckin' hell you should have been there, I was a right cunt' story. But the truth of it was that I was afraid, tearful, bitter, lonely, and I sat on me own. I wasn't an Oliver Reed character, I was like Wilfred Brambell. I wanted to take out any notion of anecdote and make it fucking boring. So we went for boredom – eleven-year-olds walking from place to place, walking into houses and sticking needles in their arms. That was it, walking and fixing. I mean, they walk in *Road* too, it's a fucking marathon, but there you have character and moving portraits of human beings and great Jim Cartwright dialogue with it. *Christine* is just kids and 'Are you alright?' We took out anything that smacked of drama. No, hold on – I left in a bit about the stylus, the needle from the record player, having gone missing. But I did wonder if that was too much. I think the budget was fifty thousand and it had to be shot in ten shooting days. And it was going to run fifty minutes, so we had fifty minutes to be boring.

JOHN WARD: I'd done a lot of the spadework on *Christine*, but didn't get to work on it. Arthur Ellis used to joke about *Christine*, he'd written a scene where she walks up steps, and Alan said, 'Don't you think the steps are gilding the lily a bit?'

ARTHUR ELLIS: I wrote the script, then did a second draft. We ended up sharing the credit – Alan didn't write anything, but he asked me to do it on the basis that we'd split the dough, and I was happy to do the script and work with Alan Clarke and get my fifteen hundred quid. Then Alan got stuck into auditioning and getting the kids – like Vicky Murdock, great little lady.

VICKY MURDOCK: I was at the Anna Scher School. And I started to get jobs, because people were always coming in looking for kids for something. And if they wanted down-to-earth kids they came to Anna Scher. So I was taken on the agency books. Alan might have seen me in a class.

I remember going for the read, it was Easter 1986, the school holidays. I'd just come back from a school trip where I'd really got in trouble. I was thirteen, let loose in France, and I was due to be suspended. Then this job came up, and I went to see Alan at Shepherd's Bush, thinking, 'I really have to behave.' Now, as I understood it, the original story was focused on a guy and three other kids. But there wasn't any script around, we just talked. And he'd just throw questions at me – he wanted to know background, things about my mum, questions about cars or wallpaper or 'Have you been to Yorkshire?' He was looking for something and I was way too young to understand, because sitting there as the actor who wants the job, you never know, you think, 'What should I try to be?' But there was no air-kissing with him, he wanted to get to the bones of people. Anyway, I walked out, that was it. Went back later – and he said to me, 'I tell ya what, Vick – I'm gonna throw it at you – and it's gonna be your number.' And I couldn't believe it – I just thought, 'God, I'm in so much trouble at school, I hope I get the time off.'

We had two weeks of rehearsal at North Acton. There was a script by now. There was me, Kelly George, Joanne Mapp. I was thirteen, they were a couple of years older. We had a guy called Paul who was the adviser on the drugs front, an ex-addict who'd cleaned up. On the first day he made us sit there and watch *Christiane F*, and I remember we cringed and cracked up a bit as she was spewing over the walls. And I thought, 'Do I know what I'm taking on here?' But Clarkey wasn't patting us on the back and saying, 'Oh, you can do this, luvvie.' None of that – he was, 'I know you're capable, so that's it.'

CORIN CAMPBELL HILL: We shot it under the flight path in Hounslow, which Alan specifically requested. Mike Jackley found the estate. Steve Saunderson shot all of the film handheld. It was a short shoot.

VICKY MURDOCK: I spent most of my time walking round these houses, you know? With my chin on my chest. He said, 'That's the way it is.' It had to be realistic, which can be a pain in the neck on the technical side. It was like there was always somebody at my shoulder, and I developed this druggy walk.

CORIN CAMPBELL HILL: Vicky walked and we followed, down the pavement, across the green, round the corner, into the flats, up the stairs, through the door, into the kitchen. If we missed the sitting-room, we had to do it all again. It was a physical feat, you had to be on tiptoes creeping, creeping behind the camera. And anybody watching us would have thought we were mad.

MICHAEL JACKLEY: It was very bleak – investigating this lower-middle-class background, in which there isn't such deprivation as in, say, *Road*. But these young people still lead desperately meaningless lives and end up sticking needles in themselves. Alan was drawn to that side of life.

VICKY MURDOCK: Alan said to me, 'This is such a dull life. Christine has no vision, so forget that you have any.' It was suburban kids who have enough pocket money, and they're throwing it away, but they want to do it, they've chosen it; they're not in a tower block having it pressed on them. It was so dull it was chilling. Just a hopeless scenario, you couldn't throw any jolliness into it. The dialogue was secondary, I always felt. Between the kids it was all just chit-chat, everything was really about the contents of that tin: 'When is that gear coming out and when is it going in me?'

TARIQ ANWAR: In the edit Alan obsessed endlessly over the lengths of these long repetitive shots, the girl walking from house to house. He changed his mind repeatedly, about whether they should be two minutes, three, four. I couldn't really see the difference myself, to be honest – it was all going on in his head. And it could drive you crazy, except that he had his own way of charming you into making these incessant changes and re-changes. He'd come in of a morning and say, 'Tariq – you'll think I'm a fookin' idiot – but . . .' And you'd end up doing it for him.

STEPHEN FREARS: I used to get depressed watching them, it was so awful, the view of life was so terrible that I often didn't watch them, I'm ashamed to say – just so bleak. *Christine* – the drug addicts on the housing estate, I couldn't watch that. The handheld camera just made it more bleak – because then he could film them walking from one house to another. So it became, oh – just inescapable. Fantastic, clearly. But it made me not watch – is that a good thing or a bad thing? I'm not sure how to conduct that argument.

ARTHUR ELLIS: When *Christine* went out, I watched about twenty minutes of it, then I got a phone call. After that I just read the reviews. They seemed to draw some kind of metaphor from the missing needle on the record player. The reviews told me what it was about, I suppose. Someone called me up to say they thought it was immoral, they wanted some judgement. Couldn't help them there.

23
'Genially dirty': *Rita Sue and Bob Too* (1986)

STUART GRIFFITHS: The contrast between Alan's personality and the darkness of his subject matter was often quite extraordinary, because he was one of the funniest men I ever met. I think the only film that really got across his own marvellous sense of humour was *Rita Sue and Bob Too* – hilarious stuff, pure Alan if you knew him as a person. He reminded me of some of the great Northern comedians, albeit a bit more sophisticated. He could remain deadpan while people would be aching with laughter at his wit. There's a line in *Twelfth Night*, 'A witty man will turn a sentence inside out like a glove.' He could do that. I told him once about a line in *Henry V*, 'Not for Cadwallader and all his goats.' I couldn't work out why it was so funny, and he immediately and acutely analysed it, it was all in the individual letters. Empson or Richards would have been interested in what he had to say there.

SANDY LIEBERSON: After our time in the States, Alan and I saw each other periodically over the next five years, and then we got to work together when I left Goldcrest and decided to produce *Rita Sue and Bob Too*. A version of the script, about forty or fifty pages, was submitted to me by Oscar Lewenstein, who was associated with Andrea Dunbar's plays while he was at the Royal Court. It was this story about two girls living on a Bradford estate who get involved with a married man who's a bit more well off. And I thought, 'God, you could make a very unusual – and very inexpensive – little film out of this. And at the same time have something very strong to say about England.' But Goldcrest were very uncomfortable with it, and I think it was too small a movie for them at the time. But when I left nine months later, I approached Oscar and we agreed to do it together. And I asked Patsy Pollock to join me – both to cast it, which would be the

Rita Sue and Bob Too (1986): Clarke and the film's co-producer Patsy Pollock

secret of doing it, and also because I felt she had something to contribute on the producing side. And she was over the moon about the prospect of working with Alan. So we invited Alan on board and he accepted, he loved the idea. He saw it as something he could get his teeth into on every level – the rawness of the characters, the open sexuality of it, the provocative nature of the story, the humour. We went to David Rose first and he was very supportive of Channel Four backing the film, and of course had a history with Alan from the BBC.

DAVID HARE: I'm a tremendous fan of Andrea Dunbar, I thought her original plays were great. She was the classic Alan Clarke author in the sense that she wrote about where she lived. She lived on a council estate and she wrote this stuff down in school exercise books, she just called them 'scenes'. And then she'd give them to Max Stafford-Clark.

LESLEY SHARP: At the time I was cast in *Rita Sue*, I was in *Road* at the Royal Court. And it was part of a double bill with a play of Andrea's called *Shirley*, I was playing the title role. She was a breath of fresh air, Andrea – an extraordinary person to find walking around the Royal Court, really, her background was so harsh, nothing to do with that stripped-pine middle-class London intelligentsia. Her writing was so full of blood and teeth, and she was brilliant in rehearsals. In *Shirley* there was a fight in this pub, and the discussion in rehearsal got very lahdy-dah, 'Oh well, when men hit each other in pubs it's very like so.' And she put us straight – 'Well, no, actually, on Saturday nights down at the Beacon it's more like this,' and we all bowed to her superiority.

DAVID HARE: Patsy Pollock had a lot to do with the shape of that script. She got Andrea Dunbar in a pub in London, and Andrea was going, 'I'm not fucking writing for any fucking wanky fucking film director.' And Alan was just loving it, thinking it was the best thing that ever happened to him. And Patsy had to virtually lock her in a room to get work out of her, it was all like that. So they had this very puritan producer, Oscar Lewenstein, and this foul-mouthed writer, and the director rubbing his hands and thinking, 'Oh good, chaos here.'

SANDY LIEBERSON: We all had something to say about the script, Alan included, but I think Patsy was particularly helpful. She has a way of connecting with people like Andrea, and I guess Andrea was comfortable with her.

There wasn't an order that the actresses had to be unknowns, they just had to be right. They didn't come off the estate, but we wanted them to represent the attitude and character.

MICHELLE HOLMES: I grew up in Rochdale on a council estate, and there was always something in me of wanting to get out and make more of myself. I was eighteen, and when I read the script I just knew I could play Sue and make her believable. So I met Patsy Pollock and then Alan. There's some people you just click with – I'm a bit eccentric, I think Alan was too, he picked people out who were a bit offbeat. I read and he jumped up and said, 'Great, fantastic. But you're too old.' I went, 'Right, stay there. I'll be fifteen minutes.' I took my make-up off, flattened my hair, changed out of my trendy bits of clothes, went back in and read it again. Same reaction. As I left, Patsy said, 'Don't worry, we'll get you back.' The long and the short of it was I went up nine times and Alan said, 'You'll never play this part.' And Patsy was ringing me on the sly and saying, 'Come up to the office.' I don't know if he was pushing me to see if I had the kind of balls and energy he was looking for. But I'd walk in and say, 'Look, Alan – I'll do the catering, I'll sweep the floor, I'll make your breakfast – I'm doing this film.'

SIOBHAN FINNERAN: I can't remember how much of the script I'd read when I was cast as Rita, but once I'd read the whole thing I thought, 'Oh my God, what are my mum and dad going to think?' I was twenty, but it was my first job really. And they weren't really any the wiser until the Brighton Film Festival when it was plastered all over the papers, and my poor mum opened up the paper and saw 'The film that turned the festival blue'. But they thought it was great fun. My grandma ended up seeing it and, apart from telling me she wished I'd stand up straight, her only comment was about the bad language. So we assumed she missed all the bonking in the first ten minutes.

We had two weeks' rehearsal and it meant that Michelle and I could build up a rapport, and with George Costigan too. The first week was just the three of us, so it was great fun. And of course there were less nerves and inhibitions about all the stuff we were going to have to do in front of the crew. I'm sure we'd have coped, but it was just better that we'd already done it fifty times on a camp-bed in a rehearsal room before we got into that car. I mean, the camp-bed didn't always do what it was meant to, collapsed at the wrong moments, but we got the work done. I remember we had to stop every day about four o'clock 'cos we all got the bad giggles and had to have cakes. Alan would shout, 'Oh God, it's cake time, can we have some sweets for these two?'

LESLEY SHARP: Rehearsals weren't just to do with the characters and 'Let's sort out the relationships and the dynamics.' Alan let you into his process as well; he'd say, 'Right, what we're gonna do, we'll have the camera here and then it's coming in here, then we'll pull back and do a big tracking shot.' It was a two-tier process, there was a melding. The energy with which he used the camera was the energy with which he spoke to you as a director, and I think the shots he put up on screen are a real testimony to his character.

GEORGE COSTIGAN: The reason Alan rehearsed, I think, was because he'd come from the theatre – he knew how to play with actors, and he knew what the value was. Alan more or less ran the entire film on the last Saturday of a fortnight's rehearsal, so that you had some overview of what you were doing. And what that means to an actor is that you can plan how you're going to shape your performance, and he can plan where he wants it shaped too – where he wants the bombs to go off.

SANDY LIEBERSON: A large part of the film was going to be shot on Steadicam. But Ivan Strasburg got worn out physically trying to wear the Steadicam rig all day and worry about the lighting. We'd been shooting at least a week, maybe more, and Ivan was happy for us to bring in John Ward.

JOHN WARD: It was the autumn of 1986, I'd just finished *Full Metal*

Jacket. Garth Thomas had put me on a warning and then he said, 'Get your arse up to Bradford now.' I was a great admirer of Alan's work, so to get to work with him was wonderful for me, I'd wanted that very much.

SANDY LIEBERSON: It was shot right on the Buttershaw estate. Andrea was living there, and her family, her mother and her sister and kids, relatives, friends. The people from the estate would come and watch us film, and offer their comments on proceedings.

SIOBHAN FINNERAN: That estate was . . . Jesus Christ. I wasn't brought up with a silver spoon, but it was a complete culture shock at the time. Kiddies running around with nothing on their feet. The crew adopted half of them. It was just a mess, really.

Andrea was around a lot of the time on set. A lot of the time she had that expression of 'Couldn't give a shit'; I'm sure she did, but it was very difficult a lot of the time to say what she was thinking. But she'd have the crack with me and Michelle over a pint and a fag if we were all in the pub.

GEORGE COSTIGAN: The sex scenes? Well, they were meant to be uncomfortable. Freezing cold in a car on the Yorkshire Moors, take seventeen, anybody who found it erotic would be a bit damaged, I think. It's just clumsy and real and fumbling about, it's not sexy and it's not shot to be. You're just looking at a bunch of people grabbing it while they can.

MICHELLE HOLMES: We had extra knickers on, even though we were pulling one pair off for the camera. When we shot it George's pelvis was on my belly. So all I got from it was a stomach-ache, it was totally non-sexual. It was, 'Let's get on with it.'

GEORGE COSTIGAN: The most direction he ever gave me was a long shot of me from the back, having a post-double-coital celebratory slash. Piece of piss, I thought. Did it. 'No, Georgie, no.' Alan, impassioned. 'No, you get him out, you look at him, "You little bobby-dazzler – didn't you play a blinder, eh?" – hold him nice and gentle, "Yissss, my son." And then you have the slash. Try again . . .' It was a tight budget, but we did six takes of that shot.

LESLEY SHARP: George and I had great fun discussing what had gone wrong with Bob and Michelle's marriage. I think one of my favourite scenes was when Michelle tries to warn the girls off in the bedroom – they both go, 'Has he done it before?' But it's sad, it happens all over the place. Obviously, in Michelle's case, she didn't want the marriage to break up but she'd lost the plot of what constitutes a good relationship. It's become all about the house and the Rover and all that.

JOHN WARD: I like the shot we did in Haworth, where the girls are on a school trip walking down the streets of the town, and one of the girls calls Sue a slag who sleeps with married men – so she slaps her. A lot of takes, naturally, and the poor girl's face got redder and redder and the make-up girl was buzzing around. You know the murderball story – the same thing happened here, he said, 'Go on, hit 'er, otherwise she won't react right.' Whallop! Ow!

MICHELLE HOLMES: I was saying, 'I can't do that. Really can't.' But that's his trademark, Alan's, isn't it? That's his little trick with actors. He played people off one another a bit. He'd stir the pot a little bit, I know he'd say things to George, he'd say things to me.

GEORGE COSTIGAN: I argued with him a few times, 'That's not what this is about,' and so on. He had a great fear – his endless direction was 'Light, keep it light, keep it frothy, keep 'em laughing.' And what you don't see – from not having his overview and, to be perfectly honest, not being as smart as he is – is that when you watch the film, that lightness and that desperation of the characters to keep having a laugh, it wears them out in the end. When Bob couldn't get a hard-on Al was laughing; I said, 'It's not funny, Alan, not funny at all.' But I'd no idea what his overview was, and what he wanted was that car with those three people still laughing in it. And if you have Bob sulking in the front seat, then you've thrown a loop in the film which you're not to know about.

Rita Sue and Bob Too (1986): Clarke directs and John Ward operates the Steadicam on location in Haworth

Rita Sue and Bob Too (1986): A bit of a domestic between Patti Nicholls, Siobhan Finneran, Willie Ross, Michelle Holmes, Lesley Sharp and George Costigan

SANDY LIEBERSON: I wasn't sure of Steadicam at first, I worried a little, but once I got used to it I loved the feeling it gave the movie. It gave it spontaneity and vitality and immediacy and energy, which was very much in keeping with the tone of the movie. I don't think it called attention to itself.

JOHN WARD: I like that final shot, travelling through the house with George. It starts downstairs in the kitchen, he wanders round the house a bit lost, then he goes upstairs, he puts a bath on. And we come to that lovely little end piece, he thinks he's lost them all – his wife and the two girls. Opens the bedroom door, and then he finds Rita and Sue in his bed – 'You took your fookin' time!' And he grins and dives at them, and there's a freeze-frame. Alan called that his 'split-screen shot' because George bared his bum for the world. I think Alan had wanted the girls without their bras there, and they were happy to do it. But it was felt to be too much.

GEORGE COSTIGAN: Alan had come to me in the middle of rehearsals and he said to me, 'How do we stop Bob winning this film?' and I said, 'I don't know, Alan, I've every intention of winning this film if I can. I mean, I think it's wrong in a quasi-feminist way, but I don't know how you do that. After all, he gets the two girls in the end.' He said, 'No, you're right, I'll think about that.' He came back about two days later and said, 'I've got it!' 'Go on then, what?' 'You go upstairs and you run the bath – and the girls have gone out. And you go into the bedroom and they've left you this blow-up rubber woman. And we have a shot of you going, 'Oh well –why not?' And then you dive in and fuck that. That'll clinch it, that makes him a shit, don't it?' And I think he was really toying with the idea.

MICHELLE HOLMES: You see, I don't think Bob did win. To my mind, it wouldn't last, the three of them. It was just a period in their lives for the girls. And how sad was he?

SIOBHAN FINNERAN: At the time there was just a huge hullabaloo, about teenage sex and all that. I remember we had this press conference at the Brighton Film Festival – Clarkey could hardly speak, I think Patsy had to do all the talking. We couldn't believe that they thought it was far-fetched, that the estate had been made to look worse and that this kind of life wasn't going on. You know – hello? What planet do you live on? Oh yeah, that one they call Down South. It was out at the same time as *Wish You Were Here*, Emily Lloyd playing a sixteen-year-old in the 1950s having sex with older men, and they weren't hung up about that one. It was just that ours was modern-day, and grimmer.

DAVID HARE: *Rita Sue and Bob Too* is genially dirty. I mean, it's quite unusual for a British film to be about sex in the first place – for it to be sexy, and for it to represent sex as something that's good fun, where everybody has a nice time while they're doing it. It's part of Alan's libertarian spirit.

PAM BRIGHTON: I hadn't seen Alan in ages and someone invited me to a press showing of *Rita Sue and Bob Too*, which was very odd for me because Andrea came from Bradford, very close to where I lived. And I walked in and Alan went, 'Oh God – if you hate this film . . .' I wasn't mad about it, actually. I thought it was sort of oddly too lightweight – very uncharacteristic of his work. I thought Andrea's writing was better than the film, bleaker than the film. And Andrea hadn't liked him at all, oh no. But Andrea didn't like anybody much.

SANDY LIEBERSON: The film sold everywhere, just about every territory in the world. They loved it in the States. And we didn't even have to re-voice it. And it went to the Cannes Film Festival. For all that he loved his television work, Alan loved cinema too, and I think he felt frustrated that he wasn't able to make more cinema films.

TIM ROTH: I was in Rome on a shoot for four or five months, and one of the videotapes we had kicking around was *Rita Sue and Bob Too*. Stuck it in the machine, got a whole bunch of people over, some Americans who'd never see this shit before – and we pissed ourselves laughing. I don't think it went down very well here, did it? Well I mean, we were crying with laughter. It's a brilliant fucking piece about kids and about sex. And it has wonderful parts for women, I mean really great parts. And that's his humour, right there, it's a sort of everyman humour and you love him for it. Now that had been a play? At the Royal Court? I had no idea that was the case. Extraordinary piece of writing.

SIOBHAN FINNERAN: Andrea Dunbar died within twelve months of Alan. She had a massive brain haemorrhage, she was something like twenty-five and she left three little kids, none of them older than six or seven. God knows where those little beggars are now. Mind you, the one good thing that came out of it is apparently Bradford Council had to do something about the estate.

24

'Who's spoiling life?': *Road* (1987)

DAVID M. THOMPSON: I remember when the BBC decided to film Jim Cartwright's play *Road*, I thought we wouldn't go to Alan because I didn't think he'd do it. But we did, and he loved the material, saw something in it and knew he could make it his own.

JOHN WARD: Alan wouldn't let me see the play, he insisted I know nothing about that. He dropped the part of the narrator, much to the anguish of Ian Dury, who'd taken over the role and wanted to work with Alan so much. We first discussed *Road* in Bradford, on *Rita Sue*. He told me, 'They're talking about doing it in the studio because it's from a stage play, but I don't want it to look like a television version of a stage play.'

CORIN CAMPBELL HILL: It was late autumn 1986 and we were due to go into the studio December or January. The designer, Jim Clay, had done a fantastic studio set – I think he'd laid tarmac – and it was all there ready to shoot. Then came a BBC electricians' strike. And Alan would go out and jokingly beg them to stay out, because he was so desperate not to go in and shoot.

DAVID M. THOMPSON: The rumour has it that Alan engineered the strike so we wouldn't have to shoot the film in the studio. As soon as it was up, he realized it wasn't to his taste, it would never work. And of course it wouldn't. So we abandoned the sets, destroyed them, and regrouped to do it on location.

CORIN CAMPBELL HILL: We thought seriously about shooting it in a quarry. We considered a very harsh estate in Oldham. And eventually we settled for Easington Colliery, which became such a key character in the film. Some houses were still occupied, there were

The dispossessed of *Road* (1987): Mossie Smith (Carol), Neil Dudgeon (Brink), Jane Horrocks (Louise), Wiliam Armstrong (Eddie)

still some people at work, but very few. It was a sad, declining place. Very harsh sea breezes. The silence and the starkness of the place and the relentlessness of the piece were just a very strong match.

JOHN WARD: We went to Easington to recce, and it felt really good to go back up north with Alan. We had a 16 mm camera with wide-angle lenses like you've never seen – a 1.9 mm, a 3.5 mm, a 5.7 mm plus the usual prime set. And we did some tests, shots of Alan looming into the camera. It added to the sense of the place, because you could go into close-up and still see the whole room behind. The 1.9 and the 3.5 were a little extreme, we looked at each other and went, 'Hmm – maybe not!' The majority were 8 mm and 9.5 mm. I think we put the 12 mm on a couple of times and Alan's comment was, 'I'm a bit worried about going telephoto here.'

The lighting became harder. I knew I'd need a Wendy light at least to light those streets for night – 192 bulbs and two generators, the budget would have gone through the roof. So Alan said, 'Well, let's shoot it in daytime. It could be a summer's evening – daylight goes on for ever up north.'

MOSSIE SMITH: We started rehearsing and Alan was trying to harden it up – it had to be taken down, less big and stagey, which was a bit hard for us, knowing it so well. But he wanted energy and edge.

JOHN WARD: It was the first time I'd ever sat in on rehearsals, I watched them all for three weeks in Acton. And I starting walking round with the actors like another character. So I knew that script inside out, every line of dialogue the day we started shooting.

WILLIAM ARMSTRONG: By the time we got to Easington the company was me, Mossie, Dudge, Lesley Sharp and Sue Brown from the first Royal Court cast, Jane Horrocks and Alan David from the second. What was weird was that Easington was this church estate, and there were these rows of back-to-backs, and what was gonna happen was that every other row was going to be demolished. The ones that were left were going to be remodelled with nice big gardens and stuff. So in every other row we could do what the fuck we wanted.

STUART WALKER: I stripped all the walls back to their original plaster, there was a quality and a texture from the plaster and broken surfaces which gave it life. Then we used colour washes. Very often we found things which really needed to be left as they were – staircases without banisters, very incongruous-looking fireplaces. And because of the vibrant colours and the objects, everything sang, there were relationships going on all over the place. Alan desaturated the film in the end, took some colour out, so it was less vibrant than it might have been. But it was a very satisfying piece for a designer, which television often isn't.

JOHN WARD: I lit and operated on *Road*. Then the BBC would not allow freelancers to be drama cameramen, their insurance policy didn't allow us to work on the premises; but we could do stuff on location. So we had a meeting with the film operations manager at Ealing and John Goodyear, who was credited as cameraman – and who did light a lot of it, to be fair. Alan sat to one side, and finally the manager said, 'OK, Alan, John Goodyear's your cameraman and John Ward's your Steadicam operator and as long as that's understood you'll be fine.' And Alan said, 'No problem, that's fine with me – just make sure John Goodyear's got a lot of books, and make one of them *War and Peace*.' And he got up and left. And I thought, 'Oh shit, we're not going to get on here.'

CORIN CAMPBELL HILL: On *Road*, as on *Contact* previously, Alan would come back to the hotel and say with great largesse, 'I'll buy everyone a drink.' And he would pay, but the signal was for me to get them in. Because always he would then go upstairs to his room, he had the video rushes delivered and a steak dinner on its way up, and he would sit and eat and watch rushes and work, night after night. It's a harsh existence to go out and shoot a tough film from early until late, then to go back to an anonymous hotel room, take your rushes and your supper, and shut the door. And he loved it, and that was what he wanted. Except for a notable night in the first week.

JOHN WARD: He didn't drink much in these years, Alan. But we went out for a bash at an Italian restaurant, and he had a few – he got drunk very easily, three beers and he was anybody's. And that night there came a point where he knew he'd had enough. He always timed his exits and entrances to perfection, he knew instinctively how to do it well. There was a hen party at the next table, and late in the evening these girls suddenly started a conga line. And the last we saw of Alan that evening was as the last member of this conga line wending its way out of the restaurant and off down the road. ''Night, fellas!' and off he went.

MOSSIE SMITH: I've got a feeling it wasn't until we got up to Easington that we saw John Ward wearing the Steadicam. I remember Al saying, 'What we do is, the man wears this camera and we all hide behind him, like a snake.' There'd be John Ward, the sound recordist and Al, all snaking along.

JOHN WARD: A lot of people think Steadicam is dead easy, but you still have to rehearse and choreograph the moves just as if you had a track and a dolly there. It's as important for the actors to know where the camera's going to be as it is for you to know where the actors are gonna be.

NORMA MCMINN: That was a good one, *Road*. Of course, Alan had *Be-Bop-A-Lula* in it, he always loved Gene Vincent.

JOHN WARD: That *Be-Bop-A-Lula* – why Alan used music so well I'll never know, because he was musically illiterate, tone deaf. It's lovely when Mossie and Jane are clacking along reciting all the names of pubs – 'Ikkey's, Swan, Ancient Shepherd, New Zealand Chief . . .'

WILLIAM ARMSTRONG: Alan wanted that sense of the characters

just pacing down the road. He kept pushing the pace, keeping up with the Steadicam, and Neil and I would stride out. And poor Mossie and Jane were fighting to keep up, just belting along in their stilettos. You can hear it on the soundtrack like an 'ack-ack' that gives a kind of real manic urgency to it.

LESLEY SHARP: On stage I'd played Louise and Clare as well as Valerie. There were loads of characters divided up between seven of us, we all played three or four each. But Alan had his own very firm ideas about what he wanted to do with it and he gave each of us one part. I was caught up at the National Theatre for a year and scheduling was tough, so they'd only allow me two or three days away. And I begged, 'Please, please, please, I really really want to be in the film, will you let me do Valerie?' Because I loved that character Valerie, and I loved that speech.

MOSSIE SMITH: When Lesley Sharp was doing her scene, we made the usual noises about 'We're filming' and so on, but people didn't seem to think anything of this girl wandering around the streets talking to herself. One woman said, 'Oh, we're used to it, everybody was like that during the strike.'

NORMA MCMINN: The bit when the girl's walking down the street saying, 'He spends all the money, he's horrible, big and ugly' – Alan told me a bit of it reminded him of me, in me hard-up days when I was having bad times with my husband John.

JOHN WARD: Lesley's scene was a *tour de force*, and probably the hardest shot I'd done in my life at that stage. It was bitterly cold, I was bundled up like a yeti. It was a quarter of a mile walk, two hundred yards on each side of those houses. We had a couple of rehearsals, then we rolled, and Alan wanted to try it a couple of sizes in case he had to cut into it. We did one from the opposite side of the road with her in long shot as this tiny figure. But the first runs, the first six or seven takes, were the set from which we got the one we wanted. They all worked, it was just a question of performance from Alan's point of view. We did it sixteen times in total –

Lesley Sharp 'relaxes' after sixteen takes and four miles of pounding the streets for her *tour de force* scene as Valerie in *Road* (1987)

about four and a half miles. There's a photo of us sitting on the pavement at the end of the street after we finished, looking knackered. And a very concerned Corin is bending over us saying, 'Are you sure you're OK?'

DAVID M. THOMPSON: Alan would sometimes shoot a maddening number of takes, twenty or thirty, but he didn't spend much money on other things like costume or make-up or design. It was all spent on footage. Every time a train went by, he'd joke about it, he'd say, 'Is that more stock for me?' Still, the film was cheap; he may sound terribly wasteful but he wasn't, he was meticulous. You felt you were in very safe hands because he'd thought through the whole concept of the thing. He might have done a lot of takes, but that was to find the real moment of truth, what he was looking for.

JOHN WARD: That was very important to the last scene in *Road* – we must have burned more stock in one day with one camera than the BBC have ever done on a drama. Twenty-five ten-minute rolls, four hours of film – I think we did more rolls than we did slate numbers.

WILLIAM ARMSTRONG: For the last scene Al did one of the bravest things I've ever seen a director do. We had five days to film it. How it was set up, Stuart Walker had knocked through the walls of three houses to make one big space. The room was painted completely black and it had a mantelpiece made out of this chrome Cadillac bumper. And there were banks and banks of car headlamps on the ceiling. We went in there and did an afternoon, filmed a bit – and he kept tutting and shaking his head and saying that it looked a bit like the Soho Poly, because it was all black. And actually it could have been fucking anywhere. So Alan elbowed the whole thing.

STUART WALKER: After shooting all that day we went down to the beach and racked our brains over what to do. And Alan decided we'd go back to a wrecked house we'd already seen, and he gave me half a day to prepare it. It was so instinctive – that was the way he worked – to respond to your feelings and say, 'It doesn't feel right.'

WILLIAM ARMSTRONG: Now I think that's fucking brave. Alan taught me the virtue of DFI; he kept saying 'DFI' and I asked him what he meant. And one of the cameramen piped up and said, 'Different fucking idea,' at exactly the same time that Alan said, 'The director's a fucking idiot.' But he had such balls to do that. The house we went to next was just this tiny, abandoned terraced place. And they spent the rest of the day dressing it, didn't do much to it really, just painted the walls – one is blood-red and another is orange. And we ended up having two days to film what we'd planned to do in five.

JOHN WARD: We did the final scene in two halves, two days, around the Otis Redding song 'Try a Little Tenderness'. The first half is ten minutes long, we went at it from the first line to the point where we knew we'd run out of film in the mag. And I'd build up the coverage on each run, from character to character, then two-shots and so on.

MOSSIE SMITH: We'd done it about thirty-six times and Al was saying, 'Yep, that's right.' But I suddenly had a bit of a flash and I felt, 'God, I've been doing this bloody scene wrong ever since I was at the Court.' And I asked Al if we could go again; by this time we were shattered and it meant all of the actors having to go again. But he said OK. It was the moment where Carol's on the point of dragging Louise out and she says, 'I want somethin' else to happen for a change.' I'd always done it rather softly, a bit wistful. But I realized no, she'd be outraged – 'Nowt's never the way you wanted. You always have to make do. *Every single thing's a disappointment.*' So we did it again and that was the take Al used – it had an edge.

DAVID M. THOMPSON: I think the last scene is one of the most extraordinary pieces of television I've ever seen. Alan was an angry person, not overtly political but there was a broadly political agenda about giving people a voice who wouldn't otherwise have it, and I think that's most effectively expressed in *Road*, in that big speech of Jane Horrocks's – about finding your own voice and becoming a person.

WILLIAM ARMSTRONG: There's this thing at the end of Jane's speech – 'I never spoke such a speech in my life. And I'm glad I have. If I keep on shouting, somehow, somehow – I might escape.' It's just that feeling, it's not terribly articulate but I know exactly what that feeling is. You can't change anything, but you can shout – and I've always thought that's a really up ending. It may sound negative, but it seems to me that all of Alan's films shout, and *Road* shouted in a big way. And I guess what I'm saying is that I became an actor to shout. What a loud-mouthed bastard. But, y'know, fuck Chekhov.

JOHN WARD: The whole film is Steadicam, aside from the final overhead shot – we cut a hole in the ceiling and I think it's handheld, the camera wedged in place.

PAM BRIGHTON: I thought *Road* was the best one Alan ever did – superbly made, as perfect a piece as you could get. The intensity with which he caught the atmosphere and the sense of those lives was absolutely remarkable. I remember sitting there stunned for an hour afterwards. If anybody needed a stronger indictment of how the working class in the north of England have had to live, they couldn't do better than that film.

25

'Should we really be doing this?': *Elephant* (1988)

DANNY BOYLE: I had been directing theatre at the Royal Court, and I wanted to get into making films somehow, but I couldn't see a way in. Then I saw an advert for a producer's job at BBC Northern Ireland, and I was interested. I had some friends there, and I knew that I could probably direct as well as produce if I got in. Well, I got the job, and one of the first things I did was write to Alan Clarke – basically because as a kid I'd seen *Penda's Fen*, incredible film, which I hadn't understood but which made an extraordinary impression on me. Only later I found out Alan had directed it. But by the time I was in London I knew his subsequent work. And for me there are only two British directors worth their salt, who have a really remarkable body of work that's truly distinctive – one is Nicolas Roeg and the other is Alan.

So I wrote and asked Alan if I could come and watch him work, 'cos I was thinking, 'Fuck, I'd better find out what you do with a camera.' He wrote back and said, 'Sure, come along, I'm doing this thing called *Christine*.' And I went out to this estate and met him – and, you know, it's a wonderful thing when you find out that your heroes are not cunts, that they're good people. I was nobody, and he was so generous with his time and in letting me watch what was happening. I followed the crew around and they were buzzing, they were excited. Because he wasn't your conventional director who's doing a wide shot, two mediums and two singles, then sending everybody home. They were clearly being set challenges, and getting that buzz from him. Having said that, the only bits of advice he gave me were, 'Make sure you get plenty of coverage, or you're fucked when you edit. And read the book of Truffaut's interviews with Hitchcock, that's the only book worth reading on film-making.' I did, though, and it was wonderful. So I went to Belfast, and I kept in touch because I wanted him to come over and direct something. I'd seen *Contact*, an incredible film. And I'd commissioned a very interesting four-part script from Bill Morrison about cocaine smuggling from the Republic to England via Larne and Stranraer. So I got Alan across to do that.

The thing was, I'd become obsessed with certain information I'd been gathering about killings in Northern Ireland. One of the things that struck me while I was there, this was the mid to late 1980s, was that there was this level of killing going on that nobody knew of in England, because they were bored or not interested, or the information wasn't getting through. And I was experiencing both sides because I worked in Belfast in the week and then flew home to my kids at the weekend. And I realized that all people in England tended to pay attention to was a particularly savage or brutal sort of killing, usually involving a figure from the 'mainland' as it's called, and a British soldier often as not. They weren't even interested in RUC men being killed, never mind local people. And I got hold of extraordinary statistics from the RUC which said that a hundred and twenty people were being killed each year, regularly. And yet the reports in London gave you the impression that it was fifteen or twenty killings, and those being mainly soldiers and people with families in Sheffield who could be contacted for comment by the newspapers. The vast majority, the other hundred – nobody gave a fuck about, basically, not in England.

So Alan and I started talking about how to do this, and we came up with the idea of a remorseless way of presentation. We drew it up for the guy who ran the place, who'd appointed me originally. We just gave him this document saying that what we were going to shoot was a series of killings – assassinations, murders. And there'd be nothing spoken, and no attempt to moralize. And he went for it, partly because of Clarkey's reputation. Also, I think it was attractive to the BBC because here they didn't have the usual considerations of 'Are the terrorists going to speak? Are they going to have the oxygen of publicity?' – as Thatcher called it. Of course, nobody was going to speak in this, you weren't to know who was who. It was abstract, in a way. The title comes from Bernard MacLaverty, who'd written in one of his stories that for the people of Northern Ireland the Troubles were an elephant in our living room. Nobody mentions it, because it's just so enormous, it's everywhere and with you the whole time, you can't ignore it. And yet after twenty years you become used to it, if not reconciled to it. I'd read that and mentioned it to Alan. Anyway, we sort of devised the piece together but there's no writing credit on it, it wasn't 'written' in that sense. And then Alan starting devising how to shoot it with John Ward.

JOHN WARD: I read a piece of paper with the ideas on it, and I thought, 'Wow – this is going to be the most amazing piece if it works, but I don't see how it can.' But there was a sense in which Alan wanted another banned movie. When we did *The Firm* a few months later, *Elephant* hadn't been shown, *Scum* was still banned, and *The Firm* had an awful lot of power in it that could have put it on the Banned shelf as well. And Alan would talk about his trilogy of banned movies, he did think in those terms. When David Hare told him about someone else who was supposedly banned from the BBC Club, he said, 'Temporary, David, just temporary. Mine's for life.' He had more pride in that than virtually anything else he'd done in his life.

But I was knocked out. I said, 'I see what we want to do, but how do we do it? If we shoot it all in one, how do we hide the pulls to jerk back the guy who gets hit with the shotgun?' In the end we had to have false walls with a hole which I had to avoid picking up. It had to be all on Steadicam because he wanted me to operate it all the time – and it is; even the statics on the bodies are Steadicam.

We sat down and we planned each killing; we got to look at three or four pieces of footage from the RUC's Black Museum in Belfast. Ken Bond was the armourer from the BBC, typically ex-Army, frighteningly simple when it came to these things. So we'd ask him, 'You hit a guy with a shotgun, what happens?' He'd go, 'Well, half the body disintegrates, depending on the distance you hit them from, but always thumping great wounds.' So we had to work on the basis that certain things had to be toned down a bit.

DANNY BOYLE: We heard the most terrible stories, none of which we decided to cover. One we were told was how the RUC were called out to a house where a man had been shot dead, and what they found in the room was his body and his four-year-old child running round screaming. You can't do that, you know, it's just too much, it's disrespectful. But I think that was what he was trying to capture, the essence of that, without basing it too closely on specific events.

JOHN WARD: But Alan wanted it as near accurate as possible; we got photographs and a film of a real shooting which a documentary crew had picked up on the streets of Belfast by sheer chance, not that close, a hundred yards or so. The police confiscated the film as evidence and figured who was the gunman – the guy was in prison. You didn't realize it had happened until the guy fell, it was like he tripped and just crumpled to the floor. It's as simple and as frighteningly casual as that, and that's what we wanted to capture in *Elephant* – like the guy who walks through the car park and gets into his car, then another guy, ordinary guy, gets out of his car and shoots him. That was the feel of it.

DANNY BOYLE: During the course of pre-production both Alan and I happened to be in London on the weekend when the Remembrance Day service at Enniskillen was bombed. And he rang me and he was frightened by that, he said, 'Should we really be doing this?' Certainly, we both felt then that the piece shouldn't be shown in Northern Ireland. And it wasn't intended to be, we thought it would only go out in England, Scotland and Wales. Of course, it was shown in Northern Ireland, and clearly it upset a lot of people, because in a sense they just don't need that kind of approach, they're familiar with it on a daily basis. But it looked like the right way for us to show it to the mainland.

JOHN WARD: We shot it in Belfast – that was a decision that was strange. Three shootings happened while we were there. But I had been to Northern Ireland three or four times, I'd been in the middle of riots and knew full well that I was in no danger whatsoever, because the IRA never touched the media in those days; they knew they'd get a bad press. What worried me was the reaction from people on the streets, because we had a minimal crew and these things looked too real for comfort. Someone wanted to do a piece on the making of the film, but Alan would not let me be interviewed; he said, 'I don't want anybody on the crew identified – just in case.' Nothing would have happened, but he felt that was one risk too far.

Alan and I got very close on that because we stayed in the Europa Hotel together, the rest of the crew were all local and we didn't see them in the evenings much. We had the occasional pint of Guinness in the Crown bar across the road.

It was bitterly cold, and quite hard work physically, and I was keeping an eye on the angles and not getting reflections from shop-windows. Normally you're on top of that, but less so when you're trying to rehearse by running down alleyways with gunmen. And not getting too close to the gun going off – we were given our safe limits, but with Steadicam you're rushing up to something and you don't always stop on a sixpence. I had to wear earplugs too, because these guns made a fair crack, and the last thing you want to do with a Steadicam is jump. But I didn't hear so well with them on.

I saw it more as a series of films than as a single film. The one that got to me was the one in the park on a very cold morning. Those others had a certain build-up but this was so casual. It still catches me out, and I shot the thing – 'Where does he come from, that gunman?' It was the whole business of one guy walking down a path, then two guys come in the opposite direction. The first guy walks past, you forget him, he's gone – then suddenly he walks back into the frame and shoots one of the other guys dead. I still jump sometimes when that comes on.

Another one that upset me was the one where it's two gunmen on one guy – one of them brings him down with a sawn-off shotgun, which is known as 'sandbagging,' apparently, and then the other walks up to him with a pistol and finishes him off. The sheer callous nature of that quite upset me. But apparently it's true, it was a standard method.

The end shot is incredible, that really does take your breath away – the long walk of a man being escorted to his own execution. But it wasn't so hard to do. It was just a long way to walk, the building's about a quarter of a mile long – it's the old Carreras cigarette factory. It was hard to get the locations, not because they didn't want you to hire for filming but because you were recreating shootings on these premises – that made the proprietors uneasy, they feared repercussions.

DANNY BOYLE: Alan's not the kind of man you're in awe of, but certainly I was in awe of him as a director, and I just watched him work and helped him wherever I could. For example, I'd tell him about certain locations I'd come across – I found the cigarette factory for him, through working on something else.

JOHN WARD: The whole point of it is that the killings never solve anything – this killing doesn't solve it, it just leads to that killing, and that, and so on. It's the inevitability of the cycle of violence that *Elephant* shows. So the moral of the story is 'There must be talks.' People who say, 'You shouldn't talk to gunmen' – well, who else are you going to talk to?

I still think *Elephant* is the best thing that's ever been done on Northern Ireland. I think as a piece of television drama it's brilliant, and it stuns me that we were bold enough to do it at the time. In essence it's a silent movie, and people watch and think, 'Surely somebody's going to say something?' Nope. There's a vague conversation going on in the football game, but it's just noise, it's peripheral.

DANNY BOYLE: The remorselessness was the thing about it, the way Alan directed, he made it mesmeric and frightening. There was nothing particularly spectacular or overly dramatic, but what was brilliant about the way he shot it was that he did create drama without trying to impress the viewer.

JOHN WARD: We flew back from Belfast and my wife met us at the airport. We ran Alan back to the Grampians in Shepherd's Bush, one of only two times I went to his flat, which he was always ashamed of – barely furnished, let alone liveable in.

CORIN CAMPBELL HILL: While I was in the office setting up *The*

Firm, Alan repeatedly made these endless phone-calls to Belfast about the ordering of the killings. He'd been over there cutting it but he hadn't finished it, it hadn't settled in his brain, he was so often re-ordering.

MARK SHIVAS: When I went back to the BBC as Head of Drama in 1988 I was confronted first by *Elephant* and then *The Firm*, extraordinary pieces of work, and things I had to look at and OK. I had to confirm I was behind them, and decide how and what time they should be transmitted, and what kind of warning they should carry.

DANNY BOYLE: I went on the BBC *Open Air* programme after the broadcast, and a man called up to say that he'd been paralysed in a shooting and the film had brought it all back to him, and how could we do this? It's true, you can't – you can't defend it really. You can just make *Ballykissangel* instead and never get into trouble. But if you want people like Alan to make films, then you've got to touch on stuff that's very sensitive to people. But I think the film is handled with dignity, it isn't sensationalized. It wasn't trying to be some sort of moody thriller made out of people's tragedies. It was trying to speak to an ignorant mainland, really.

DAVID LELAND: In many ways I think *Elephant* was the best film Alan ever made – the essence of what he did. It doesn't conform in any sense to what we think of as conventional drama. But that forty minutes is such an intense ride. You sit and write a screenplay and you know you're aiming for ninety minutes to two hours. Why? It's only IMAX that does it differently. I wish *Elephant* could be screened as IMAX – that would upset the applecart, wouldn't it? 'An all-round experience of paramilitaries at work.' I remember lying in bed watching it, thinking, 'Stop, Alan, you can't keep doing this.' And the cumulative effect is that you say, 'It's got to stop. The killing has got to stop.' Instinctively, without an intellectual process, it becomes a gut reaction. And if it didn't have its feet in the mud, then it wasn't right for Alan.

DANNY BOYLE: When we started working together Alan always read the *Sun* every day, no other newspaper, whereas I was your typical liberal-left *Guardian* reader, and I asked him why. And he said, 'Well, there's no point in reading the *Guardian* 'cos you know exactly what they're gonna fuckin' say. I read the *Sun* because sometimes you can't quite predict which way it's gonna go. You still get all your information out of it.' That was interesting about him, he wasn't a fixed man; he was non-conformist in every respect. He would look at everything freshly and without prejudice, which I loved in him.

PAM BRIGHTON: I always hated *Elephant*, I thought it was absolute bollocks. It was Alan at his worst, with lots of feeling and passion but just no analysis, which meant that he could do something like that – which just embarrasses me, the thought of it. You know, sometimes I think that his instinct was so good and so strong that it didn't matter, he just went in where angels fear. But living in Northern Ireland as I do, I felt that his thinking about here was absolutely wrong. We'd argue, and he saw it in that very common way as a hopeless sectarian problem with too many guns. I'd say you need to have an analysis of here which includes the British state, and the nature of that power and the reaction against it. I didn't see *Contact* – again, I suspect I wouldn't really like it. Well, I just don't care for dramas about British soldiers. They shouldn't be here and that's all there is to it really, you know what I mean?

26

In a mean little country: *The Firm* (1988)

DAVID HARE: It's with the arrival of Steadicam – which he falls madly in love with, doesn't he, in the 1980s? – that Alan believes in a style which I describe as being a sort of democratic camera; it was a decision that the only way of shooting the lives of the people, so to speak, is to be in among the people – not judging them by keeping your distance or using montage. It's a profoundly political way of using the camera, but different from Ken Loach who is, you might say, the other working-class poet of the period. With Ken there's a documentary feel to his work – the identification isn't complete. And Ken is always an artist, holding off, observing. But Alan wants to get right in there. *The Firm* is plainly the climax of the style, and I think the masterpiece – one of the few authentic television masterpieces. And it's where he refines the style to an incredible degree, partly through finding this great actor who also understands the style, and who appears to be just behaving off the top of his head in the most terrifying manner.

GARY OLDMAN: Alan was the guy who had the real balls. He used to say to people at the BBC, 'Do you come with no balls or did you have to have them removed to get the job?' And he was always fuelled by what was really going on – they're very political films, Alan's. He was a great football fanatic. And partly *The Firm* was a response to that moment when Thatcher wanted to make it harder for the so-called hooligan to get into football matches – there was talk at one time of making football hideously expensive, season-ticket holders only. And she'd really got hold of the wrong end of the stick, because she imagined that it was fifteen- and sixteen-year-old kids on the dole who had nothing better to do and thumped one another at the weekend. Whereas, of course, it was thirty-plus

The Firm (1988): Nick Dunning (Simon) and Gary Oldman (Bex) take a breather

so-called respectable people who were holding down good jobs, with homes and cars and gold American Express cards.

PHIL DAVIS: Those firms, they were the face of all that – popular Toryism. They were the result of Thatcher's Britain. I mean, it's always gone on, people have always been beaten up on street corners. But these guys all had jobs and were 'upwardly mobile' – they weren't kicking against the system or the bosses, they were kicking against each other and just generally indulging themselves. You look at *The Firm* and it really sums up the 1980s.

DAVID HARE: If you say what are the great implicitly anti-Thatcherite films of the 1980s –well, that's the best of them, I think. The great joke, the best thing in *The Firm* I think, is that at most you just about see the edge of one football throughout. That's the ultimate indictment of these people – they're not even interested in the bloody football.

JOHN WARD: No, you never once see a football in the entire thing.

Someone asked Alan why and he said, 'It's not about football, nothing to do with it. It's about tribes.' As a football fan I felt the same, we were concerned with tribal conflicts between gangs. As Steve MacFadden's character says, 'If they stop the rucks at football, we'll go to boxing, we'll go snooker, darts.'

By the time *The Firm* came along Alan and I had become an item; as far as the BBC were concerned they could not separate us. And I know Alan said to the BBC, 'If John doesn't do it, I don't, and that's the end of the matter.' So, of course, I was really very chuffed at that point. I saw *The Firm* much like *Elephant* in many respects, that sort of non-judgemental piece. Let them do as they do, and it's up to the audience to decide whether these guys are evil monsters, or whether this is just how they live and how they justify themselves, rightly or wrongly.

DAVID M. THOMPSON: I never thought we'd get Gary to play Bexy, but it was due to the power of Alan that we did.

GARY OLDMAN: Alan, judging on his past record, he was a great one for discovering people. So, in a sense, I was already a bit of a name and he fought a bit shy of getting me in. But we bullied him. I got a meeting with him and I think we got on famously, we liked one another almost immediately. We didn't read the script, but we talked around it, about those chaps – who I believe he never met. I was never a member of a crew but I was born within the sound of Millwall supporters; you could see the top of the old stadium from my back yard. And I'd followed football quite fanatically when I was younger, so I'd been in the company of those guys.

JOHN WARD: The writer, Al Hunter, wanted Alan to meet the guys he'd used for his research. Alan said, 'No, I'm a football fan, they're the guys who are ruining the game, I don't wanna see them.' So, in that sense, he judged them – he hated them, he thought they were scum of the earth basically.

PHIL DAVIS: I know Al Hunter quite well; he's a good guy and a good writer and a great admirer of Clarkey's films, but he doesn't

The Firm (1988): Phil Davis (Yeti) and Clarke pose beside the Prince of Wales pub, location for the shooting of the climactic fight scene

quite feel *The Firm* is the film he wrote. Things were changed as the drafts went on that were not always to his liking. But that was the thing about Alan, he shaped everything to his own wishes, he was utterly ruthless about getting what he wanted. And that's part of the deal of being a film-maker, sadly, and it's sometimes very difficult for writers when you don't see eye to eye.

CORIN CAMPBELL HILL: We shot it in Thamesmead in the spring of 1988.

PHIL DAVIS: The opening shot of Bexy at work – you think he might go straight in with Oldman's face, but it's all three-quarter profile, from behind the ear, as he's pacing down the street. And of course it's wonderful, it says so much, the way he's trying to sell the house by telling the punters it's a load of crap – you see the hideous confidence of the guy.

JOHN WARD: That shot, it's like Tim Roth says, 'This is your man.' Alan can take you through a person's landscape by using the

Steadicam, he can place people very firmly in their environment. Bexy's an estate agent, the scene has him showing the punters this house, and Alan said to Gary, 'You're taking the piss out of these people, send 'em up.' Gary went off, we walked the scene. He says, 'If this house don't sell itself I'm a monkey's uncle.' He shuts the door on them – and does a monkey-walk back down the garden path, making chimpanzee noises. Alan watched and went, 'Bloody hell.' Gary's the fastest-thinking actor you'll ever work with. He's such a performer, and he made things happen on that film.

GARY OLDMAN: The atmosphere was so actor-friendly that you felt you could go for stuff and make a fool of yourself if necessary. So the bits and pieces that I would ad-lib or throw in off the cuff, Alan encouraged that. He'd say, 'I like that.' Those chaps, a lot of their friends are black and they kind of get into that culture and the music and the vernacular; that was something I remembered, so I'd throw a bit of patois around. And the character was, in a way, larger than life – a bit of a showman was Bexy. A bit like Barnum, he was running a big circus.

PHIL DAVIS: For a lot of film directors, the shot is the thing, but for Clarke it wasn't, it was the event. The thing that he was shooting, he would get that right and then he'd send his Steadicam whizzing in, and then sort it all out in the cutting room. It was getting the sniff of real life in there.

GARY OLDMAN: Ordinarily, film-making is so fragmented and it's so made up of many pieces, but you could get a real energy and momentum going because you knew there would be no cuts, and that you had great freedom. Alan would light the room for 360 degrees, and he hated that thing where, as he'd put it, 'Y'know, Oedipus comes home,' and the doorway is lit for Oedipus to walk in and say, ''Ello, Mum, I'm home.' And then, of course, because you're lit, you're still on that same angle when Oedipus says, 'See ya later, Mum,' and leaves. But in that time between going in and out, there's a huge scene that's supposed to have taken place. So Alan gave you the freedom to come in, go ''Ello, Mum', play the

The Firm (1988): producer David M. Thompson and Gary Oldman in a respite during the shooting of the final fight

whole scene, and it'd be a continuous take that would get you to the door and out. The other thing about 360 for Alan is that it enabled him to say that producers couldn't come in. It kept the suits out. He didn't want the set overcrowded with people looking over his shoulder, so he'd say, 'Eh, sorry, guys, it's lit for 360. No room for any more in here.'

DAVID M. THOMPSON: On *The Firm* I really felt like a total outsider. Sometimes producers do, and it's not a bad thing in a way – why interfere when it's going really well? But you just knew something was going on there that was rather electric, between the cast and Alan. It was like a gang, that whole ensemble of blokes, and it was just a little bit unnerving. The level of latent violence on set was interesting – and a bit beyond just acting. They were really in their parts.

PHIL DAVIS: We were rehearsing the hotel scene where all the firms converge – mine, Gary's, Andrew Wilde's. And it was the only scene where we were all together – all the different crews, all the lead actors. And Clarkey would just sit there in amongst it, in an old flat cap, biting his nails, watching and joining in, under his breath – 'Go on', all that, like he was part of it. He was always pretty cool, but when he wanted a bit more heat he'd start ad-libbing stuff – 'Fucking bunch of cunts.' And the guys would start 'Oh, yeah, fucking bunch . . .' He played us like an orchestra, you know. He'd make a sign and it would get more and more lairy.

JOHN WARD: The gathering of the rival firms was shot at the Tower Hotel on Tower Bridge. There was a fight, a real fight, two guys ended up almost at each other's throats. Alan had got everybody up so far, just like the murderball scene in *Scum*. Everybody was jeering and pushing, and maybe one push was a bit too hard. And one guy pinned another to the wall, I wasn't looking until Alan came hurtling past me and leapt in and separated them.

PHIL DAVIS: Y'know, it happens with actors – film-making, you spend a lot of time hanging about, waiting for them to light it or whatever. And while you're doing that, you're not rehearsing as such, but you're sort of one foot in character and one out, and so it's bound to happen. In some way you take on a bit of all that and you enjoy it, you enjoy the badinage – it's great to insult people and swear at them, wear the gear and chant your chants. You do it in some ways to warm up for the scene. In others . . .

DAVID M. THOMPSON: There's an extraordinary moment as Bexy's firm are leaving the hotel, pacing down the corridor and chanting, and one of them, Charles Lawson, punches a panel right out of the ceiling. That wasn't planned, it was a spontaneous piece of destruction on the part of the actor.

GARY OLDMAN: Funny old guy, Alan, because he abhorred violence, was appalled by it. And he was very conscious of those big fight sequences – they were very specific and very detailed in the choreography – trying to make sure that no one really got hurt. But we did a bit, inevitably. The director says 'Action!' and that was a full-blooded bunch of chaps he had there, so we went for it and a couple of us took a few knocks. I think I got a cracked rib.

JOHN WARD: A whole other side of the film was Bexy's domestic life with his wife Sue and their kid. I think a lot of embellishments came from Gary and Lesley Manville there, because of course they were married at the time. And Gary was quite reticent about their onscreen fights because Lesley was pregnant at the time with Alfie, who's now nine years old, born late 1988.

LESLEY MANVILLE: The role felt quite close to my own upbringing in terms of her class and her interests – I could recognize her, I wasn't worried on that score. What was new to me was the violent side of Sue's relationship with Bex, which was something we evolved in rehearsal. I suppose the key to Sue was that in her own way, she was just as violent as the men in the film. In fact, a scene was cut from the film, which caused a huge battle with the BBC. It's when Bexy has come back home very late from his trip to Birmingham, where they've had a rumble. There were lots of cutaways to me in the house, waiting for him, anxious. And he comes in and wakes me up, and starts acting violently, so it looks like he's beating me up and raping me. My hair was being held very tightly, my head was being bashed against the wall, then we fall on the floor and he's pulling up my nightdress. Then we both start to giggle – like it's a joke, a routine we've done before. And you were very thrown by it – it was a way of showing that this woman, this wife and mother, had her violent side. It was a brutal scene, every bit as gruelling as the fights between the men.

DAVID M. THOMPSON: It was me rather than Alan Yentob who felt very strongly about that sex scene, though others were worried. It was an apparent rape of his wife and then it turned out she got off on it. She was colluding in the violence. And it seemed to me to be really interesting territory but such a dynamite subject, and so under-explored in the film that it would seem gratuitous. With hindsight, I think we'd have gone with it and risked it. But again maybe not. Maybe it should have been in the video.

GARY OLDMAN: I think that scene showed that football was not the only arena for that kind of testosterone, if you like. Alan was making a point that you can't be that character and just go out to football for two hours and just sort of turn it on and off – that it must in some way influence and bleed into your everyday life. All that machismo, there's a certain attractiveness to it, and I think that certain women find it very sexy. But, ultimately, it's a selfish existence and it affects other people around you – obviously in the scene where Bexy's kid gets hold of his Stanley knife and cuts his mouth open.

JANINE DUVITSKI: That was my son in *The Firm*, with a Stanley knife in his mouth. Typical Alan. I got a phone-call from his office and I thought, 'Finally! I'm going to work with Alan again.' And they said the child Gary and Lesley were using wasn't very happy and they'd been asked if there was a baby they knew well. And they knew Albert, my son. And I said to Alan, 'It's not going to be violent, is it?' knowing his penchant for realism and violence. He said, 'No, just involves a bit of strawberry jam.' Which was true, all he had to do was just like sucking a lollipop. They only did it once. And Albert knew Gary very well, so he went happily off and I stayed out of the way so he wasn't looking at me. And when I saw it, of course – he starts to cry, and my sister was scolding me, saying, 'How could you have let them? He was obviously upset.' But no, it was just the force of Gary's reaction in character, when he sees what he's allowed to happen.

JOHN WARD: For the final scene, the big clash between Bex and Yeti in the football boozer – at one point we were going to have Bexy's mob nicking Yeti's Golf and driving it through the doors of the pub. But Alan was against any Ramboesque antics. He said, 'No, let's just have them march in and smack 'em.'

PHIL DAVIS: What was shot was far more violent than what went into the final cut. That last fight was a massacre, really, when Bex beats Yeti up. It's hard to watch now, and I think there were producers hopping from one leg to another suggesting that there might be a little less claret on my face. Bexy's firm were tooled up with baseball bats – some of them balsa wood, some of them real. And Charlie Lawson was fighting on one leg because he'd hurt himself at a party John Ward had thrown. But it was great when they charged in. Bex hits me and my glasses fly off. And after that I just had to be covered up for most of it, just taking all these blows. But I was well padded, and Gary's quite good at all that, very skilful at all that stage fighting, so while it looked pretty tasty I got away without too many bruises. One bit that didn't make it into the final cut, he slashes my buttocks with the Stanley. That was really nasty; I was there lying on my stomach and the fight was over and he went – slash! – up from behind.

JOHN WARD: The only thing I don't like is the gun at the end – Yeti shooting Bexy dead. I don't think it works, it's just out of keeping. I don't think football hooligans pull guns on each other. Artistically, it was a good device but it was a step out of reality, I think.

DAVID M. THOMPSON: One of the most powerful scenes, and Al Hunter admits this, is the end scene, which was in fact improvised, where all the lads are in the pub being interviewed for a documentary and shouting over each other direct to the camera. It was brilliantly true to the spirit of the film, and not in the script. It was a savage sort of ending, and it gave the thing a great kick. Alan had just got inside the skin of those characters, and I think finally made rather a moral film out of potentially amoral material. It was a serious study of violence, of people doing it for the buzz. At the time some people at the BBC were very jumpy. Gary Bushell had written in the *Sun* about people being injured on the set. There was a problem with West Ham, they were vaguely identified with it in some of the photographs and the colours, and they were a little unhappy that we were suggesting their fans were especially thuggish. I think Alan thought it was going to be banned, I felt there was a gloom and doom about him on that score.

GARY OLDMAN: He had a real honest voice, Alan. Even *The Firm* he was thinking of shelving when the business of cuts came up. It was just 'Here we go again' for him – same old bullshit.

DAVID M. THOMPSON: There were some agonized meetings, and I suppose in those days I was rather more nervous about things than I am now. The BBC hierarchy and Alan Yentob were worrying about how to handle the press. We prepared a defence and wrote a press release explaining the film but, in fact, the film spoke for itself, it didn't need all that crap. I was probably too tame with it, I should have pushed harder and let it go to extremes. I think Alan got very angry about some of the cuts we were trying to make on it. We had some transatlantic phone-calls where he was quite tense. He did threaten to take his name off, and we did cut a bit but his name stayed on. There was some political horse-trading. We cut a close-up of a Stanley knife going through Andrew Wilde's eye, that was unnecessary. And we slightly mellowed the soundtrack by lowering the volume of the kicks in the pub scene. I think in the end it was the version we all accepted which aired. I'm not one hundred per cent sure that's how Alan saw it.

The Firm has been on television two or three times, and it was released on video very successfully. It's one of those films where certain people seem to know every line of the dialogue. That's a bit scary, I suppose; it has a certain hooligan cult following. But what the hell. You never know quite how a film will go down.

PHIL DAVIES: Later I directed *I.D.*, about an undercover policeman who joins a firm. And I was doing a big crowd scene at the Rotherham ground, quite nasty, difficult to shoot. We had to have two sets of supporters going at each other, so we were filming right on the axis where the barrier was. We had six hundred extras – a lot, but not enough – and we were trying to make 'em look like six thousand. They'd all been sitting there a while with their cups of tea and breakfast buns, so I went down to the front with my megaphone to get the ball rolling. And this cry went up, this sort of chant - 'Yeti! Yeti! Yeti!' I felt like a living legend that had walked into their midst. That was the power of *The Firm* – I thought 'How did these kids catch it, on BBC2 one night of the year?' But they got it. And it had a big effect on football fans.

GARY OLDMAN: We used to drink cups and cups of tea, Alan and me, we both loved a cup of tea. You know the big tea urns that you get on the catering trucks of movie sets? When we were making *The Firm*, some days were like double-urners – 'I think it's a double-urner today.' And he was a generous man, great spirit. But I only really knew him as a fellow worker, and at the end of the day that was it. He'd pull up his collar, tug on his cap and sort of disappear into the night. Until the next morning.

TIM ROTH: At one point Alan had wanted me to play Yeti. But the part that I liked was Gary's part, and the actor that I liked was Gary, and it was his turn. I'd had the pleasure of working with Alan, and so now Gary had that pleasure. And Phil Davis did a good job. It's only that – it could have been me and Gary working on a film with Alan, and that's – ah! That would have been the best thing for me. But that was the last shot.

DAVID M. THOMPSON: It was during the shooting of *The Firm* that Alan complained of backache. I remember vividly driving him to his osteopath. Of course, it wasn't backache at all.

27

Leavetaking: *An American Murder* and 'Croucho's' (1987–1990)

DAVID HARE: At the end for Alan, there was a lot of hatred of the English and a lot of yearning to go to America. Therefore he has the romance which all left-wing English artists and Celtic romantics have about America, the dream of a people who are generous, who are free, who are classless, who are not hung-up, who are emotional, who are warm – unlike, you know, Alasdair Milne.

JANE HARRIS: He certainly got very tired of England in the 1980s – well, weren't we all? – but before a lot of people, he could see what was coming. It was becoming a mean little country and he didn't like that. But while I think he had a kind of dream in his mind of going over to Hollywood, I don't think in his heart he ever really wanted to. He really was too much of his own country.

DAVID YALLOP: *Assassination on Embassy Row* was a film he wanted desperately to make. If there is a tragedy about Alan Clarke's life, it's that a man with that consummate ability and talent should have been obliged to spend so much of his life's span trying to get things off the ground – it's a common tragedy, of wasted time. And because of the nature of the work Alan was attracted to, it was always this way.

ROSILYN HELLER: I always thought about Alan and missed the fact that we had never spoken. I knew he wasn't mad at us, and that he knew we wanted to make the same movie, and that movie didn't have Robert Redford in it. Some years later, maybe 1985–1986, I was in London. I happened to be at the agency which also represented Alan. I asked after him and left my phone number. He called me right away and we met in a pub, and it was like nothing had ever happened. He asked me about the project and I said, 'The truth is it's still available and I'd still love to do it more than anything.' And Alan said, 'Yeah, it's the only project that's ever interested me in the US. And we never talked about this, but what I'd really like to do is the anatomy of an assassination. I don't want the central character to be an FBI guy, I want it to be the killer – Townley.' I said, 'Fine with me.' It was a much more interesting and less conventional idea. And he had a writer in mind, a friend of his, Tony Clarke.

I went back to the US and, as I usually did whenever I was in between producing movies and needed money, I took another executive job. I went to work for Kings Road and, as crazy as that operation was, they had a couple of interesting projects. They needed a director for one of these, and I talked them into hiring Alan. It was all very clever of us, because it got Alan over to the US on somebody else's dime to work on a new script for *Assassination on Embassy Row*, which was now going to be called *An American Murder*.

Then we brought Tony over and put him to work in my beach house. We tried to get money for Tony to develop it; Tony did a treatment of what Alan wanted and we tried to set it up but we couldn't – again, it was too political, nobody wanted to touch it. This was still prior to the independent sector opening up. So initially we went to a lot of studios, but finally we went to Hemdale, which was a company with a terrible reputation. But Alan and I knew that John Daly was crazy about Alan and had offered him everything in the world without success. We had a script by now – this was happening between fall of 1987 and March 1988.

At the end of 1988 I left Kings Road, because we actually thought this movie was going to happen. We moved into offices and started prepping the picture. The summer of 1989, July/August, Alan and I went on a recce to New York and Washington, and then to Mexico and Cuba. We were going to shoot our 'Santiago' scenes in Mexico for a week to ten days. But Fidel literally was offering to bomb Havana for us in order to replicate the 1973 coup, he wanted desperately to have us there. But I knew we could never shoot in Cuba, because we'd never get the actors there, it was outlawed. I couldn't imagine any US movie actors being allowed by their lawyers to come down there. We did go, and we had a great time, Alan was fun to travel with. But he wasn't feeling well. He had a strange couch, and a pain in his right leg which he said was sciatica.

We were back in the US at the end of August. One weekend Alan was in his hotel room and he ended up in Cedars-Sinai emergency room. He said he had coughed, and felt as if he'd broken a rib – he was in excruciating pain. They didn't see any broken rib and they sent him home. And after a couple of days I guess the pain in his chest eased a little, but he was still suffering terribly and mainly staying in his hotel room. And I said, 'Listen, y'know, I think there's something the matter. Do me a favour, please go to my doctor.' This was Labor Day weekend approaching, nobody was around, but we didn't go down to the beach because Alan couldn't move. I called my doctor before the weekend and explained about this friend of mine from England, and he said, 'What do you think is the problem?' And I remember saying out of the blue, 'I think it's respiratory,' just because of that cough – and some bizarre intuition, I had heard his voice kind of changing a little bit. So my doctor referred him to a respiratory specialist, who immediately sent him to Sinai to have his lungs checked. At which point what they saw was – unbelievable.

Alan called me because they wanted him to come back the next day, and I went and spent the weekend with him. They drew so much fluid from his right lung, it was incredible. I spoke to the doctor after this, and the doctor said, 'This man has no more than three months.' His lung was totally gone, and the suspicion was that this wasn't even the primary site. So Alan had to go back to England to be taken care of; he didn't have the money to spend on doctors here. But he insisted that I not tell anybody. Now you realize we were prepping a picture, and John Daly was very into the project and adored Alan. So we did tell John that Alan wasn't feeling well and he was going back to be checked out. And we kept up an illusion that it was emphysema, but that he was being treated and it would be fine. But we knew better.

JOHN WARD: I was going to do his American film with him when he had to fly back to England – the beginning of the end. There are wonderful, incongruous shots of Alan standing being interviewed on La Cienega before that. He must have seen the funny side, standing there knowing he wasn't the Hollywood director and would never be, really. I called John Daly's office in September and was told Alan had gone back to England. My suspicions were roused, and I spoke to Molly. Alan was then in the Brompton hospital having tests, chest X-rays and so on, and Molly was staying in his flat. She said they still weren't sure what they'd found.

ROSILYN HELLER: In England he found out that the original cancer had been on his spine, which is what had really affected his leg all that time and put him in so much pain. But the main thing was, we never discussed it as if he was dying. And he just took to his room in Shepherd's Bush and didn't tell anybody. His daughter Molly knew because she was staying with him. However, we continued to talk as if he was going to get better, we still discussed revisions in the script and so on. But I knew he could never direct this movie. The fact that he lived as long as he did would have surprised the doctor at Cedars-Sinai.

ARTHUR ELLIS: I knew he'd come back from the States and holed up in his flat in Shepherd's Bush. And he wasn't answering the phone, and he wasn't putting in appearances at the Ritz. You knew something was up.

JOHN WARD: I got back to England just before Christmas and saw him and he looked dreadful. But I saw him again one or two times in January and he seemed to be getting better. In January I went off to Berlin for four months, and not long after I left, Molly phoned and said, 'Dad wanted me to tell you, it is cancer.' I said he must have known that when he was in hospital; she said he wouldn't tell me face to face.

STEPHEN FREARS: I was in America and I heard a rumour that Alan was ill. And then I got back and called Patsy Pollock, and she said Alan was in the Cromwell Hospital. I might have been one of the first people allowed in to see him.

SANDY LIEBERSON: I found out that he was ill, that he was at the Cromwell Road Hospital and that he didn't want any visitors. And I just turned up there. I could see how distressed he was. He couldn't walk really at that point. So I put him in the wheelchair and we went outside, and he was so relieved. But as we went along, the pavement was uneven and bumped the chair, and he was in terrible pain. We had to go back in. But still he wouldn't admit how bad it was – he was going to beat it, his spirit was fantastic.

ROSILYN HELLER: He was getting radiation treatment there and it had diminished the cancer in his back. And so he had some news that he could get better, or at least he talked as if he would get better. But I couldn't believe that was possible, I knew his lungs were gone. But he was in better shape, he did improve; obviously the radiation kept him alive longer than the doctor had predicted. But at a certain point he became immobile and couldn't stay in the apartment, and that's when he went into the nursing facility in March.

CORIN CAMPBELL HILL: He was transferred to a clinic on Hornsey Lane up towards Crouch End.

STEPHEN FREARS: Alan invented this club called Croucho's, because it was in Crouch End. People came out of the woodwork to tell him they loved him.

SANDY LIEBERSON: There was nothing formal in the way it started, just that a few people were going back regularly, and more came and other people heard about it. Before you knew it, it was the place to go to. I think Alan loved that, really. Every evening, it seemed, we'd meet there, smoke a joint, somebody would bring wine. And it became something that I think all of us looked forward to doing.

DAVID YALLOP: It was an extraordinary production. He directed and stage-managed it brilliantly, because to confront the death of somebody you love is no easy thing, and a great many of us were facing it here. People would be out there chatting, and my wife said to me,

'It's very seductive, isn't it?' Because he had created this ambience. So many people wanted to see him that he created a rota.

MOSSIE SMITH: Jane Horrocks and I went to see Al when he was dying. We walked in and he said, 'Right, Mossie, pour two glasses of wine for yourselves, and get yourself on the veranda and have a cigarette.' Which I did. And looking down on the veranda there were hundreds of dog-ends down below. And then he told us. He said, 'The doctors have looked at the rushes and they don't like them.' His legs weren't working, and his arms weren't great but he was still so sharp. He said, 'You wanna get yourselves down here, girls. It's the best casting couch in the world, I've got everybody coming in.'

The Cannes Film Festival, May 1987: Alan 'Scruff' Clarke tries on Stephen Frears' dinner jacket for size, with Patsy Pollock on his arm

SANDY LIEBERSON: Half the time Alan would be asleep, because he was so drugged by then, but he'd come in and out of consciousness. But I think the fact that people were there gave him so much pleasure and joy, to see faces and hear talking, made it seem in some way normal and less frightening. I haven't experienced anything like that.

DAVID HARE: It's an extraordinary story, this late flowering of his social side. Patsy Pollock got closer to him in the last years than anybody and loved Alan, and he loved her. Patsy was 'den mother', as it were, to all of us who were trailing through this room, which he loved. And I think he found a side of himself he didn't know existed – he thought of himself as asocial and a loner and all that, and on the contrary he loved this long party at the end of his life.

JEHANE MARKHAM: He was in Room 101 in the clinic, the significance of which wasn't lost on him one jot. I feel quite strongly that if someone is dying you should be there and acknowledge that and talk through it with them. But interestingly enough, Alan didn't want that; he said, 'I don't want to get involved with a dance of death.'

ROSILYN HELLER: It was like total denial. But as I say to people now when they're facing the prospect of the death of their friends – 'You have to take the lead from the person who's dying, how they want to handle it.' So with Alan, nobody talked about his dying. They talked as if he was going to get up and do this movie.

DAVID YALLOP: I had written a draft screenplay of my book *In God's Name* – far too wordy, you needed a calendar to time it, as usual. But Alan was going to direct it, I was trying to give him something to think forward about and trying to be positive. It was never going to happen. But it was a big book, and we discussed ways of doing it, as a four-parter or which stories to tell, what structure to use. His energy began slipping away, and we talked of it less and less.

ARTHUR ELLIS: In the home we'd watch TV and talk, and there was nothing that couldn't be said for the sake of a laugh. We had black jokes, anything was game. He did like male company. And a lot of the women didn't know how to handle him. If anything got too soppy, he wasn't comfortable. If people were on a down, they wouldn't go in, 'cos the last thing he wanted was people sitting around saying, 'Oh, poor Al, he's going.' He wanted to talk about football and films.

STEPHEN FREARS: The World Cup was on, the one in Italy, a very good World Cup. And all through the night there'd be these replays of the World Cup going on.

GEORGE COSTIGAN: He was fierce when it came to football. Especially when we were watching Argentina in that World Cup. I remember I marvelled at some piece of skill by Maradona. 'He's a cheat' was all the breath Alan would waste on Diego. When Cameroon stuffed Argentina in the first match I thought Alan was going to get better on the spot, he was that pleased.

STEPHEN FREARS: It was like an extended party, except that there was also a man dying there. And at the same time that the levity was going up, I imagine the terror was also going up. On the one hand, you thought, 'This is the most wonderful way to die, surrounded by all these people telling you that they love you.' But he must have been absolutely terrified. And I suppose that to go and tell a man you love him is a wonderful thing to do, but I suppose it was also selfish in some way because the thought of him dying was so awful.

DAVINA BELLING: My last memory of him in hospital I'll never forget. There he was looking completely grey – but so excited, because he'd got the transcripts of the complaining phone-calls that had come in from a screening of *Rita Sue and Bob Too* on Channel Four. And he was so amused by this, it was great. 'Look at this! Outraged from Manchester.' Patsy Pollock and several others started sleeping there on a mattress overnight, because the one thing Alan said that he found upsetting was waking up in the middle of the night or early in the morning and being alone. That's the one thing that frightened him.

ROY MINTON: It was Paul Knight who told me Alan was ill, that he was in this clinic up in Highgate. I hadn't seen Al for a long time, we'd had rucks. The rift was over *Scum*, a bit bad, and we just left each other alone. But when I came to see him, we fell back some years, you know? So I stayed in town for about two months to be with Al during his last days, spent a lot of time up there, on the rota system, all that. Clarkey had the phone by his bed and I said, 'Anytime, just give me a call.' And several times, two in the morning, he'd call and say, 'Can you get over?'

PAM BRIGHTON: I think the good thing for Al's kids was that there'd always been that difficult thing of their not spending enough time with him. And I think they both kind of idolized him, maybe felt they'd not had enough of him. And yet they had so much of him in those last months. And that was an up side, one of the very positive things about it.

DAVID YALLOP: When he was dying, Alan would often stimulate or provoke me to recount anecdotes about him, often to Molly and Gabriel and Jane. And one was actually filling in colours for them of their own father, or their own husband, of things they'd not been part of, around the bedside of a dying man. Very amusing anecdotes – nothing solemn. Laughter came very easily near Alan.

GRENVILLE MIDDLETON: He was only two weeks away from death, and we had such a laugh reminiscing. Dave Yallop was very good to him. Jane was there with her bloke; Alan would introduce him saying, 'This is Brian Harris, he's everything to Jane that I wasn't,' and it was true – he's a gentle, quiet man where Alan was totally the opposite.

NORMA MCMINN: I didn't know he was ill at all, and afterwards people told me that he hadn't wanted me to know. On 15 July he phoned me up and said, 'Can you sit down?' 'Why?' 'Just sit down, I've got something to tell ya. I've got cancer.' I said, 'What!?' He said, 'Oh, it's just me back, I'll be all right.' But I could tell by his voice, he sounded terrible. I could hear someone in the room, a nurse or something, knocking something over and I heard him going, 'Will you effin' well behave yourself?' So he was directing to the last. He was sort of saying, 'I'm gonna be all right, don't be worryin'.' But he said he'd send me some money to come up and see him in the nursing home. 'Buy yourself something to wear.' And sure enough he sent me three hundred quid. It dawned on me later – I'm almost sure he knew I didn't have much money, he knew he was dying and that I was gonna come up. But in his mind I would be coming up for the funeral. It was his way of doing it. And I could understand that's the way he'd want it to be.

STUART WALKER: Just before he died, he was slipping down in bed all the time, it was very uncomfortable for him. And he wanted something he could rest his feet on to stop him sliding. So I designed a footrest to fit at the end of the bed and went to one of the senior contractors and persuaded him to build it very fast for me, which they did. It was padded. He was very pleased with that.

GEORGE COSTIGAN: At one point in that last week I put some Mozart on, because I'd got the idea that it might be useful for soothing his vibes down. And he listened to it for about ten minutes and then he said, 'Listen, can we elbow this crap?' So I knew he didn't like classical music. Then three or four days later we were sat there watching some cricket and an advert came on for Mahler's Second Symphony, and I nudged him and said, 'Hey, Al, the Resurrection!' and he opened one eye and said, 'I'm not fuckin' dead yet.'

DAVID LELAND: It was only a day or so before he died, only then that he said, 'Y'know, I thought I was getting back, I thought I was all right but I dunno, I felt so knocked back today – I almost wondered if I was gonna beat this or not. I don't know if I can.' It was the only time he ever said anything to me about that. Everybody else knew he was dying. But such was his force. That day when I kissed him goodbye, his lips were cold. And Roy Minton was with him the last night – the mystery of the last night.

ROY MINTON: What I would say about Clarkey, a man who was so full of life – he handled his death fucking courageously, he was a courageous bastard the way he went, he really was. He died something like eight in the morning. At two or three o'clock it was getting worse, he was propped up in the bed and finding it difficult to breathe and get words out. He still knew who he was, who I was, and he knew he was on the way out. I was stroking him and mopping his brow. Typical, typical remark he made, the bastard – he said, 'Hold me hand,' and I held his hand, and he said, 'Not too fucking tight.' He went away for a bit and came back. And he said, 'This is getting really fucking serious' – he knew it in some way. I must say for someone like Clarkey who lived life so much – I'd like to think I'd have the strength and the courage to go the way he did. He was a bit good, a bit good.

JOHN WARD: Corin phoned me about ten on the morning of Wednesday the 24th and told me he had died. Between six in the evening and midnight he had just gone downhill. The doctor said he had taken so much out of his body, there was nothing left to fight with. It was pneumonia in the end that got him. It was frightening when he died, I don't remember the rest of the day after I found out. And I was going to be with him that night.

DAVID YALLOP: The funeral service was a very sad affair, at Golders Green crematorium. I asked if I might choose a hymn, and I chose 'Imagine' by John Lennon. Suddenly, in the middle of this rather alien service, officiated by a man who'd never met Alan, we stood and Lennon's voice filled the room, and I burst into tears, as I think others did. Because that song's very poignant, it means an awful lot to an awful lot of people. And I knew how important Liverpool and Lennon's music was to my friend.

RAY WINSTONE: Phil done a blinding thing at his funeral, bless him.

PHIL DANIELS: I got him an Everton shirt instead of flowers, bunged it down where all the flowers were laid out. I thought that would be sort of – appropriate. I should have put a murderball down there, shouldn't I?

PAM BRIGHTON: The wake was at David Yallop's – an endless party, every hour somebody else making a trip to the off-licence to replenish the stores. Everybody pouring drink down their necks and saying, 'This is what Alan would have wanted, to see us all drinking ourselves senseless.'

DAVID YALLOP: Then in January 1991 we had a memorial evening service at the Questors. We needed to raise quite a bit of money to hire the theatre, lay on some food and drink. People were extremely generous, friends and colleagues, actors he'd worked with once or many years ago. It said a lot. It fell to me to open the speeches, and it's difficult to bat first, one doesn't want to pre-empt anybody. What I did say was, 'They tell me Alan Clarke is dead, but I don't have to believe it.'

JEHANE MARKHAM: He should have been buried at sea – that would have been the right way for him to go, I felt. His funeral couldn't possibly measure up to him. I wrote a poem in that spirit fairly soon after he died, it came all at once. And having written it, I thought I'd like to read it at the memorial. I was nervous but I thought, 'Sod the nerves, just let's do it, for Alan.' And I think people really liked it, especially the women.

ANNA SCHER: I read this rather flirtatious poem at the memorial, Yeats's poem for Anne Gregory:

Never shall a young man,
Thrown into despair
By those great honey-coloured
Ramparts at your ear,
Love you for yourself alone
And not your yellow hair.

I don't necessarily know what was going on in my subconscious there. Maybe it's because Alan had this way of communicating with people which made anybody who came into his realm feel really very special. He had such a deeply appealing combination of flirtation and genuine affection. Women felt that, of course, but then so did all of our young actors who worked with him. So I suppose what the poem is really saying is. 'Yes, you flirt. But we like it.'

MICHAEL JACKLEY: When I was talking at the Questors they had two big blow-ups of Clarkey on the stage, and when I was speaking, one of them blacked out. And I realized it, so I said, 'Don't worry, Clarkey, I know you're still here.'

DAVID YALLOP: We all lost Alan very young, and I grieve for that loss. I miss him as if he had been a brother, he was the best friend I ever had. I don't know if his other close friends are as preoccupied with Alan as I am; I do know that when I meet with those people, we talk about him, and often at some length. It's right that we should talk about people after they've died, because while we speak of them, a part of them is still alive – like our conversation today, like this book.

Coda: The legacy of 'Clarkovsky'

DAVID RUDKIN: Alan's was a strong generation, there were fine practitioners. I still think that Alan was arguably – well, if the word 'greatest' means anything, I would say he's a very strong contender for that rather idealized status. If there was a greatest TV-film-play director of that time, I would put in a plea for Alan.

GARY OLDMAN: Alan had a very unique vision and a very clear voice and when he left, it just left a very big void, and there's no one who's come along since with that edge. It's just the balls of it.

GEORGE COSTIGAN: There are days when you think, 'Oh God, I miss him.' And you get in the middle of work and find yourself thinking, 'Hang on, what would Alan have done here? Which line would he have taken?' And the answer is, 'The hardest, the toughest – whatever the truest line was, he'd have taken it.'

DAVID M. THOMPSON: Alan Clarke was really the defining figure of authored television pieces, I would say. I can't think of another director quite in that way, who had the hold over the number of productions that he did. He always chose things that stretched him, things that hadn't been done before.

MARK SHIVAS: Absolutely, he was an *auteur*. Clarke may not have written much of his own stuff but he worked heftily on the scripts, and the choices he made show somebody who had a particular view of humanity – on the side of the underdog, to put it in one line. If Clarke isn't an *auteur* I don't know who is. But they didn't ever pick it up during his lifetime, really. Why did *Sight & Sound* never write about him? Absurd. While he was alive, I told him that had he been called Clarkovsky rather than plain old Alan Clarke, he would have an international reputation. And he was amused, but didn't seem to think that critical acclaim really mattered.

CORIN CAMPBELL HILL: After he died I felt that there had to be a celebration of his work; it had to be captured, what he'd achieved. I went to Alan Yentob and he sanctioned a documentary, which I directed, which led to a short season of his work on the BBC in 1991. And as part of that season we finally prevailed upon the BBC to broadcast *Scum*, which clearly would not have happened otherwise.

JOHN WARD: The Royal Television Society gave an award for the body of work after his death, which Molly went up to collect.

STEPHEN FREARS: We've got this BAFTA award that's named after him, and I thought, 'Of course, what that award's really for is unsung heroes.' We were always going on about Alan rather publicly, and people would look at us and wonder why this award was named after this man. Who was he? I mean, you can see why an award was named after Richard Dimbleby. No one had heard of Alan. And I remember thinking, when I was given the award, 'I'll just talk a bit about Alan.' And then I watched it on the television afterwards, and they just cut all of that. So there is an award named after him which is completely mysterious.

JANINE DUVITSKI: There's a whole thing about Alan that the actors have, whenever a few of us who worked with him get together we end up talking about him. In the documentary that was done about him, you just couldn't help wanting to see more of him, just because he was like a star, really. The only problem with Alan, he spoiled you – it's downhill all the way afterwards. I thought all directors were brilliant and sexy like that. What a disappointment.

MARK SHIVAS: I was lucky in 1993 to go to the Telluride Festival, where Tom Luddy arranged a retrospective and got myself and Corin Campbell Hill and Molly to attend with Corin's documentary. Tom had heard about Alan from Stephen Frears the previous year. Then via the British Council, those films went across America, including the Museum of Modern Art in New York. And yet still in this country it's been a small band of us who've carried the torch. Though I suppose that is poised to change as we speak.

CORIN CAMPBELL HILL: There are lots of people in this country who don't know anything about who makes television or what films are on, but you mention one or two films and they know them – they know *Made in Britain*, they know *Scum*. They're currency, they're kids' currency, and he did touch that generation.

DAVID HARE: I was in San Francisco a couple of years after his death and walking down a street I see a hoarding saying, 'Alan Clarke Festival' – and it was so unlikely it actually took my breath away. Clarkey would have been astonished. Now we think of popular culture as what everybody's looking at and concentrating on all the time, and yet in those days you could have the irony of working in a massively popular medium and yet being culturally almost entirely overlooked. And that's how Alan worked, and so there weren't books like this one, or theses, he wasn't on the list – when you go 'Ken Loach, Mike Leigh' and so on, the English shopping list of directors. It's only after his death that his reputation has grown, and yet we all knew about him and we were all saying – as with Stephen's remark, 'Clarkey became the best of all of us.' I can remember Stephen saying that way before Alan was ill, and I thought – absolutely. He's the only bloke going his own way, completely not knocked off course, and not influenced by the wrong influences – reputation, success, failure, the judgement of your peers. So it was unbelievably moving to walk down this street in San Francisco and see 'Alan Clarke Festival', 'cos you thought, 'There is some justice at last – a bit late.'

LESLEY SHARP: His legacy is so strong. I think what he left behind in his work has filtered down, to people who worked with him and have influence in the business now. There's part of Alan, the tradition of Alan, the way he wanted to make films and his vision has carried on. I'm thinking of Tim and Gary, really. Seeing *Nil By Mouth* I just thought – you know, Alan Clarke would be so proud of Gary.

DAVID HARE: If you say what influence did he have, *Nil By Mouth* is clearly a great tribute to Alan, you couldn't make that film without Alan. I think it's a fantastic film, but it's no coincidence that Gary wrote and directed it and Ray Winstone acts in it.

GARY OLDMAN: He was a great inspiration, Alan. I have a clapperboard, in fact, from *The Firm*, which I put in a frame. And I glance up at that every once in a while, here in the office. I started to write *Nil By Mouth* and then I thought, 'This is a very good part for someone that I've got here. God, who could do this?' And I thought of Ray Winstone and from there it was easy, because I started to write the part for him. And I'd never met Ray before or worked with him, I only knew him through a few of the things he'd done and specifically his work in *Scum*.

RAY WINSTONE: I met Gary for the first time at Clarkey's funeral – just a second, we looked across the room at each other, said, 'All right?' He phoned me out of the blue about *Nil By Mouth*. There's no compromise there, same as with Clarkey.

TIM ROTH: Alan was the best. He gave me the confidence to be an actor, and he made me feel that it was possible for people who weren't from the upper classes to be actors, that their stories were important. And I've never ignored what he taught me and I've taken it everywhere else. People go, 'Oh, you're waxing lyrical about a man 'cos he's dead,' but it's the truth. And that's why I'm directing now, a film called *War Zone*, about incest. And Steadicam's a big part of it – different part, but it's there. And already I'm thinking, 'What would Alan do?' One thing that Alan taught me is that absolute generosity is possible, even in the film world. And you have to remember that. I'm casting a sixteen-year-old kid in a very distressing situation. And he's in every scene of the film. So he'll be going through what I felt when Alan was directing me. Warnings have to be made – this film will be with you for ever. Your mates are gonna see it, your mum and dad – this is gonna be part of your world. But if you want to go through with this, if you want to go further, if you want this to be your life, I can help you. Because Alan helped me.

GARY OLDMAN: It's just a shame he didn't make more films for the cinema. I mean, a movie's a movie's a movie; I don't look at Alan's work and think of them as 'films for television'. But it crippled him a bit. And I know he had a battle. It's a sad loss now, because of this resurgence or renaissance or whatever one wants to call it of British cinema. And you know, something like *Scum*, the cinema version – it was just great to see Alan with the gloves off, and I would have loved to see a bit more of that.

DANNY BOYLE: If he was around now, his work would be championed in the cinema much more. You know, he'd have needed a Miramax to sell his work in America, and it just wasn't available for him at the time – partly because the fucking British film industry were a load of wankers, in my opinion, Puttnam and people like that, who were basically in this kind of closed shop, in terms of a particular approach to film-making. It was in Alan's nature to do things with an absolute originality, which would certainly have got people into cinemas to watch. I'm really sorry he never saw *Trainspotting* because I think he'd have liked it, just because it was trying to tell the story in a different way. Of course, he'd probably have directed it had he been around, I wouldn't have got the job.

DAVID HARE: He made some very, very boring work, I think some of the things are unwatchable, but they are the means by which he's working towards the good stuff. And what was great was that television gave him that sense of turnover, which you can't now get from cinema. Presumably you could still get it from television, I don't watch the series, but presumably there are directors who are aiming at that. I just don't know who they are. I think David Thomson was the first critic to make the large claims for Alan. Throughout that *Biographical Dictionary* he argues for British television directors. Then there's the Pauline Kael counter-argument that you can't make a great film for television, there's no such thing as a great television film, and it's stupid, it's just a snobbery. Because if you actually look back, most of the best British films have been made for television.

MARK SHIVAS: Alan was making several things a year, evolving his style, with a pretty free rein as to the kind of scripts he was doing, which were commissioned by the producers. And generally speaking, he didn't have to have the heavy imprimatur of the Head of Department. I cannot, with the best will in the world, see those circumstances being repeated today. For a start, there aren't so many singles made, nowhere near the number. So the chances of taking risks have got less and less. More feature films are made, the financing makes them easier and more attractive than single plays. And the more you have multiple financing, the harder it is to make something individual. And his work was not designed to get ratings, whereas much of the work that goes out on BBC1 now is tailored to have somebody in it who the mass audience have heard of, say a Robson Greene. And that requires a rating of six to eight million. Alan didn't work that way, and I can't see how he could possibly reach that position now.

STEVEN BERKOFF: I think Clarke came at the end of that reasoning about TV and drama that started with Sydney Newman. There was a species of director the BBC developed then, because the material they used was developed to a level far superior to today – incomparable. It was driven by the pure drama of the piece, and by the actors. It produced people like Alan, Ken Loach, in the early days Philip Saville.

ARTHUR ELLIS: *The Firm* was the last gasp of BBC Drama, that was pretty much the end, good-bye BBC Drama. You have the serials now; I like *Pride and Prejudice* and *Martin Chuzzlewit*, but they're commodity series with a brand-name value. If you go into the BBC to flog a one-off, it has to be seen as a film first, it can't be a play. And if it's a film, it has to have a bit of a name director, it's gotta be a certain length and it's got to hit certain demographics if someone's going to pay for it. If I want to do something now about England and my own sensibilities, I can't, I have to tie that up with some other format. I'm meeting people now who have never heard of Alan Clarke, people who are in a position to hire and fire and don't have any heritage. So you can't talk to them. *Christine* was a walking film and I used to say, 'No BBC, no walking film.' They won't make one now unless it has Richard Gere in it and a Bee Gees soundtrack.

DAVID M. THOMPSON: Were Alan working now, he would have been in the movies. In the new world of low-budget British features, he'd be the champion of it all, the king out there. Or maybe he'd get very pissed off with the financiers and the co-production set-ups. But he certainly could have flourished in a commercial mainstream environment, he was just so talented and visual. And visceral. I think he would have really thrived with the Ewan McGregors, he'd have been brilliantly suited to working with them and they'd have all flocked to him.

It's total bollocks to talk about the grand old age of television drama when it was all brilliant, inspiring stuff. It's the rose-tinted approach to say everything in the past was brilliant and it's all formulaic now. There were lots of good things but a hell of a lot of crap and boring old stuff, as anybody who was around and is honest will remember. It's inevitable when you're making forty or fifty dramas a year. There was fantastic stuff then, there's fantastic stuff now. The authored piece, the risk-taking original drama has never been so alive and well on British television; it just so happens that it's also involved with feature film production now, because that's where the talent is, where it's naturally drawn now.

DAVID LELAND: In the time that I knew Alan, everything he did was coming out of current affairs, even *Danton's Death*. He was digging into what was happening here and now, which is always the most uncomfortable area to explore in drama. Real contemporary drama has become a thing of the past on television. I don't think that politically they want to deal with it now. Thugs like Norman

Tebbit led attacks on that kind of drama, direct personal attacks. And they've managed to frighten the BBC out of doing it. *Prime Suspect* is no substitute for the kind of drama Alan used to do. His space has been taken up by documentaries, but it's not the same thing because drama always has the freer voice. That's something we've lost, something to be mourned – it's a fight we lost, one that Alan was engaged in all the while. There have been a lot of eulogies about his work, and that's quite right. But I think it would be very wrong for people to hold the idea that Alan was properly acknowledged when he was alive. In my experience of working with him, every time he wanted to do something, he had to throw another six to start. He'd convince someone to give him a desk and a telephone at the BBC, and then try to evolve what he wanted to do. He paid a price to get the films made. If people were so keen to have that kind of drama on our screens, they would be encouraging the talent to do that now. The great loss of Alan is that we haven't followed in his footsteps.

Alan Clarke (1935–1990)

Index

References in bold denote illustrations